D1528265

LETTING GO OF THE REINS

the true story of a man who left the Amish
and the woman who helped him

by

Vicki M. Botner

Mecan River Press, LLC

Letting Go of the Reins. Copyright © 2013 by Vicki M. Botner

ISBN-13: 978-0615794532
ISBN-10: 061579453X

Mecan River Press, LLC
12701 Rivercrest Dr.
Little Rock, AR 72212
MecanRiverPress@gmail.com

Printed by Createspace, Charleston, SC

Cover photograph by Karrie of Ooto Photography

Author photograph by Amy Hazel

Truthful lips endure forever,
but a lying tongue lasts only a moment.

Proverbs 12: 19, *The Holy Bible,*
New International Version (NIV)

One

Karrie

"I left."

Those two words are seared into my memory; the moment frozen in time. Two words, spoken with such weight and conviction, as if they were being chiseled into stone. While the significance of the words was obvious, I didn't immediately understand their meaning.

When I picked Bill up for work that morning, I could sense that something was wrong. He was waiting outside on the snow-covered, gravel driveway, two red gasoline jugs beside his feet, just as always. His head was tipped forward into the wind, leaving only a sliver of his bearded chin visible between the black stocking cap and the top of his denim jacket.

A blast of wind straight from the Arctic entered the car along with him, nearly drowning out his mumbled greeting as he settled back in his seat and stared out the window. Bill is usually quiet, not like our co-worker, David, who sat in the front seat next to me. David never runs out of things to say. It was the same routine as yesterday, and the day before, but today seemed different. I kept checking on Bill in the rearview mirror as I drove down the twisty, country lane, but it wasn't until I pulled up next to the old camper that we used for shelter at the logging site that Bill finally spoke.

"Hey, Karrie...I need to talk to David...alone."

It was an unusual request, and I turned in my seat to look at him. Something in his dark eyes kept me from asking, What the hell for?

Instead, I said, "Yeah, okay."

Probably a guy thing, I told myself while I sat in the car with the engine running and the heat still turned up on full blast. The three of us, along with Ferman, another co-worker of ours who hadn't come today, spent many hours inside that camper sharing our lunches, our cigarettes, and our lives. Even though we had our differences – three Amish men and a lapsed-Catholic woman – we had developed a close friendship.

At least I *thought* we were close.

Glancing over at the camper, the windows beginning to steam up from the small propane heater one of them had lit, I wondered what was going on in there. It was probably either my gender or my faith that had excluded me from their private meeting, but I still didn't like being left out in the cold.

They were gone only a few moments before the door opened and Bill waved for me to come in. Entering the camper, I glanced at David. As usual, he was sprawled across his tipped-back chair, his long legs challenging me to find a place to sit, but he was strangely silent with a dazed look on his clean-shaven face. The camper offered us protection from the biting January wind, but a chill lingered deep in my bones causing a shiver to rattle through my body.

"I left." It was at that moment that Bill had spoken those two words that continued to echo around us.

"You left what?" I snapped, plopping down into a chair and reaching for the pack of cigarettes on the table.

He answered simply, "The Amish."

My eyes flew to his face and locked with his. We seemed to stare at each other for hours, but it was only seconds before I could speak again.

"Holy shit, Bill! I can't believe it...I'm...I'm happy for you, if that's what you want," I said, trying to be encouraging and supportive, but the whole time my mind was under siege with a million questions, bouncing around my head like a frenzied pinball.

After a pause when no one seemed to know what else to say, David stubbed out his cigarette and said with a sigh, "Well...I guess we'd better get to work." He got up from his seat slowly, and Bill and I followed him out the door.

David and I walked into the woods, our boots crunching over the frozen pine needles and ice-coated leaves, each of us lost in our own thoughts. On any other day, we would have been laughing and giving each other some good-natured ribbing or just bullshitting. But not today. Except for the sound of the wind whistling through the tree branches, even the woods were hushed.

The two of us did the hand-cutting of the timber. This begins with felling the trees, trimming off all the limbs, and then sectioning the trunks to a specific length. Bill did the skidding. Skidding, or moving the wood, was done in the early days by the use of strong draft horses.

Bill uses a machine called a forwarder, although it is commonly referred to as a skidder as well. It has a large grapple claw that loads the logs onto a large bed, or the bunk. The timber is moved out to the roadway where the logs are sorted into various piles by wood type, trunk diameter, and quality, and from there it is eventually loaded onto semi-trailers for transport to the mill.

Bill has left the Amish.
Bill left.

It kept going around and around in my head as I selected a tree to fell and not even the ear-splitting whine of my chainsaw could quiet it.

I knew he was frustrated with the restrictive Amish life, but I never imagined that he was seriously thinking about leaving, especially since he was a church member with a wife and child. All three of the guys, Bill, David, and Ferman, had complained at one time or another, once they knew that it was safe to talk openly in front of me. We had discussed many times how difficult it would be for someone to leave the community. Leaving meant being shunned and ex-communicated. Leaving meant being cut off from family and friends and everything you had ever known. Leaving meant learning to adapt to a world that you had been intentionally kept apart from.

The discussion always ended there.

By leaving, Bill was choosing to drastically alter his life in a way that few people can completely appreciate. I respected his decision and admired him, but I didn't fully understand or realize the impact his leaving would have on his community.

Standing in the wintry woods that day, I was utterly clueless as to what lay ahead for him…and for me.

4

Two

Karrie

Across the road from my house, at the bottom of a steep and wooded slope, countless trickles of cool water come bubbling out from deep underground. These springs blend into streams and then gather into a small lake before rambling southeasterly for nearly thirty miles where the Mecan River merges and becomes part of the Fox. The Fox River continues to the northeast, spilling into the south end of Lake Winnebago and then out from the northern end for nearly forty miles until it reaches the Bay of Green Bay and Lake Michigan. Water that could eventually reach one of the Great Lakes, perhaps even the Atlantic Ocean, begins its journey only yards from my home.

How many people have ever stood at the very spot where a river is born?

I have, more times than I could even try to count.

When I was young, I would tramp around in my rubber boots in the river's icy water having races with twigs and leaves, hunt for abandoned nests, or move rocks around making a dam or changing the flow of a small stream.

Living across from the Mecan was like having my own private wildlife refuge and every visit offered the chance to see something new and different. Maybe today it would be a doe with her spotted fawns or maybe a beaver chewing on tender new branches. A honking flock of Canada geese might take a break in their migration and paddle around in the water, or bald eagles might circle overhead finding the best place to make a nest.

The head of the Mecan has always been both a playground as well as sacred ground. Every time I visit, I feel the magic all around me.

No wonder that I told my Aunt Cork, when I was about eight or nine years old, that I was going to have my wedding at the river some day.

"What kind of guy is going to marry you down there in all those weeds?" Cork is only two years older than I am, and her attitude and sarcastic tone made it clear that only a church wedding was acceptable to her, God, and everyone else.

"Well, if he doesn't want to get married by the river, then I don't want him anyway!" I retorted with the simple wisdom children often possess.

My river wedding was going to be as elaborate as any church wedding. Along the north side of the Mecan headwaters, in an area that appears to be nothing more than a clearing, is what used to be the old ice road. Back before homes had electricity and refrigerators, people would take their carts along the dirt path in the wintertime and cut up blocks of ice from the river.

That was the river's history, but it was my future wedding that I had on my mind when I imagined the old ice road making a perfect aisle for my wedding. White ribbons and flowers would decorate the oaks and other hardwoods lining the grassy pathway. My guests would be seated between the naturally formed rows of trees, watching as my dad escorted me to the bottom of the trail, all the way down to the river's edge, where a stand of birch, with the striking white bark of their trunks, formed a natural sanctum. That was where I would exchange marriage vows with the man I loved.

When I got married in 1988, it wasn't at the river. It was a typical proper and traditional church wedding with just one transgression: I was pregnant. My wedding may not have been at the river as I had planned so many years before, but it wouldn't be long before I would return to it.

After high school, I moved out on my own and rarely made it down to my special place at the Mecan for many years. But that all changed just before Christmas of 1997, when my parents decided to move to Neshkoro, a small town about twenty miles away and offered to sell the house to my husband and me. Some people say that you can't ever go home again, but I've never been one to listen to what people say.

Not only was I returning to the Mecan, but I always loved the property with the gray, two-story farmhouse; a large, old-fashioned red barn with several other storage buildings, including a dog kennel; and the forty wooded acres.

I need space. A lot of space.

My nearest neighbor should be a few miles down the road and not so close that I can look out my kitchen window into theirs and see what they're having for supper. It makes me crazy being cooped up inside for too long. Maybe it is the Native American blood of my dad that also drums in my veins. Maybe it's some genetic coding that predetermined my passion for hunting and fishing. Maybe I'm just a country girl. Whatever it is, for me there's nothing better than being able to go hunting on my own land or to go fishing anytime I want by simply walking across the road to the Mecan. Returning to my river was both a blessing as well as a chance for my children to explore it, and love it, as I did.

Buying the home where I grew up was a great opportunity for us, although it was strange moving into what had always been my parent's bedroom. In those first few weeks, there were several times when I caught myself walking into my old bedroom, now my daughter's, instead of the room that I shared with my husband.

There was another benefit to the move that I hadn't expected. I was back in a place where I had so many happy memories; back in a place where I felt grounded and strong. Perhaps my returning to my childhood home, now with my own children, helped me to realize that I was truly an adult and responsible for making the right decisions, no matter how difficult or daunting they might seem. Whatever the reason, it wasn't long after moving back home that I knew my marriage was over. It was the death of the happily-ever-after dream; however, as it so often seems to happen in life, as one dream dies another comes along to take its place…and mine came in the shape of a horse.

One early spring morning in 1998, I noticed a young Belgian draft horse in the paddock of a neighboring farm. He was a stunning sorrel and impossible to miss with his glistening red coat and white-blond mane and tail. Belgians are large and powerfully built, typically weighing about 2000 pounds: a ton of bone and muscle. They are one of the strongest draft horses with the ability to pull loads as heavy as they are.

Each time I drove past that farm, I looked for him and watched while he matured and became even more magnificent. As big as he was, he was amazingly graceful with a regal attitude to boot. He was the king of the land and loved to show off by throwing back his head and shaking his ivory mane. I fell deeper and deeper under his spell. That horse had charisma, and every time I saw him glowing like a flame, I vowed to find a way to make him mine.

Why shouldn't I have something special, something just for me, I wondered. Nearly every weekend, I was traveling somewhere for a dog show. On the rare weekend that I didn't have a show, then there was always plenty of housework to catch up on and caring for my kids, Kelsey and Clayton, as well as the constant dog training. My ten-year marriage had been deteriorating for years and by that time, my husband and I had become not much more than two people sharing the same address. I knew that he had found other ways to keep himself busy while I was gone, but I didn't even care anymore. In fact I was relieved, but it wasn't the life I imagined for myself. The end of my marriage had been looming on the horizon like a big summer storm, blue skies surrendering to tall, dark clouds until finally one day, the rain began to fall.

In the spring of 1998, I told my husband to move out, and I filed for divorce. I was on my own with two children, various animals, and a mortgage, but I wasn't worried. I had a talisman. That Belgian draft horse that I had been watching for months was the epitome of strength and perseverance. He had come into my life exactly when I needed him and now more than ever, I had to find a way to make him mine.

It wasn't very long before I saw my chance.

One evening as I was driving past the Belgian's farm, I noticed an Amish buggy coming up the driveway. Without even thinking about what I was doing, I turned my car in to meet it.

"Hi, I'm wondering if that horse might be for sale," I asked the young, bearded driver as I pointed toward my obsession standing in the paddock, his head high, watching me.

"I'm not sure," he said, "This isn't my farm. I came over to chore for my brother-in-law...but I think he wants to sell it." I had to restrain myself from screaming with the hope and excitement that filled me while the man continued, "He'll be home later tonight. Come over tomorrow to talk to him, if you're interested."

Please let that Belgian be mine.
Please let that Belgian be mine.

The chant looped through my mind all night long and was the silent prayer I sent out to the cosmos. As soon as I'd gotten my kids off to school the next morning, I was off on my quest.

The Belgian lived at a farm that had been the home of my childhood friend and classmate, James Wood. While I was growing up, I never minded the isolation of living in the country. There was always something, either work or play, to keep me busy. My playmates were the many and wide variety of animals we had, from the typical dogs, cats, and horses, to the more exotic raccoons, geese, and even a deer. But country life was even better after James moved in nearby.

James and I often met midway between our homes at the Mecan's boat launch area. We would ride our bikes along the hilly country roads or run around in the woods, but most of the time, we stayed by the river, taking our fishing poles and hoping for a nibble from a bluegill or maybe even a bass. Other times we would tromp around in the shallow water or find a rock or a bog that was safe to sit on, talking and listening to the sounds of the river.

After turning sixteen, we got our drivers' licenses and took turns driving to school. It was a practicality, considering the extra-curricular activities we were both involved in, but it also marked a turning point. Driving ourselves to school gave us a taste of the independence of our impending adulthood. We felt free, even if it was only deliverance from riding the school bus.

James and I lost touch after high school. His former home had been sold several years earlier, yet as I drove down the driveway that morning on my mission to get the Belgian, it was still strange to see a horse-less, black Amish buggy parked beside the barn.

The Amish surrounded me, but it was a horse that had finally brought me back into contact with them.

My initial exposure to the Amish, as it is for most people, was limited to staring at them as their horse-drawn buggies went rattling by. They lived a separate existence from the rest of us because of their religious beliefs, but I didn't really know what those beliefs were. I knew they didn't use anything powered by electricity or any of the other modern conveniences most of us consider necessary to our daily lives. Their desire to live in a simpler time seemed curious and quaint, but also illogical and impractical. I admired their willingness to work hard and the way they took care of each other, even though I thought they dressed funny.

The Amish began moving into Central Wisconsin in the early 1980s when the farming crisis forced many family-owned farms into foreclosure. Chris Herschberger, Bill's father, co-founded the Wautoma Community in 1983, and it was a year or two later when I came into contact with my first Amish person. It was not long after I graduated high school, and I was training and fitting show horses for a family only a few miles from my home. One early summer afternoon, my boss' wife came out to the arena where I was hot-walking the last horse of the day.

"Karrie, could you do me a favor and pick up the Amish girl who works for us on your way over tomorrow? She lives just down the road from you, at the corner of Cottonville and B."

"Sure, not a problem," I answered and clicked my tongue to keep the horse moving through his cool down.

Most of the Amish in our area are allowed to ride in automobiles, although they're supposed to travel as much as possible by horse and buggy. I know that I gave that young Amish woman a ride a few times but don't recall anything about our initial meeting or any conversation we might have had. She may not have spoken to me at all; I honestly don't remember.

But there was a second young Amish woman, named Ada, who I remember very well. She also worked for the same family that summer and one blistering day, I talked Ada into going for a swim with me after work at the family's private pond.

"Do you have a swimsuit?" I'd asked, suspecting that she probably didn't.

"I don't, but it's okay, I'll just wear my *ruck*." Ruck is the word for dress in their German-Amish dialect.

"Well, I brought an extra one...just in case. You can wear it, if you want," I offered, "It'll feel a lot better than having your dress weighing you down in the water and that way, your dress will still be dry for you to put on afterward. Besides," I continued, "no one is going to see you since it will just be the two of us."

It didn't make sense for her to go swimming in a long dress, but I wasn't sure if she would wear my spare swimsuit either -- it was a bikini! I don't know which of us was more surprised when she took the black bikini from my hand and went into the mudroom at the back of the house to change. When she came out a few moments later, her plain, solid-color dress gone, I was shocked! Not because Ada was wearing a bikini, but because she looked so completely normal, just like any other young, American woman. It was her Amish clothes that always made her seem so foreign and strange.

Those were my first encounters with the Amish. They wouldn't be my last but at that point in my life, I didn't have time to worry about the Amish. I was busy making my own plans and that included leaving Wisconsin.

Not long after I met and gave rides to those two young Amish women, I moved to Georgia. In addition to my work with horses, I had also been training dogs for field trials, a competition for hunting dogs. I was ready for a change, so when an opportunity came to get away from everything that had become routine and too familiar, I took it.

For two years, I gave being a Southerner my best shot, even taking an office job when the field trial work ended, but it wasn't meant to be. I never mastered saying "y'all", and the plural, "all y'all", always cracked me up. "All y'all?" I'd repeat and get either a questioning or a nasty look. When someone asked if I wanted "bald" peanuts, I was completely clueless and my wisecracks about giving peanuts a comb-over were not appreciated.

Eventually the heat and humidity wore me down. I missed having four distinct seasons, and not just weather that is hot and not-so-hot. I was ready to go home, back to where we say "you guys" and where no one else has heard of "boiled" peanuts either.

After returning to Wisconsin, I decided to work exclusively with horses and rented a barn to set up my own stable, breaking and training horses for both pleasure-riding and racing. I met my husband when he brought his horse to me for training. During the summer, I also jockeyed some of the racehorses that I trained. I've always loved the thundering speeds of a competition pairing human and horse. Racing is an exciting sport, but also dangerous...something that I learned the hard way one June weekend in 1989.

Our daughter, Kelsey, was born in February 1989, just four months before the racing accident that fractured my pelvis in twenty-seven places. To complicate things even more, I found out while I was in the hospital that I was pregnant again! It was a horribly painful injury, but I recovered, the baby continued to grow, and I even returned to finish the rest of that racing season. I planned to race the next year, but my husband never liked me being a jockey. After the accident he became more and more insistent, until finally, grudgingly, I agreed to quit.

After the birth of our son, Clayton, in March 1990, I shifted my focus back to dogs. Dogs have always been a part of my life, as both pets and business. My mother became a groomer while I was growing up and would have me help her with that and with the breeding and training of our Chesapeake Bay Retrievers.

When I got back into working with dogs after the birth of my son, I bred a few, very select litters, but I worked primarily as a professional AKC handler. Over the next several years, I attended dog shows in practically every state and in several foreign countries, including the prestigious Westminster Show held annually in New York.

Dogs will always be a part of my life, as will horses. And there was one horse, more than any other, consuming my thoughts.

Please let that Belgian be mine, I thought, once again, as I got out of my car at the Amish farm.

Answering my knock on the kitchen door was a plump woman about my same height. The somber clothing she wore, from the stiff white cap on her head to her long brown dress and black leather shoes, contrasted with her lively, sparkling brown eyes and her warm, welcoming smile. I guessed her to be about my age, in her early thirties, even though the bit of brown hair not covered by her cap had a few gray wisps mixed in.

"Hi, I stopped by yesterday and was told that the Belgian out in the paddock might be for sale?"

"Are you Karrie Dollar?" the woman asked, leaving me speechless and confused. I didn't recall introducing myself to the man I had spoken to the night before, and even if I had, the woman used my maiden name, a name I hadn't used for over ten years.

"Um...maybe...it depends on what you've heard!" I joked, attempting to hide my uneasiness.

"I'm Verena."

The name meant nothing to me, no matter how hard I tried to place her, but her broad smile never faded.

"You used to give me rides when I lived at that house over there." She pointed toward the east, and I finally made the connection. She was the first Amish girl I picked up when I was training horses! Verena was the first Amish that I had ever met and now she was my neighbor.

"You'll need to talk to my husband, Amos," she told me and stepped outside. As we walked, we chatted as though we were long-lost friends, catching up on what had happened in our lives since we last saw each other. Verena told me about her six children who ranged in ages from seven-year-old, Edith, to the newborn.

"When did you move in here?" I asked.

"Oh, it's been several years now. Here's Amos," then to him, she said, "Amos, Karrie used to give me rides when I worked for that family in Richford. She's here to talk to you about Rex."

"A man I met last night said the horse in the front paddock might be for sale," I added.

"Yes, that's Rex. He's for sale," Amos Lambright immediately struck me as an easy-going guy. He has a short, stocky build with reddish blond hair and bright, clear blue eyes. "He and my favorite mare don't get along too good, so one of them has to go."

Without any hesitation I made him an offer, and we soon had a deal.

The Belgian was mine!

My wish had come true.

I was thrilled to get Rex, but I got more than a horse that day: I got two new friends as well.

Not long after that, Amos and Verena took me up on my offer to help them with the haying. It's a hot, messy job, but I don't mind hard work. I'll take physical labor and the freedom from a monotonous routine over being cooped up inside or dealing with petty office politics. Working with the Lambrights also gave me the opportunity to learn more about my new horse, and Belgian draft horses in general which are used by many of the Amish for farming.

As I spent time with my neighbors, I also found out more about their way of life. I discovered that they really do call non-Amish people "English", because that is the language we speak. I learned that men only grow beards when they are married, or more specifically, when they are "published." A couple is published when their intention to marry is announced during church service. At that time, at least in the Wautoma Community, the man must quit shaving and cannot ever again trim his beard. An Amish beard doesn't include a mustache and runs along the chin-line, but that rule will vary slightly from one community to another. Each community sets its own specific rules in what is called the *Ordnung*. When a young person in the Wautoma Community is sixteen and a half, he or she is eligible to become a church member by reading over and agreeing to the community's *Ordnung* and being baptized during a church service.

Not everything the Amish did or believed made sense to me, but I'm an open-minded person and try to keep a live-and-let-live attitude. There were times when I envied what I thought was their simpler way of life. For those of us living in the modern world, with all the quickly changing technology, it's easy to get overwhelmed. It can feel as if our lives are speeding up while we struggle just to try to keep up with it all. It's understandable that we would look at the Amish, and their pastoral life-style, and yearn for a simpler time, a time that we feel has passed. But as I got to know them better, I began to realize that their lives are just as complex as ours, and in some ways, even more so.

The family and community bonds of the Amish continually impressed me. We "English" have so many methods of communication, but it seems as if it only gets harder for us to stay connected to each other. Without the use of telephones or computers, the Amish can spread the word of butchering day at someone's farm and a dozen people will be there to help. That in itself is impressive, but there's something more, something intangible...something in the way they speak to each other, or the way everyone will set to work without needing to be told what to do. The strong commitment they have to each other is like an invisible quilt, wrapping all of them up inside, all safe in the shared warmth. It was a connection that I had been missing in my life, and I was very thankful to be increasingly welcomed into the Amish fold.

When Verena and Amos invited me to help with butchering, I was reimbursed with fresh meat, which I appreciated, especially after becoming a single parent. I received canned goods and fresh bakery items in exchange for occasionally giving rides to them and some of the other Amish I met through them. I was happy to help the poor Amish, as I thought of them, and didn't mind that the loaf of bread that someone gave me didn't begin to cover my gasoline expense. It felt good to be needed and part of a community.

By 2001, I knew practically all of the Amish in the Wautoma Community and that spring, I became a driver...an Amish taxi service. I made a map to help me find the farms of the fifty-four families in the community as well as their stores and the three Amish schools. Whenever possible, I would try to combine riders and trips, but that rarely worked out, and it seemed that I was always on the go, especially with Kelsey and Clayton getting more involved in various activities. Once word got out that I was available, it seemed as if someone was constantly calling to schedule a ride.

Many people assume that the Amish never use the telephone, but that simply isn't the case. Everyone within the Wautoma Community does, usually by visiting the home of an English neighbor or in recent years, it has become much more common to see an Amish phone shack. Phone shacks, which look a lot like outhouses, are permitted because the telephone is located outside the home and considered to be communal, although it seems that a lot of phone shacks are mostly found on the property of someone who has a business. Incoming calls need to be scheduled in advance since the telephone ringer is supposed to be turned off. Answering machines are forbidden.

Cellular phones are also allowed within the Wautoma Community Amish if an employer requires one and provides it. The phone is to be used only for business, never for personal calls, not even in an emergency. Ironically, there is no rule against the cell phone having voice mail.

The following summer, in June of 2002, I ran into an Amish friend, Jerry Yoder, at the big, annual Amish auction at a nearby farm. He asked me to consider driving his logging crew full-time. Since working the past year as an Amish taxi service had proven to be a bit too hectic and unpredictable, I accepted Jerry's offer on the spot.

The next afternoon, I went to pick up Jerry and his crew after what had been a sweltering day with the temperature soaring up and over 100 degrees. It had been as hot and humid as any summer day that I experienced when I lived in Georgia, but at least in the north, that type of heat doesn't last. Wisconsin summers are changeable and within just a few days, it could cool off to the point where the furnace might need to be turned on.

Even though it didn't have air conditioning, I took my van to pick up the men after work that first day since I needed the extra space. Five men climbed in, and the smell that came with them was worse than anything I have ever experienced in my life. I've mucked out stables, spread manure, and changed some nasty diapers, but all those things--together--could not even begin to compare to the stench of those men. It was truly a physical attack, making my eyes water and my stomach roll.

The crew had been laboring all day in that sizzling heat. Anyone would smell bad, but this was more than just the unpleasantness of dirty, sweaty men and there is no use in tiptoeing around it: even on good days, the Amish stink.

Part of the reason has to do with the way they live. Most of their homes have indoor plumbing with the unheated water being gravity-fed from a tank in the attic or an upper floor. Some of them might have a wood-burning water heater, but in the majority of Amish homes, the water either has to be heated on a stove or used as is. A cold shower might sound nice and refreshing during a summer heat wave, but most of the time we English still long for a nice long soak in a tub of hot water to soothe our aches and pains. The thought of going home to a hot bath, or even a hot shower, never enters the Amish mind partly because it would involve much more than simply turning the faucet over to the "H" setting.

The Amish use laundry detergent that they make themselves or they buy Amish-made detergent at an Amish store. Amish detergents don't have the cleansing or deodorizing qualities of our commercial brands, which leaves their clothes smelling musty even after they have been freshly washed and hung out on the clothesline to dry. Added to that are the other odors that saturate their clothing, from the kerosene of the lanterns to the pungent aromas of horse, cow, and goat manure: a whole smörgåsbord of scents to assault your nostrils.

All of these things explain the practical reasons why the Amish stink, but it is also important to understand that they have a very different mindset regarding what we consider to be proper personal hygiene.

Cleanliness is next to godliness. It's a common phrase, and something that many of us practice whether or not we truly believe it. But this is simply not the case with the Amish, in either belief or practice.

Cleanliness comes from within. That's what the Amish believe and live by. It's an expression that I'm thankful my children never heard when they were young and hated bath time.

Since cleanliness is definitely *not* next to godliness for the Amish, they feel that it is only necessary to bathe once a week. Anyone bathing more often than that would be questioned, teased, or possibly even required to publicly confess for wastefulness and vanity. They don't have any rules against using deodorant, yet no one ever seems to use it.

Five fetid Amish men got into my van that day; I couldn't open my mouth for fear that I would vomit. As soon as the door shut, I sped off. But I couldn't drive fast enough, not even with every window open, and the fan blowing on the highest setting, to keep the stench at bay.

What the hell have I gotten myself into? I asked myself. No way could I do this again tomorrow!

Luckily, it turned out that Jerry wanted me to become the driver for Bill Herschberger's crew since Jerry had recently hired Bill's driver away from him. What a relief! Only two stinky Amish men, Bill and his friend, David, instead of five! Even after Ferman joined Bill's crew a little later, it was fine with me since I was still able to use my car, which thankfully had air conditioning.

"You're not going to like driving David and William," Verena predicted when I told her about my new job.

"Why not?"

"David's just like his father, and William never says anything...and he has a terrible temper."

All of the Amish, except for David and few of the other young ones, call Bill by his given name: William. It seemed too stuffy to me, but I wasn't sure which he preferred.

When I got to David's, my first passenger to be picked up my first day as their driver, I asked him, "Do I call him Bill or William?"

"I don't know, you should ask him," he said with a shrug. David was no help.

"So...which is it? William or Bill?" I asked, looking in the rearview mirror as my second passenger settled into the back seat.

"Bill," he answered simply, and that is what I've called him ever since.

As the crew's driver, I shuttled them to and from work each day. I also had to be available in case they needed anything. When the forwarder broke down, Bill would call me to take him to get repair parts. Something always seemed to be breaking on that old, heavily used machine, so the two of us spent quite a bit of time together.

I'm usually a talkative person and will easily chat with anyone, while Bill is reserved and not as likely to initiate conversation, at least not with someone he doesn't know well. It took him a few weeks before he opened up but after that, we never seemed to run out of things to discuss, from what was wrong with the forwarder to the big buck with the many-pointed rack we hoped to get that hunting season. There are some people you connect with, even when you initially seem to be exact opposites.

As Bill became more comfortable with me, he would sometimes vent his frustrations with his Amish life. He didn't understand why he had to rip the perfectly good carpet out of his home, or why they couldn't use electricity since it was cheaper than kerosene. There seemed to be a lot of things that didn't make sense to him. It was fascinating to hear the inside scoop of the enigmatic Amish. I was glad that Bill trusted me enough to share his personal thoughts and feelings.

This certainly wasn't the William that Verena had warned me about, and I couldn't help wondering if I was the first person who had ever really listened to him. Verena's comment about Bill's temper still puzzles and amuses me. In all the time that I've known Bill, I've never seen even the slightest bit of temper, not even when it would have been completely justified.

"Why don't you work with us as a logger? You know how to use a chainsaw, and it would be handy to have our driver with us all the time."

One of them, Bill or David, made the suggestion one day a few months after I became their driver.

"Why not?" I asked myself and nothing came to mind to stop me.

My first day as a logger was January 1, 2003. It was the first day of a new month and the start of a whole new year. In only a few weeks, on the very last day of the month, we would find ourselves pondering another new beginning as well.

Bill had left the Amish.

Three

Karrie

"How about an early day, today?" David asked as we neared the camper for our lunch break.

"You know I'm always ready to quit early," I agreed instantly. Thanks to Bill's shocking declaration, my mind had been on everything except work all morning, which is not a good thing when you are handling a chainsaw.

We all quickly loaded into my car, and I cranked up the heat. The sun was now high overhead, shining a cold, silvery light but providing no warmth.

Bill's house was my first stop.

"Call me later if you want," I said as he got out. Even though I didn't completely understand what his leaving meant at the time, it didn't matter. Regardless of the situation, I knew that he could use a friend, and I would be there for him, as he had been there for me only a few months earlier when I needed a friend.

My dad was diagnosed with cancer in October of the previous year. It was stage four; the final stage. Dad had complained for several years about some pains, especially in his legs, but he would attribute it to the physical nature of his work, or getting older, and refused to see a doctor. When he couldn't stand it anymore and finally went in, the cancer was all over his body: in his lungs, in his bones, and in practically every organ. A few medical treatments were available, but Dad opted out.

Without undergoing any treatment, we were told that Dad probably only had a few months to live. There was no hope. It was a very difficult time for me, even harder than my own battle with breast cancer that had been caught very early a few years before. It had only been a few months since starting as Bill's crew driver when we found out about Dad, but Bill was there for me to help me get through it.

One day, probably in November, I took Bill to Wautoma to pick up a part that had been ordered for the forwarder but when we got there, it still hadn't come in.

"I might as well run you home," I said as we got back in my car, "then I'll go visit Dad for a bit before I have to go back to get David and Ferman."

My dad was on my mind constantly. If I had any free time during the day, I tried to go see him, even if it meant the drive to and from his house took longer than the actual visit. I knew that our time would run out all too soon.

"I'll go with you, if you want...to see your dad."

"Are you sure?"

"Why not," Bill replied in his simple, practical way, "It's not like I can do any work until that part comes, and it'll save you making an extra trip."

He was right. It was out of my way to take him home first, but I didn't want him to come along strictly out of convenience.

"He's pretty sick...so we don't do much...mainly just watch TV."

Of course I forgot that the Amish don't have televisions and having the chance to watch one might be worth the depressing atmosphere. Even so, who really wants to spend time with a terminally ill person? It was my dad, I had to go, but that didn't mean it wasn't difficult. Death had latched onto him like a tick, swelling up bigger and fatter each day as it sucked the life from him.

After spending time with Dad, and seeing how very sick he was, it was hard not to cry the whole way home, dwelling on the inevitable, and thinking about how much I was going to miss him. I appreciated having company the handful of times Bill went with me.

Bill was there one time when Dad complained, "Those goddamn pigeons are shitting all over the barn. I'd take my gun and shoot them, but I'd probably break my shoulder."

He wasn't exaggerating. The cancer had weakened all of his bones, and the recoil of the gun would have seriously injured him.

"We'll do it for you," I jumped up from my chair, glad to have something to do besides watching another hunting show, and went to find guns for Bill and me.

Shooting pigeons while they roost is too easy and not at all sporting, so Bill and I took turns going out into the barn to shoo the birds so the other could shoot them in flight. For me, it was similar to shooting trap or sporting clays, both of which I've done competitively.

It must have been torture for him, but Dad was there the whole time, watching from just inside the doorway, barely able to stand without his walker. He took pleasure in pointing out our mistakes and gave us a hard time if we missed a bird on the first shot. It was one of the last happy memories I have with my dad. I was with him again, not long after that, and just two days before Christmas, when he died.

Even though he wasn't supposed to use his cell phone for personal calls, Bill called to apologize because he hadn't been able to attend Dad's funeral.

It meant a lot to me, and I was glad that Bill had the chance to get to know my dad even a little.

Now it was my turn to be supportive.

Bill knew quite a few English people, including other drivers and people who do business with the Amish, but I suspected that I might be the only English person that Bill knew he could trust. I didn't realize then how important it was for him, or for anyone who leaves, to have someone on the outside to help. Of course, there was a lot I didn't know then about the Amish, including how they respond when someone leaves and how they treat anyone who helps.

Four

*I have given them your word and the world has hated them,
for they are not of the world any more than I am of the world.
My prayer is not that you take them out of the world
but that you protect them from the evil one.*
John 17:14-15, *The Holy Bible*, NIV

Bill

"Call me later if you want."

"See you tomorrow, Bill."

I watched for a moment as Karrie and David drove away then took the empty five-gallon jugs over to the fuel shed. Part of my job driving the forwarder was to lug these same two jugs back and forth from work every day. After refilling the jugs, I carried them over to the house and left them outside by the kitchen door. They would be ready to go in the morning.

Just inside the house was a wooden rack with pegs where I hung my jacket and vest. I took my insulated lunchbox over to the kitchen table, pulled out a chair, and unwrapped a meat sandwich. Almost the same as any other day, but today was different.

Amish kitchens are usually warm, sometimes too warm, because of the cooking fire that is kept burning throughout the day. On a winter day such as today, I would have been glad for some heat, but there was none in my kitchen…only a chilly emptiness.

Had this been any other day, my wife, Ruby, would have most likely been in the kitchen when I got home. Our seven-month-old daughter, Frieda, might have been playing on the floor nearby.

Had this been any other day, I might have thought that Frieda was down for an early afternoon nap. I might have thought that Ruby was busy elsewhere in the house.

But today wasn't any other day.

I knew they weren't in the house.

They were gone.

Ruby left me because I left the Amish.

The night before, I was out in the fuel shed filling the jugs after work, pacing and stomping my feet to stay warm. Nothing different from any number of other nights until a single thought came into my mind.

It's now or never.

An icy chill went through my body. It settled into my spine, making it feel like a long, fragile icicle. If I moved, would it shatter?

Where did this come from? There hadn't been any major or even minor incidents lately, so why did I feel this way? Why now? Why today?

It's now or never.

This time it was like a mighty old oak crashing down on me, trapping me completely beneath it. I couldn't move. I couldn't breathe. I could feel only my heart beating violently inside my chest, as if it was trying to burst out.

I knew what needed to be done.

I knew what I had to do to survive.

But could I do it?

As far back as I could remember, I felt out of place. Always questioning things. But learning quickly that my questions weren't the kind you were supposed to ask. The kind you weren't allowed to ask. So I kept them to myself. Kept them inside.

Now for each of those questions and for every doubt I had, it seemed that a seed had been sown. Tucked away in the soil and forgotten. I hadn't noticed over the years while those seeds had sprouted and grown tall and strong. Until today. Today was the day that I looked out and realized that I had planted an entire field.

My field of doubt.

And it was time to reap.

Now or never.

With a sigh, I knew. Knew what I had to do.

The crushing weight of that oak seemed to be lifted from my body. My lungs filled and then sighed heavily. My heart beat normally again, no longer needing to abandon my body.

I was no longer Amish.

It was a typical evening, at least on the surface. Inside, I continued to feel relieved since making my difficult decision. Finally doing what I had always wanted to do. Choosing the path that I was meant to follow.

But I dreaded telling Ruby.

I put it off until we went to bed. In the darkness, I wouldn't see the hurt or anger in my wife's eyes. Between us lay Frieda, already asleep in the middle of our king-sized bed where she always slept.

"I need to tell you something…something that I should have told you a long time ago…even before we got married," I said to Ruby in our German-based dialect that Amish usually speak at home. Amish don't learn English until they are six and start school.

"Whatever it is, tell me," Ruby said, her voice flat and controlled.

"I don't want to be Amish anymore."

"Is there somebody else…or what?"

"No. I just don't want to be Amish…I haven't since I was a little boy."

"Well, I don't want to leave," her voice had that familiar stubborn tone. After a pause, she continued, "I wish you wouldn't. What are you going to do? How long are you going to leave for?"

"I don't know."

It's not uncommon for someone to leave the Amish but then return. Sometimes people leave as a way to protest a change or a new rule in the community. Sometimes people plan to leave permanently but find they miss their family and friends too much. Sometimes they can't adapt to the outside world after being kept sheltered and being told since birth to never trust the English.

Anyone returning to the Amish must confess publicly at church for all wrongdoings and make amends. Making amends usually means being put in the ban. For most offenses, that means about two weeks. Someone in the ban is not considered to be a full church member and would not be allowed to stay for the members-only part of the service.

Being in the ban also means that you have your meals served separately. Your food is scooped out first. After the meal, your plate and utensils are washed last. This keeps your sins from contaminating the others.

While you are in the ban, you should also make it clear how much you regret your sin and act properly repentant. The Amish are very strong believers in telling the truth and confessing all sins. No matter how big or small. As long as you publicly confess and complete your punishment, the incident is forgotten and never spoken of again. It doesn't matter if your sin is smoking cigarettes or something much worse. Anything and everything is handled within the Amish community. Nothing is taken to the English and their outsider ways and laws.

"Maybe you should go talk to Monroe Schmucker…maybe he can help you," Ruby suggested.

"I don't think he…or anyone…can help me."

Monroe is her uncle, as well as a bishop. As the Wautoma Community grew, it needed to be divided into three church districts: the East, which was my district; the Middle, where Monroe was a bishop; and the West, which had been Ruby's district before we married.

A bishop holds the highest rank and authority within a church district and there is usually only one bishop in a district. Bishops are selected from the preachers in that district and once a bishop, always a bishop. If a bishop moved to another district, he would still be a bishop in his new home. That district would have two. Each district also has a deacon who is the assistant to the bishop. There is typically only one deacon per district.

The church districts in the Wautoma Community, as well as the surrounding areas, usually have two preachers. There can be more depending on the district's size or if a preacher moves in from another community. It's called a "full boat" when there is one bishop, one deacon, and two preachers.

Preachers are married men and selected during the members-only part of a service. Nominations are made by both male and female church members. If you're nominated, you are expected to accept. After all the nominations are made, each of the men come forward and select an *Ausband*, the German songbook used during regular service. One of the songbooks has a slip of paper in it. The man finding the slip of paper in his book is the new preacher. There is no additional training or any special qualifications required to be an Amish preacher, only that he is a married male church member in good standing. To be an Amish preacher, you just have to be nominated and find a slip of paper in a book.

Deacons are chosen the same way as the preachers, but bishops are selected from the preachers in that district.

The elders are another significant group in the church. They are the older men in the district whose opinions are respected and valued. When several of them band together on an issue, they can influence the church leaders and the community.

I knew the bishop, as well as everyone else, would do their best to talk me into staying, but my mind was made up. The last thing I needed was to have them telling me that I was wrong.

Being Amish was killing me.

I wouldn't ever go back.

I couldn't.

Frieda's deep breathing was the only sound in the room for several minutes, until Ruby finally broke the silence, "What are you going to do about work? You can't keep logging with them. Maybe you could go drive truck?"

"I don't know…" I hadn't thought about all of the details of my leaving. There would be a lot to figure out in the weeks ahead, including my work situation. I knew there would be a lot of changes to deal with including being shunned by my community. No Amish would be allowed to work with me, at least not directly. David and Ferman might be able to continue doing the hand-cutting as long as it was at a separate site from where I was skidding. Even so, they would be strongly discouraged from having contact with me. I might lead them astray.

I didn't like to think about any of this. No one wants to be cut off from his family and friends. But if you are Amish, it's all or nothing. Shunning was the price I would have to pay for my freedom.

But it didn't make any sense.

Why did things have to be this extreme? Why did it have to be this way?

"William, promise me that you won't shave your beard."

"Huh?"

"Don't shave your beard…and I don't want Frieda seeing you in English clothes, either."

"Okay," I agreed without thinking. Now that I left, I wouldn't have to follow those strict Amish guidelines, that was true. I would be free to shave and dress however I wanted. But it was so unimportant, I hadn't even given it a thought. At least not until Ruby brought it up. Was it really that important to her? Is this all she cares about?

I lay there, feeling as if my arm had just been cut off, and I had gone to her, holding on to the bleeding stump, needing help. And instead of caring for me, instead of trying to give me comfort and aid, she was fussing over whether or not the fingernails on that severed arm were clean.

Where would I work? My beard. My clothes. This is what she was worried about? What about me? Why wasn't she worried about me?

But I knew the answer.

Typical Amish. Focus on the little crap. Don't consider the big questions such as why I was leaving. Didn't she want to know? Or didn't she care.

"I'll go stay with my parents for a while," Ruby stated.

I hadn't expected that.

In the Amish world, the man is the head of the household and the spiritual leader of the family. I hadn't given much thought to how my life, and the lives of my wife and daughter, would change once I decided to leave. I assumed that Ruby would stay with me. She took a vow. She made a promise. She was supposed to let me to lead the family the way that I thought best. I never thought she would leave the Amish with me. Honestly, it never entered my mind. But I thought she would continue to be my wife.

Maybe she just needs some time to adjust, I reasoned.

"Okay," I told her, "and if you talk to my parents let them know not to come over right away. I don't want to talk to anybody."

We both lay there for a few minutes, neither of us saying anything. Finally, I rolled out of the warm bed and headed for the basement.

Smoking is forbidden in our community but as with other things, many Amish do it. After we got married, I usually smoked outside. When it was too cold, I would either go in the bathroom and open the window or go down to the basement near the chimney draft. Ruby knew I smoked and every now and then, she would tell me that I should quit. Not because she was worried about my health, but because it was against the *Ordnung*. Now it would be one more thing I could do openly and not feel like a hypocrite.

Taking a seat on an old wooden stool, I lit a cigarette and drew deeply. The smoke filled my lungs. The warmth from the wood-burning stove was soothing, but my stomach was still in knots. My mind kept replaying everything Ruby had said. I never expected any of this to be easy, but was it wrong to have hoped that it might have been different?

Young folks, anyone sixteen and a half or older according to the Wautoma Community *Ordnung*, get together Sunday afternoons or evenings in someone's home to sing and play games. Dating is allowed at this age with many first dates taking place after a singing with a boy giving the girl a ride home. Maybe not the first time but eventually, she will ask him to come in for a visit.

Amish boys tend to be careful when they ask a girl for a date. The Amish don't believe in casual dating as the English do. It's not that you have to marry the first person you go out with, but it does seem to happen a lot. If a boy and girl have gone out a couple times it may become assumed that they are heading for marriage.

When I was about nineteen, I asked someone for a date. She was the daughter of the Bishop. In our group, you asked the girl for a date at the end of the evening. Before I ever got a chance, my friend and future co-worker, Ferman, jumped the gun and asked her earlier that afternoon. But I wasn't upset. I was in no hurry to date anyone, although I did ask one other girl. She turned me down since she had just broken up with someone. After that, it would be about three years before I would ask anyone again.

Ruby's family moved down from Amherst after the Wautoma Community became more established and was already divided into three districts. I don't remember exactly when we met since she attended a different church district than I did. It was probably at one of the singings.

Someone new always stands out, especially in such a small community. But I would have noticed Ruby anyway. She was very pretty with dark hair, deep blue eyes, and a nice figure, very petite, barely over five feet tall. Whenever I stood next to her, I felt bigger and taller than I really am. She always seemed happy and cheerful. I noticed how helpful she was to everyone, especially her own family.

Before that night at the singing, we had never talked to each other. I didn't have any idea what she would say, but I knew that if I didn't ask to give her a ride home, someone else would...very soon.

I asked.

She said yes.

It was the first date, ever, for both of us.

After dating about six months, or maybe a little longer, I asked Ruby, "What do you think about getting married?"

"I'd like that," she answered quietly.

And that was that.

For the Amish, there is no proposal made on bended knee with a diamond engagement ring. Everything is kept plain.

Getting engaged seemed to be the right thing to do. Ruby and I had been dating for awhile. We'd gotten to know each other. We got along. That's the way things are done.

Our wedding was September 26, 2001.

We quickly settled into married Amish life.

Until I shook everything up.

By the time my cigarette burned down to the filter, my stomach felt better. I opened the door of the wood stove and flicked the butt into the glowing bed of coals. It burned brightly for an instant and then it was gone.

With the stove door still open, I tossed a couple more logs in. The fire began to claim them. They crackled and hissed in protest. A loud pop sent sparks shooting everywhere and a red, hot ember landed near my toes. I watched as the color slowly faded from that escaped coal until it lay on the floor, cold and black. Dead.

As I closed the door to the stove, I wondered if I was going to be like that ember. Had I escaped. I had finally gotten my freedom. But what next? Could I make it in the outside world?

Five

Do not conform any longer to the pattern of this world,
but be transformed by the renewing of your mind.
Then you will be able to test and approve what God's will is—
his good, pleasing and perfect will.
Romans 12: 2, *The Holy Bible*, NIV

Bill

Telling Ruby that I left had been difficult. I hated hurting her, but it felt so good to know that I was out. I was free!

After finishing my cigarette, I went back into bed. I couldn't tell if Ruby was asleep or if she just didn't feel like talking anymore. I lay there, my body feeling relaxed and light, and I realized that I was excited. Tomorrow would be the first day of my new life. It wasn't going to be easy. Ruby had reminded me of that. But my life would finally be mine to live the way I wanted. No more rules that didn't make sense. No more confessing for things that didn't matter. No more Amish life.

Morning came and we both got up as usual. Ruby made my breakfast. While I ate, she packed my lunchbox. It was all perfectly normal, just the same as the start of any other day. Until she spoke.

"Did you change your mind?"

"About what?" I looked over at her. She was wearing the blue dress that matched her eyes.

"About leaving."

"No."

Her question surprised me. Why was she asking? Maybe she decided not to go over to her parents after all. Maybe she was staying. Maybe she wanted to be with me no matter what. Maybe everything was going to be okay. I finished eating and got up from the table to get my jacket and vest from the peg by the door.

"You'd better go give your daughter a kiss good-bye."

Hope snapped inside me like a dried-out old twig. My stomach twisted into knots. I didn't usually kiss either of them when I left for work.

Ruby was leaving.
She was taking Frieda and leaving.

Shrugging into my jacket, I went into the bedroom where Frieda was still asleep. Her tiny hands balled into fists on either side of her head. I kissed her forehead and my whiskers tickled her, causing her to stir but not waken.

Walking back to the kitchen, I took out my wallet.

"Take this," I said, handing Ruby about eighty dollars, it was all the cash I had, "And use the checkbook if you need to."

I hated this. Hated that my wife and daughter were leaving. I didn't want them to go. But I didn't know what else to say. It would only be for a short time. Everything would work out.

I went out, shut the door behind me, and without looking back, grabbed up the fuel jugs. After only a few minutes, a car pulled into the driveway. David sat in front by Karrie, as usual, jabbering on about something. As usual. I stowed the fuel jugs and slouched down in the backseat, staring out the frosty window. The early morning sky was a cold, lifeless gray giving no hint that the sun existed in anything but memory.

Ruby's voice came into my head, the way it had sounded when she told me to go kiss Frieda. Once again, I heard the chill in her words. I felt terrible about what I was doing to her. Really terrible. But I figured that we would find a way to continue our life together even if I wasn't Amish. She would go to her parents' for a few days, and then she and Frieda would be back. We were still a family.

But then I heard the way her voice sounded when she said that she was going to go stay with her parents. There had been that stubborn tone of hers. And something else. Something that sounded...final.

I wasn't sure about anything.

As we passed a small clearing, I caught a glimpse of an orange glow. The sun was finally rising. The icy branches caught some of the first rays and began to sparkle, and that was when I saw it: a snowy owl gliding across the field toward a stand of pines. For a moment, I had the feeling that I was up there in the sky with it. I was free! No matter what happened, I was free. Instead of feeling sad, I began to get angry. Angry again about the stupid Amish rules.

If Ruby was leaving me...permanently and not just going to her parents for a visit...life wasn't going to be easy for her. There is no divorce for the Amish. Not ever. Not for any reason. Whether or not I'm Amish, Ruby is married to me under Amish law. She can't ever remarry as long as I'm alive. She would live the rest of her life alone.

By leaving me, Ruby was ignoring one of the most basic Amish beliefs. We were always taught that the man is the head of the household. Period. The man is the spiritual leader of the family. What reason did she have for leaving since my spiritual beliefs hadn't changed? I was still a Christian. I wasn't asking her to leave the Amish with me.

Besides that, how could she leave me? How could she ignore her marriage vows? How could she justify leaving but remain married to me under Amish law? How the hell does that make sense? It was all so idiotic and a perfect example of Amish hypocrisy.

I was out of all that bullshit now, I reminded myself. I was free! Let her go home to her parents. Her father, and the preachers, and even the bishop, would tell her that she needed to honor her vows.

They would remind her that her duty was to me. To be my wife.

Within a few days, she would come home.

She and Frieda would be home soon.

I was sure of it.

"I need to talk to David...alone," I said to Karrie when we pulled up to the camper at the site. She twisted around in the seat to look at me.

Something about Karrie always reminds me of a mountain lion. Maybe it's the tawny hair. She is medium height and slim, but extremely powerful with an agility and gracefulness of a cat. She can work as hard as any man, but no one would ever mistake her for one. She's tough without losing her femininity. Her hunting and fishing skills seem to come naturally, as with any good predator. Seeing her with her children, or with the Amish children she used to drive, she is gentle and playful. But if something threatens or upsets her, she won't hesitate to show her claws...or to use them.

Only her eyes didn't match the golden brown of a mountain lion. They are a vivid blue-green, and they stared into mine, assessing me. It seemed as if she was going to say something, but then she looked away and said, "Yeah, okay."

She was irritated, that was easy to see. She probably wondered why I was excluding her. We had become friends over the past few months, but I felt that I should tell David first.

I've known David since he was a toddler. When the Wautoma Community was just getting started, there were only a few families. There weren't many kids my age to play with, so I was excited when David's family moved in. Another boy to play with! I didn't even care that he was four years younger.

David and I got to be good friends once he was old enough to hang out with the Young Folks. Actually, it was as if I had been waiting for him and the other boys to get old enough so there would be a Young Folks group. A few of us started calling ourselves the Bachelor Boys, and I was the unofficial leader since I was the oldest.

When he was eighteen, David came to work with me doing the hand-cutting. It was about a year before I got married. After Ruby and I got married, I couldn't hang out with the Bachelor Boys as I used to, but I stayed close to David because of work.

Once we got inside and closed the camper door, I didn't waste any time, "I just wanted to let you know that I'm leaving the Amish."

David's brown eyes widened with surprise, "Is Ruby going with you?"

"No, she's going to go and stay with her parents for awhile."

He nodded and turned away to light the heater. When he finished, he looked at me. He had a strange look on his face, as if he was embarrassed about something, "Just between us, Bill, you aren't leaving for Karrie, are you?"

I couldn't believe it…just like Ruby! Why did they both immediately think I was leaving because of someone else? Did they really think that I was cheating on my wife? Didn't they know me better than that? How could they think that I would do such a thing? I expected the people I was closest to to know me better. Why would they assume that I was having an affair? Both my wife and best friend knew how frustrated I was at times with our way of life. Why did my leaving surprise them?

But as much as the question irritated me, I understood. Maybe it was easier for them if there was someone else to blame. Karrie was certainly an easy target since she is an outsider. Blame everything on the English female that I work with. Make Karrie the scapegoat. If they can do that, they don't have to think about the real reasons.

"No, I just don't want to be Amish anymore. I haven't wanted to for a long time," I answered honestly, just as I had with Ruby.

Ever since I was a child, I've known that I didn't want to be Amish. It had been growing inside me for years.

Feeling that I didn't belong.
That things didn't make sense.
That we were all only half alive.
Doing what we were told to do, whether or not it made sense.

How many times had I felt that I was a hypocrite because I did something that I knew was against the rules? How many times had I been reprimanded for things that weren't important, like wearing shoes that weren't plain enough? If I wore plain shoes, did that really make me a better person?

The Amish seem to think so.
But I don't.
And I could no longer be Amish.

It's going to be different now, I told myself, as I sat in my kitchen finishing my lunch. I was out. No more following rules that didn't make sense. No more humiliation of public confessions over stupid little things.

But once again, my emotions swayed like a sapling in the wind as I glanced at my empty lunchbox and remembered Ruby packing it for me that morning. Would she ever come back? Would we ever be a family again? Had I just eaten the last lunch my wife would ever make me?

Leaving everything on the table, I went over to the desk. It took me a few minutes, but I finally found the old bill. I pulled out my cell phone and dialed the power company's number.

Many people are surprised to learn that Old Order Amish are allowed to have electricity, at least for a while. When Amish buy a house from the English, it is often newlyweds who are just setting up their own home. There are a lot of modifications that need to make the house a proper Amish home. In the Wautoma Community, the new homeowners are given nine months to make the required modifications.

Sometimes a young man will move out of his parent's home before getting married, especially once he is twenty-one. Twenty-one is considered to be "of age." While the young man isn't forbidden from moving out, it isn't encouraged or celebrated. There's nothing in the Ordnung that stops a young woman from moving out when she's twenty-one, but it never seems to happen.

I was twenty-two when I decided to move out on my own.

"That land between us and Lewis would be good for you," my father suggested at the time, "You buy those ten acres. We'll make you a house there, William."

The parcel he was referring to belonged to my brother, but Lewis couldn't farm it because it was heavily wooded. It would have made a nice place for a home. But just as I was beginning to consider it, my father continued, "Now I don't want you building a little shack out there, and hanging out, and doing stuff that you shouldn't be doing."

I didn't say anything. I learned long ago that it was best not to argue with my father. It wasn't worth the effort. Instead, the first chance I got, I found a house and bought it. It was four miles from my parents. That may not sound like a lot...unless you usually travel by horse and buggy.

After I moved into my new home, in June 2001, I was in no hurry to have the electricity disconnected, or do any of the other things that I was supposed to do. I had nine months. Nine months that were officially allowed in the *Ordnung*.

Since I had my own place and electricity, I hooked up the TV/VCR combo that I had purchased several years earlier but had kept hidden in my father's barn or in the logging camper. It was not, and never would be, approved in the *Ordnung*. Since there was practically no television reception out in the country, I had videos...lots and lots of videos. Even though my little TV was color, I like the old black and white movies best. Westerns, especially anything with John Wayne.

Ruby and I got married four months after I moved into the house, and I continued to put off making the required modifications. What's the rush? The deadline was five months away. Plenty of time.

One day, not long after she moved in, I came home to find that Ruby had ripped up the carpeting in the living room. I couldn't believe it! All the carpet was gone, except for a small patch under her heavy curio cabinet. Instead of the nice, relatively new carpeting that had been there that morning when I left for work, there was only sub-flooring. It was ugly and rough. But now it was proper for an Amish home.

Whenever I saw my father, he would ask about the other modifications that my house needed to be proper. His biggest concern seemed to be, "Have you fixed your furnace yet?"

"No, haven't got to it," I would answer, stalling.

The furnace used fuel oil. Fuel oil, at least in diesel form, is allowed by the Amish. It is what my logging machines use. The problem was that the blower on the furnace ran off electricity. Electricity is, of course, forbidden.

In order to be proper, I was supposed to convert to heating with a wood-burning stove. I was lucky because there was already a wood stove in the house when I bought it. It wouldn't be too difficult to switch over. But that wasn't the problem. Using a wood stove meant that I would have to carry in wood every day. Why should I? My nine-month grace period, I figured, should get me through the worst of the Wisconsin winter. I could deal with the wood stove next year. At least that was my plan.

"Your father was here today," Ruby announced when I got home from work one day about mid-October.

"What'd he want?"

"He was downstairs. He said he got everything fixed for us…the well and the furnace and the pump."

"He converted the pump?"

"Yeah...he ran the line through our closet."

"Oh, shit!" I uttered and rushed to see what the damage was. "Why didn't you move it?"

"Move what?" Ruby asked, following me down the hallway.

"The TV and all my movies!"

Dad had already caught me with this TV and made me confess before I got married. If he found me with a television again, especially since it was the same TV that I was supposed to have gotten rid of, the punishment would be even more severe!

I snatched open the closet door expecting the worst. Surely he would have said something to Ruby. She would have seen him carrying everything out. But how could he have missed it?

The new line was at the front of the closet, right next to the door frame and on the side where Ruby's dresses hung. I slowly reached in, my heart pounding. I pushed the dresses aside and there was the TV, shoved into the back corner, still sitting on top of the box of videos. Just as I left them.

He missed them! Somehow he ran the water line right next to my contraband and hadn't seen any of it!

It shouldn't have surprised me that Dad had taken it upon himself to convert my house. He likes to be useful. In his mind, he thought he was helping. That's his way. But instead of being grateful to him, I was irritated, and not just because he nearly found my TV and movies.

I admit that I had been stalling, but I was still within my *Ordnung*-approved modification grace period. Maybe I should have felt a little guilty for putting it off, but I honestly didn't care if my house was proper or not.

I think my dad may have known that. Sensed it. He did what he thought was best to get my house proper. To make sure my soul was safe.

It took one phone call to start undoing some of my father's work.

Only a few hours after calling, my electricity was back on. I hadn't expected it to happen that fast.

It was a good sign.

I was reconnected to the world.

Out in the fuel shed, I got the TV from its latest hiding spot along with the box of videos. I was going to watch *Big Jake*, one of my favorite John Wayne movies, as soon as I got everything hooked up. But when I got back in the house, I decided there was another modification to make first. There was more of my father's work to undo.

I was in the basement priming the furnace when I thought I heard a buggy come into the driveway. As soon as I heard someone knocking on the kitchen door, I quickly flipped off the light. I stood there in the dark basement. Waiting. Hoping they wouldn't come in. Hoping they wouldn't find me.

It was probably my father or one of my brothers out there. Come to talk to me. Come to find out if it was true. Come to talk me out of the terrible mistake I was making.

It didn't matter who it was. I didn't want to talk to any of them.

Not right now.

I waited several minutes. There was no sound. Whoever was out there must have given up and left. I had avoided them. For now.

When I went to bed later, the king-sized bed seemed enormous without Ruby and Frieda. I told myself to just turn off the light. Just go to sleep. But I knew it wouldn't happen. My mind was full of questions and doubts. Would my wife and child ever come home? Could I find work outside the community? Was I really doing the right thing?

Everything seemed to hit me all at once. I felt very much alone.

"Hello."

"Hi, Karrie, it's Bill. Is it too late?"

"No, what's going on?"

We talked for a long time. I told her about Ruby leaving with Frieda and about someone stopping by to talk to me. Even though she couldn't really understand what I was going through and what I would be facing in the coming weeks, Karrie listened and was supportive.

"How 'bout we go to Wautoma tomorrow after work so you can get some new clothes and whatever else you need?"

"That'd be good," I said, feeling better.

"No western shirts!" Karrie commanded when we got to Pamida the following afternoon. Work that day had been typical, except that I had to make my own breakfast and pack my own lunch. But I didn't mind. Everything was easier when you had electricity.

"And you aren't getting skin-tight Wranglers, either! I swear, every ex-Amish guy that I've ever seen goes out first thing and gets tight jeans and a western shirt. It's like they all want to be cowboys."

I smiled. I couldn't help it. She had a point. Guess all of us ex-Amish guys just want to be John Wayne.

We picked out a pair of Wranglers that weren't too tight. They were only my second pair of real jeans. Wautoma Community Amish men are allowed to wear lightweight denims for work, but they don't have a zipper. Zippers are not allowed under any circumstances. Zippers aren't plain. In place of the zipper, the jeans have a flap in front with buttons. The pants must also be worn with suspenders. In other communities, young men might be allowed to wear regular jeans during *rumspringa*. Not in ours. But I had a pair anyway. I picked them up at Pamida one time and kept them hidden under some other clothes in my dresser.

Proper shirts for Amish men are button-down, made of cotton, polyester, or a blend. They can only be solid colors: blues, greens, and yellows. Nothing bold or what might be considered fancy.

Along with my new jeans, I picked up a camouflage baseball cap with an American flag on it. No more worrying about whether the hat had the proper width and fold to the rim. No more worrying about whether it had the proper hat band. No more black felt hats. No more straw hats in the summer. No more black or blue stocking caps in the winter. I could go out without a hat at all if I wanted, although with my hairline already starting to recede, that wasn't likely to happen.

When we got back out to the car with my purchases, Karrie asked, "Is there anything else you want to do while we're here?"

I thought for a moment. "I don't know…would you want to go bowling?"

Six

Karrie

"Want to go bowling?" Bill asked.

Bowling? It wasn't what I expected him to say when I asked if there was anywhere he wanted to go. But why not?

"Sure," I shrugged and turned the key in the ignition. A bowling alley is such a typical small-town Wisconsin hangout. Granted, it's a bar...but in Wisconsin, bars are family-oriented gathering places where people also eat and spend time together.

Bill wanted to go bowling. Thinking about it made me smile. After leaving the Amish, and their extremely rigid way of life, the first thing he comes up with is to go bowling? The game that makes you wear those funny shoes!

Of course under Amish rules, Bill was really living it up. Bowling is forbidden. The shoes alone were enough to get him into trouble since they weren't plain.

Several months earlier, I took Bill, David, and some of the other guys, bowling. If they had been caught, they would have all been in trouble, but only the ones who were church members would have had to publicly confess for their sin and be put in the ban.

The Amish play volleyball and a game similar to baseball called *round-town*, so they aren't completely against sports, and while bowling may appear to be just another game that uses a ball, it isn't really the game that is offensive to them. Besides the fancy shoes, the Amish consider a bowling alley to be filled with all kinds of evil things, from smoking and alcohol, to what they call "loose women".

By Amish standards, I was a loose woman because I was divorced and smoked. They undoubtedly thought that I showed far too much skin in the summer when I wore shorts with halter or tank tops. Of course to them, even a short-sleeved shirt is considered too revealing and except for Middle Eastern countries that require women to wear head-to-toe covering, most of the women in the world are "loose" according to Amish standards. A man wearing shorts and a t-shirt, or maybe even no shirt at all, might not be living up to their ideals, but I never heard the Amish call a man "loose." It was all just typical bullshit and patriarchal double standard.

When we got to Dogger's in Wautoma, all the lanes were busy with bowling league teams.

"Why don't we try Omro?" I suggested. We made the 20 mile drive but when we got there, that bowling alley was also busy with the league teams.

"Sorry, Bill. We picked the wrong night."

"That's okay. Maybe we can get a drink or something."

We found two seats at the bar. Bill ordered a beer, I got a Coke, and we placed an order for some cheese curds and two burgers. Cheese curds, or squeaky cheese as it is sometimes called, is cheddar cheese that hasn't been aged. The nuggets will squeak when they are eaten fresh or at room temperature. A lot of bars and restaurants in Wisconsin serve them battered and deep-fried, like mozzarella sticks. They lose the squeak, but are gooey inside and sinfully good.

"I hope no one comes by again tonight. I don't know why they can't just leave me alone."

"If you avoid them long enough, they'll give up, won't they?"

Bill shook his head wearily, "No. They'll keep at me...as long as it takes...and in as many ways as they can...to get me to come back. It's their duty to save me from hell. Hell--that's where I'm headed now that I've left."

"So, you only get to heaven if you're Amish?"

"Pretty much, since I was born and baptized Amish."

"And the rest of us are all going to hell since we're not Amish?" I hated religions that preached that way. Follow their rules or you were damned for all eternity.

"I don't know about that," Bill said, "The Amish don't really talk about what happens to others. But if you're born Amish, and get baptized when you become a member, you've got to stay Amish to get to heaven."

"Do you think you could go back?"

Bill paused for a moment, lifted his glass and took a swallow of beer, "I guess if someone could explain to me a good reason why we do so many things that don't make sense. If they could prove that there's a good reason for those rules...but that won't happen. Did I ever tell you about how I had to confess when I left my cell phone home for Ruby when she was pregnant?"

I shook my head and snagged the last cheese curd from the basket.

"The baby was due any time. I didn't like leaving Ruby home alone, since it was her first time being pregnant. We didn't know what to expect. I wanted her to be able to get help right away if she needed it.

"We were working up near Almond then, not as far as some of the jobs, but it would have taken too long for me to get to her if something happened. I'd have to call for a driver...and hope I could find someone...then wait for the driver to come get me. It could have been an hour before I finally got home. That's a long time. It's too long.

"What's the point in me having the cell phone anyway? Ruby was the one who needed it. If something happened, and she didn't have my phone, she'd have to get somewhere for help. She'd have to hitch up the horse and ride several miles to an English neighbor or a phone shack. That's ridiculous. What if she was in labor? What if she was too weak? Or worse?

"Maybe she could've got to her parents' or somewhere for help, but there was no way that I was going to risk it. What kind of husband leaves his pregnant wife like that? What if she died? I could have lost both her and the baby.

"I didn't care if it was against the *Ordnung*, I left my phone at home with her...and then I had to confess," Bill spoke with an intensity that was rare for him, obviously still upset about the incident.

"Wait..." I said, "you had to confess...for what?"

"I sinned."

"What?"

"According to the *Ordnung*, I committed a sin," Bill took another drink of his beer, as if the liquid might dowse some of the heat he felt inside.

"You sinned...because you left a phone with your pregnant wife in case there was an emergency or she went into labor?"

"Right."

"But it's okay for you to have that phone for work?"

"Yup. For business use only."

"So you were supposed to go off to work, worrying the whole time, leaving her to face whatever might happen alone. She could die...but that would have been okay?"

"Yeah, because it would have been God's will," Bill answered, his tone flat.

"It would have been God's will for her to die?"

"Yup."

I didn't say anything for a few moments while my brain tried desperately to make sense of it all...but it was futile. There was no logic in any of it.

"Unbelievable. Sorry, Bill, but that's just screwed up."

Bill nodded, "I know. I confessed...mostly for Ruby's sake...since she got feeling guilty, but I don't regret what I did. And I'd do it just the same again...if I was still Amish.

"There so much crap like that," Bill continued, "stuff that makes no sense but somehow those rules make us better people? I wouldn't have felt too good if my wife died having our baby! Let us have a phone for business but don't use it to save your family. Let them die! That's God's will!

"There's no way in hell any of them can come and explain to me how that makes sense," Bill spat out the words with such force that it surprised me. He had never been this worked up about anything.

We sat silently while Bill finished his beer and I tried to absorb everything he had just told me.

"I guess we should get going," he said, glancing at the clock on the wall. "It should be too late by now for anyone to be waiting at the house for me."

"You think they'll try to come by to see you again?"

"I asked Ruby to tell them not to, but someone came last night anyway. I'm just glad that I was in the basement. They probably tried again tonight after they finished with chores."

It wasn't that I didn't believe him. It made sense that his family would be wanting to talk to him...just as any family would if they thought one member was heading in a different direction or doing something dangerous. What I didn't know was how stirred up an Amish community gets when someone leaves. A real hornet's nest. At that time, I didn't understand the desperate lengths they would go to get someone back.

That was about to change.

"You think we'll finish up with this job by next week?" I asked, pulling into Bill's driveway. On the way home from Omro, we kept the conversation light, mainly talking about our favorite topics of hunting and fishing.

Before he left the Amish, I used to get Bill and some of the other guys to go shining for deer. Bill would hop in front, since he and I really got into locating the best spots where we could find and watch the deer. The others just seemed happy to be riding around, not caring where they were going or whether we saw anything. I got in the habit of taking them home first, and then Bill and I would swing by the places we knew we'd find the bucks with biggest racks.

"If the weather stays good, I think you and David should be able to finish the hand-cutting."

"And after that…" I was about to ask about our next job but never got the chance. The words evaporated from my lips the instant I sensed something was wrong.

Being the skilled hunters that we were, even in the darkness, Bill and I detected something outside, a slight movement over between his fuel shed and barn. Something wasn't right. We were both instantly alert. Then the shadows moved again...and began to come toward us.

"Shit, Bill, what do I do?" I asked, regretting that the car was already in park. In seconds there would be no time for us to escape.

"It's okay. I'll deal with them," Bill's voice was nonchalant and resigned, but I wondered if he was as calm on the inside.

I wasn't.

Even though I probably knew all of these guys, there was something sinister about them waiting for Bill on a cold, moonless night. What were they up to? Were they going to haul him out and beat him until he agreed to return? Were they that desperate to get him back?

"William!" One of the shadows said with forceful authority as the passenger door was flung open. An angry presence filled the car, along with the familiar Amish odor, and I watched as a hand reached in and grabbed Bill's shoulder.

"Bill!"

Seven

My brothers, if one of you should wander from the truth
and someone should bring him back, remember this:
Whoever turns a sinner from the error of his way
will save him from death and cover over a multitude of sins.
James 5: 19-20, *The Holy Bible*, NIV

Bill

I don't know why I asked Karrie if she wanted to go bowling. I'd gone a few times and liked it. I guess mostly I just wanted to do something... anything...instead of going home. Bowling was the first thing that popped into my head.

If I went home too early, I knew someone would be there to talk to me. News travels fast in an Amish community even without telephones. It had probably been one of my brothers stopping by last night while I was in the basement. They were sure to try again. I didn't want to see any of them right now. Ruby was supposed to tell them to leave me alone.

I wanted to be left alone, but I didn't want to go home to an empty house. It didn't make sense. Having supper in Omro was good. It might be only bar food, a burger and a beer, but it sounded better than anything I could fix at home.

Taking a seat on the barstool was a first...not my first time at a bar...but it was the first time I sat at a bar without feeling like a hypocrite.

Even before I was legal, I would sneak into the bars in Richford with my friends, the other Bachelor Boys. Richford is between Coloma and Wautoma just off Highway 21. Richford isn't really a town...the sign only says "Unincorporated" where the population number should be listed...and about all you'll find there are three taverns all on the same side of the road, a church that sits behind the bar furthest from the highway, a cemetery next to the church, and a baseball field across from the cemetery. Johann's, or the middle bar, is where I usually went.

I wasn't married when I started going to the Richford bars, so I was still clean-shaven and if I put on clothes that looked English, I could pass for a regular country boy. But if I wanted to get free drinks, I would go with my buddies dressed in our Amish clothes. English people seem to get a kick out of it. They enjoy getting the poor Amish boys drunk.

One visit to Johann's is unforgettable. I was still living at home with my parents and a friend from another community had come to visit. We waited until everyone went to bed and then we snuck out. We hitched up the horse and buggy and headed for the bars.

When we got to Richford, I tied up the horse at my usual place…on the handrails of the Lutheran church that sits back from the road, a little ways away from the tavern. I figured it was better than leaving the buggy in front of the bar. That would have got some people talking!

Several hours and quite a few beers later, we left the bar. We got to the church to get the horse and buggy, but there was only a buggy. No horse.

Shit! Now what?

There was only one thing to do. We each grabbed one of the shafts and started walking…three long, dark, hilly miles. We had no choice but to haul that buggy back home. It was a miracle that no cars came by. The sight of two Amish guys staggering down the road pulling a buggy might have sent someone into a ditch.

But there was one person who saw us. My brother Monroe was just getting home at the same time we were. As soon as I saw him, I panicked. He'd tell on us for sure.

"Your horse run off on you?" he asked, laughing. Monroe was laughing at us! He thought that we were just getting home from a Young Folks gathering. He didn't know that we were at the bar when the horse ran off.

"Yeah," I answered, relieved and without feeling guilty for lying since it was true. My horse had run off.

Monroe kept laughing, but I didn't care. At least I wouldn't have to confess.

I set out to find the horse and finally found her across the road in the schoolyard. The harness had gotten damaged so I had to re-braid and patch it up. When I finally crawled into bed, I only had a few hours to sleep before my mother started calling for me to get up to chore.

After that, whenever I went to the Richford bars, I always checked and double-checked that the horse was secure before leaving her tied to the church railing.

By the time Karrie and I finished eating and drove home from Omro, I figured it would be too late for anyone to be waiting for me.

It wasn't.

As we pulled into my driveway, I noticed dark shapes moving by the hitching rail between the barn and fuel shed. For a split second, I thought about telling Karrie to back up and get us out of there. But I knew that I might as well get it over with. Might as well face them.

"Shit, Bill, what should I do?" Karrie asked, sounding a bit spooked as the familiar outlines of my brothers moved toward us.

"It's okay," I sighed. "I'll deal with them."

"William!" My brother Adlai called and opened my door. Even before hearing his voice, I knew he was one of those shadows. We've always been close, even though he's six years older.

"Bill...?" Karrie asked, her voice rising with alarm.

"Yeah, I'll see you tomorrow."

Her concern was understandable. The shadows had startled me at first. But I wasn't surprised to find them waiting. Part of me had been expecting them. It was time for preaching and pleading. I might as well get it over with.

"Call me later if you want," Karrie told me as I got out. Her car crept out of my driveway, as if she wasn't sure that she should leave. I should probably call her later, I told myself. First I had to get through the ordeal.

Four of them came to talk sense into me. Four of them! My brothers Adlai, Lewis, Monroe, and my brother-in-law, Toby. They had all stood out there in the cold for who knows how long. My older brothers came to get me, the youngest of the family, back in the fold. Back in line. Now I would have to listen while they lectured me on all the harm I was doing to everyone by leaving.

It had begun, just as I knew it would.

Knowing they would follow, I went into the house without any greeting and took a seat at the kitchen table. My brother Lewis came in next, and still standing, started right in.

"Is it true, William? Have you really left?" Lewis is the fourth of my siblings and also a preacher.

"Yeah, I left." I thought of my cigarettes in my shirt pocket and wished I could get one out right now. But I couldn't. It would be disrespectful.

"Why? Was it something I did?"

There were a lot of questions that I knew would be coming. There were a lot of questions that I expected. But that one took me by surprise. And it was one that I would be asked many times.

If I hadn't already been tired and my head a little fuzzy from the couple of beers, I might have had some fun with them. I might have said something just to get them going. But I didn't. I sat there, my usual quiet self, responding only when necessary.

"No, you didn't do anything. It wasn't because of you. I just don't want to be Amish anymore."

"What if you go to another community?" Toby asked. Toby is married to my oldest sister, Millie, "You and Ruby could take Frieda and move somewhere new...a whole different environment. Have you thought about that?"

Sometimes the Amish will leave a lower, or more restrictive, community for one that is less restrictive. Going to a higher community was acceptable. My brothers wanted me to consider it because it would keep me Amish. I would still be Old Order Amish, and that was the most important thing to them.

"No. I don't want to move."

"Think about it, William. You wouldn't be put in the ban. You can still visit your family. Just think about it."

It went on. Over and over again. Adlai, Lewis, and Toby took turns asking the same questions. Why did I leave? What about Ruby? What about Frieda? Each time they got the same answer. But it never seemed to satisfy them. They would ask again and again. Was it something they did? They needed to make sure they weren't responsible for my descent into hell. Only my brother Monroe didn't say much. He's only a few years older than I am and has always let our older brothers take the lead.

"I've got to go out and check my water pump," I said finally, needing a break. Adlai followed me outside.

"William, are you sure there was nothing that I did to make you leave?" he asked with a pained look on his face, "I'm afraid that I was a bad influence."

"No, it wasn't anything you did." I told him again and meant it. Sure, I saw him do things...stupid little things that were nothing...but they violated the *Ordnung.* There was never anything Adlai did that I wasn't already doing...things I could do openly now that I wasn't Amish.

Before they all left that night, Lewis made his final plea, "What would it take to get you to come back?"

What would it take?

I tried to think of an answer.

It was more than being able to trim my beard or wear regular blue jeans or have carpeting in my home. It was more than driving myself or listening to the radio or watching TV. It was more than smoking a cigarette or having a drink. It was more than having electricity or being allowed to leave a cell phone with my pregnant wife.

All of those minor things came to mind, but it was something much, much more.

"What would it take, William?" Lewis repeated.

"I don't know," I answered.

More than anything, I was tired of feeling like a hypocrite and following rules that didn't make sense. I wanted to make my own choices, good or bad. I wanted to live my life honestly. I wanted freedom.

But I didn't know how to say that to him.

Or maybe I knew that he could never give me any of those things.

"I'll give you everything I have…you can have everything…if that's what it'll take for you to come back."

I was stunned.

He meant it.

The English probably don't understand it, but Lewis would have given me anything. His farm. His house. His animals. *Everything.* Anything I wanted, just to have me Amish again. Getting me back was that important to him. More important than anything he owned. And he would have done it. Lewis would have gladly given me anything and everything with no hesitation. That's how concerned he was for me. That's how badly he wanted my soul to be safe from everlasting hell.

I was deeply touched, but I shook my head.

There was nothing he could give me.

There was nothing he could do.

My brother's shoulders sagged in defeat, and he bowed his head. He knew that was the best he could do. He had nothing else to offer. There was nothing else he could do to get me back.

When they finally left, I crawled straight into bed. I was so tired and almost didn't have time to miss Ruby and Frieda.

My cell phone woke me the next morning. It was Sunday, so we weren't working. I was making the most of my day off by sleeping in.

"Hello," I answered, dreading that it was someone from my family. Leaving my cell phone home for Ruby when she was pregnant wasn't allowed, since it would have been God's will if she died. But it was okay for the Amish to call me, since it was God's work, to get me back. God sure has precise rules. Good thing the Amish always know what He's thinking.

"Are you okay?"

Relief. It was Karrie.

"Yeah, I'm fine."

"I've been wondering how went it last night. I couldn't believe the way Adlai yanked you out of the car..."

"Huh?"

"Last night!"

No wonder she looked so worried.

"Adlai didn't touch me. He just opened my door."

"I know he opened the door," Karrie said, "but then he reached in and grabbed you!"

"No, he had one hand on the door, and the other was on the roof…or maybe he put it on the back of the seat…I don't know…but he didn't touch me."

"I swear that I saw him grab you, Bill…I thought they were going to beat you up!"

That made me chuckle.

"They wouldn't do that. They just wanted to talk. They stayed here for hours trying to convince me to come back."

There was a long pause of silence before Karrie asked, "And? Are you?"

"No. I'm not going back," I answered.

I'm not going back.
I'm not going back.
I'm not going back.

Those words continued to echo in my head even after Karrie and I said good-bye and hung up.

What happened last night was only the beginning. I knew it as clearly as I know how to fell a tree so it goes exactly where I want.

There would be pressure. There would be so much more pressure coming in the days ahead.

But my decision was made.

I'm not going back.
I was determined.

I'm not going back.
But if I listened carefully, I could hear the faint whispers of doubt.

Eight

Bill

Non-church Sundays are a day of rest. Except for the chores that have to be done. Every day. There are always chores to be done. A lot of Amish use non-church Sundays as a day to go visiting. Ruby and I usually stayed at home. Non-church Sundays were my favorite day of the week.

Now that had changed as well.

I found myself dreading the long day that stretched before me. Not that I wanted to, but even if I did, I couldn't go visiting any of my family or friends. If I showed up, they would probably get the wrong idea and think that I was returning. As soon as I told them that I wasn't coming back, the lecturing and convincing would begin. No matter how lonely I was, it wasn't worth dealing with any of that.

There was no one outside the Amish that I could visit either. The only non-Amish friend I had was Karrie, and I didn't want to bother her too much. She had her own life and that already included a boyfriend and her two kids. Only one other person came to mind, so I decided to spend some time with him. My good friend, John Wayne.

While I was sorting through my box of videos, I heard a horse and buggy come into my driveway. I went to the kitchen door and recognized the buggy right away. It was my father-in-law's. Ruby stepped down and walked to the house while her father stayed in the buggy. There was no sign of Frieda.

"Hello, William," Ruby came into the kitchen, glancing quickly around, her fingers plucking at her skirt.

"Are you home? Where's Frieda?" Everything seemed brighter. Everything seemed better now that she was back.

"Frieda's with Mom. Dad brought me over to talk to you. Are you coming back?"

"No. No, I'm not coming back."

I wasn't going back.

Not ever.

It would be a death sentence. But I admit, I was tempted. There were times when I was tempted.

Especially with my wife standing next to me in our kitchen once again.

It felt right.

It felt normal.

Part of me just wanted normal back.

I wanted my wife and daughter home.

Ruby moved past me and headed for the bedroom, saying, "I need to get a few things…"

I followed. While she opened the dresser drawers and pulled out her things, I wanted to ask her so many things. Were she and Frieda doing okay? Did they miss me as much as I missed them? Were we ever going to be a family again?

"Why can't you and Frieda come back? Don't you think you could live with me and be Amish and I'll be English? What do you think about that?"

"I don't know..."

"Ask your dad. Have him talk to the bishop. Find out if we could do that, okay?"

"Okay," she agreed, but there was no enthusiasm in her voice. She didn't sound as if it was something she really wanted to consider. "I'd better go, Dad is waiting for me."

"Call me tomorrow...and try to find out, okay?" I said, hugging her to me tightly.

"Okay."

With a quick kiss on the lips, she was gone. Again.

After Ruby left, I started a John Wayne movie but fell asleep. The rattle of a buggy coming into my driveway woke me, and I glanced out the window. Now who?

My first thought, when I recognized the horse and buggy, was to pretend that I wasn't home. But I would have to face them sooner or later. Might as well get it over with.

"Hi," I greeted my parents and held the kitchen open door for them.

"Hello, William." My father and I are about the same height, but he always seems bigger...taller...and just larger somehow. Even though he isn't officially a church leader, he has always been given a lot of respect in our community, partly because he is the co-founder, but mostly because of his strong personality.

My father is a model Amish. He has always seemed so comfortable in his life. Sometimes he didn't agree with things. When some new families moved into the community, the community that he founded, and they tried to change the *Ordnung*. Sometimes the church members would vote to keep things the way they were. Sometimes they voted to change, which usually meant making things stricter. Whichever way the vote went, whatever change was made, my father accepted it. He accepted it as the Lord's will.

But he would not accept his son leaving. That was not the Lord's will. That was the work of the devil. It was the evil in the outside world. My father would do whatever he had to do to bring me back. To save my soul.

Of course, having a child leave the Amish doesn't look too good for the parents either. And he had been down that road already.

My second oldest brother, Lynn, left the Amish when he was sixteen. I was only three or four at the time. I don't remember much about any of it, but I do remember my father yelling a lot. I remember the ranting and raving. I remember other when times when Dad would beg and plead with Lynn to come back.

After only being gone a few weeks, Lynn came back. He even got baptized and became a church member. But then he left again. He stayed away a lot longer the second time. And then he returned again. I don't think he stayed long. In the spring of 1982, Lynn left a third time and has never gone back.

We were living in Milton, Iowa, on an amazing piece of property at that time. The large, white farmhouse sat among gently rolling hills with woods all around. There was a pond at the front of the house and a stream that ran out from it toward the west. The soil was dark and rich. For a farming family, it doesn't get any better than that.

Our family had lived in that house since April of 1973. Rachel, Monroe, and I were all born after the family moved in, so it was the only home I knew. In 1983, after Lynn hadn't come back, my father packed us up, and we moved to Wisconsin. Whether it was to punish Lynn, or whether he just couldn't bear the humiliation of having a child leave, I don't know. But there has always been one thing that I did know. I knew exactly what to expect from my father if I were to leave. If I was ever brave enough to follow Lynn out of the Amish.

It was about to begin.

My parents came into the living room and took a seat. My mother cried. My father started right in, doing his best to convince me of the terrible mistake I was making. Dad is a great speaker and could have easily been a preacher, maybe even becoming a bishop at some point. It has always been said that he was never nominated because of his great singing voice. Amish don't allow any instruments during church, only voices, and if my father had been selected as a preacher, or any church leader, he would have been in their meeting at the beginning of each church service. His strong, deep voice, leading them like the steady beating of a drum, would have been missed during those opening hymns.

Somehow I managed not to hear a lot of what he said to me that day. Maybe sitting through all those countless Sundays of monotonous, unending sermons had taught me a useful skill after all.

My father rambled on about how we were leading a holy life because of our simple ways. He reminded me not to trust the English. We were meant to live separately. If I didn't return, I would be lost forever.

I sat quietly across from my parents, the image of a good, obedient son. They never asked why I left. They didn't want to know what had driven me to that extreme. It was understood that my leaving was wrong and they, and all of the Amish, were right. I had strayed. I must return. That was all that mattered to them.

When he finally finished preaching on my terrible ways, Dad asked, "William, will you pray with me?"

"Sure," I said, grabbing the prayer book from a side table and handing it to him. I was happy to pray. My faith had not changed. I hadn't left my faith, only the Amish.

The three of us knelt. Dad found several verses that he thought were appropriate. Of course they were ones that I had heard so many times before. The ones he felt supported everything he had been saying to me. The ones he thought would get me back. Amish classics.

Then they left.

But it wasn't over.

Not yet.

The next few days passed slowly, but I kept busy with work. Karrie arrived each morning with David and Ferman, who was back working with us. Once I got out of the house, things seemed pretty normal. While we sat in the camper taking a break, we would get Karrie to read us the good parts from a romance novel. David could always be counted on to ramble on about something. Amusing us. Keeping my mind off other things.

Ruby called me every day. The first thing she asked, each and every time, was always, "Have you changed your mind?"

"No. Have you found out if you can live with me if I'm English and you're Amish?"

Her reply was always the same, "I don't know..."

There were several nights that week when I went home with Karrie after she dropped off the others. It was nice having supper with a family again. Kelsey and Clayton, both teenagers, were full of gossip. News about their friends and complaints about their teachers. It was strange. At their age, I was already out of school, working at the mill or with Toby. After supper, we watched TV and then Karrie or her boyfriend would run me home.

One night about a week after I left the Amish, I got home and found a sign from God.

Nine

Give ear to my words, O LORD, consider my sighing.
Listen to my cry for help, my King and my God, for to you I pray.
In the morning, O LORD, you hear my voice;
in the morning I lay my requests before you and wait in expectation.
Psalm 5: 1-3, *The Holy Bible*, NIV

Bill

The Sunday before I left, January 26, was a church Sunday for Middle church. Church was held at my parent's house.

Hard wooden benches were brought in for the service. I sat on one side with the other young, married men. Ruby was across the room with the women and Frieda. My uncle Levi was the guest preacher that day. He is married to my father's sister, Lydia Mae. They live in the West church district.

Uncle Levi's sermon began with a story about our way of life and the way we do things. Then he asked, and I'll never forget it, "How do we know we're on the right path?"

He sounded so sincere. As if he was having doubts about the way we do things. He seemed to want us to think about it as well.

"How do we know?"

Uncle Levi is a good man, very kind, and gentle. Many times I have wondered how my life might have been if he had been my father. Would he have been more understanding of my doubts? Would he have been able to offer me guidance instead of demanding obedience? Would I have stayed Amish?

My mind drifted during most of the sermon, as it always did, until Uncle Levi asked once again, "How do we know?"

"How do we know?"

His question hung there in my parent's living room, as if it were a balloon that grew bigger and bigger and bigger each time he asked, until it seemed to fill the room. But then an answer came to me as if it were a sharp, swift needle.

Well, if you don't know, at your age, how the hell am I supposed to?

That's what I wanted to say. That's what I wanted to shout. But it was not the response Uncle Levi was hoping for, there's no doubt about that.

I hate to think that he might feel that his sermon drove me away. It didn't. Leaving was a path that I had been heading toward for a long time already. His sermon didn't make me do anything that I hadn't been considering. Considering for a long time.

But his sermon affected me.

My Amish life had become like that of a tree being felled. Year after year, stroke by stroke, a deep notch had been cut onto one side of the tree trunk. That face cut left the tree unstable and weak, and had firmly established which way I would fall. Uncle Levi's sermon was the back cut, when the chainsaw goes into the trunk from the other side, grinding through that last bit of wood holding the tree upright. There's a crack and a groan. Everything is inevitable. It's done. Nothing can stop the tree from falling.

That night after church, I prayed. I prayed for God to give me a sign. I needed Him to show me the way. I needed to know if I should remain on the path that I had been born to. The path that I was expected to follow. Or could I choose the other one. Could I choose the path that I wanted to blaze for myself. If I took the new path, was it truly headed for heartache and hell as I had been told my whole life?

I wanted a sign.
I needed a sign from God.

On Thursday night, only four days after Uncle Levi's sermon, I made the decision to leave. Even though I decided to leave, part of me still wondered. Was I doing the right thing? I still hoped for a sign.

Was that too much to ask?
Or just as with Ruby, had God also forsaken me?

About a week after I prayed, I came home after work and discovered that my water pump had gone out.

It was my sign from God.
God had not forsaken me.

In the Wautoma Community, the water tank is gravity-fed so it is typically placed in an upper room or an attic. If space is tight, or to make it easier to fill the tank, some Amish build a shed for the water tank outside that looks like a two story outhouse. In our community, a gasoline-powered motor can be used to pump water to fill the tank.

54

My water pump was in a small, heavily insulated hut, about the size of a child's playhouse, and was located a short distance from my house. Every winter, I dreaded the cold since that was when the pump was more likely to freeze up. Sometimes I left a lantern burning out there overnight for added heat. All my precautions paid off. In the years that I lived in that house, the pump had never gone out. There had never been any problems before I left the Amish. Never.

It had been much colder the previous week. The pump hadn't frozen then. Why now? It didn't make sense. There was no reason for the pump to go out now. Today. But it had. In fact, the pump had frozen so hard that the metal casing had cracked open.

Had I still been Amish, I would have tried to repair the pump. If that didn't work, I would have gone to buy another one which would have meant first tracking down someone to drive me to Wautoma or Stevens Point. Either way, it would have been time consuming and expensive.

My father, when he Amishized my house, had disconnected the electric pump that had been used by the previous homeowners. Even though I couldn't use that electric pump while I was Amish, I figured that it was worth holding on to and had stored it in a nearby corncrib. And that was where I headed. Had I still been Amish, I would have been violating the Ordnung. Had I still been Amish, I would have had to confess my sin in church.

But I was no longer Amish.

I got that electric pump out and had it hooked up in no time.

For most people, having a pump freeze and break would seem to be bad luck and a nuisance. They would probably curse and complain about the situation.

Not for me.

For me, it was an answer to a prayer. It had Biblical power. It was the same as a burning bush or a lightning bolt.

It was my sign.

It was the sign that I was making the right decision.

God had answered my prayer.

On February 6, my Bachelor Buddy Willard stopped by for a visit. He was curious and asked a lot of questions about my leaving. I told him about my uncle's sermon and about praying for a sign. I tried to explain everything to him. But none of that seemed to be what he wanted to hear.

I like Willard and have always considered him a good friend, but his questions that day made me uncomfortable. He kept at me. He would ask the same question different ways. But I wasn't fooled. He was waiting for me to tell him that I left for Karrie. He seemed to *want* to hear that I left for Karrie. Willard acted disappointed, as if he had come on a fishing expedition hoping to land a trophy bass but all he hooked was a bluegill.

Around that same time, my father called. He started right in on me, asking the same questions that Ruby always asked. He got the same answers that she always did.

"I'm helping move a house on Friday," he told me after he finished with his preaching.

The Amish are always moving something or building or adding on. As the family grows and more space is needed, a room or even a whole wing will be added to the house. Sometimes a small house can easily be moved and attached to the main house. This is done a lot of times when older people want to slow down and go live near a grown child. It lets them have their own home while still being close.

I don't think I've ever felt comfortable talking to him. He always kept such a tight rein on all of us. His way was the only way. The Amish way. I've always known that he would never understand or support my decision. He didn't care what I needed. All I heard from him was about my duty to my family. My duty to my church. My duty to my community. He didn't want to know my reasons for leaving or give me any helpful advice. Nothing mattered to him except that I return.

Before I left, I would have offered to help him move that house.
Before I left, I would have at least asked who was getting the new home.
But I had left.
So I didn't ask.

Not too long after that, I found out whose house my father helped move barely a week after I left. It turned out that I knew the person who got the new house. It turned out to be someone that I knew quite well.

That someone was my wife.

Ten

Karrie

"I can't stand it anymore!" Bill said, tired and exasperated.

"Do you want me to come get you?" I asked. It was Friday night which usually meant taking it easy and watching TV at my house.

"I just want to get out of here! Every day they're stopping by or calling me. Ruby. My parents. My brothers. The preachers. Sometimes I don't answer the phone. Now it's the weekend. They'll all be stopping by for sure. On the way to church. On the way home from church. They won't leave me alone!"

He paused for a moment before continuing, "Freddie Yoder stopped by the other day with Eli Yoder."

Freddie was a preacher in Bill's church district, and Eli was the deacon. While they share the same last name, a very common Amish name, they are not related.

"What did they want?"

"I saw them coming. I figured the bishop would be sending them to see me sooner or later." Eli Byer was the bishop of Middle church.

"Harley was already here," Bill continued. Harley was one of Bill's Bachelor Buddies, "We were just sitting at the table talking, but I didn't want Harley to get in trouble for being over visiting me, so I stepped outside and asked what they wanted. They said they wanted to talk to me. I told them that I didn't have anything to say. They gave me this look, like they couldn't believe that I was talking to them that way.

"Then the deacon says that he's counting on me to be in church next week, to put things right. He said again that they wanted to talk to me and suggested we go in the house. I told them that it was my house and I say who comes in!

"I don't think he expected that, and then he sort of stuttered, saying 'well...I...I guess that is your right.' I didn't want them to come in and lecture me, but I really didn't want Harley to get into trouble. When they were leaving, the deacon yelled, 'Hope to see you in church!'

"I can't believe them. I've left! Why would they think I would want to come to church? They just want me to come so they can put me in the ban!"

"What?"

"Yeah. That's how they think they can get me back. 'Come back so you can make things right.' It's a trick they use. How the hell does that make sense?"

He was asking the wrong person if he thought I would know the answer. My own religious experience with Catholicism hadn't gone much better.

One of my more memorable Catholic episodes happened about the time I started catechism. I entered the church, swinging my yet unblessed rosary wildly back and forth, and then I intentionally let it splash into the holy water.

"There! Now it's been blessed," I announced loudly.

Ushers rushed forward, scrambling to surround the large, main basin while keeping everyone back until it could be refilled with uncontaminated holy water.

I had a lot of questions during catechism and got a lot of dirty looks, but it was after I repeatedly pointed out things that didn't make sense that the nun kicked me out. No one ever seemed to have an answer for the questions I raised, such as if we're not supposed to have any idols, why do we have all those statues of people around the church? I seemed to have a knack for pointing out things and asking questions that I wasn't supposed to ask and would get really frustrated when no one could give me an answer. It all seemed so phony and contrived.

But the worst was the time I washed my face in the holy water. That got me run out of the church by the priest. I'll never forget him. His face had turned the color of an eggplant while he yelled at me to get out and to never come back. I've often wondered if being kicked out of church by the priest carries some sort of "doomed to hell for all eternity" type of punishment.

The thing is, I'm actually a very spiritual person. Put me down at the Mecan, sitting on my special fishing rock that I swear has a groove worn into it over the years from my butt, hearing the wind rustling the reeds, and the geese honking as they glide across the water. That's where I feel connected to something bigger and more magnificent.

Put me in a small, stuffy room with a cranky old woman who looks at me as if I'm Linda Blair in the *Exorcist,* and it makes me mad. I don't intend to be disrespectful, but it's pretty obvious that I'm not a "lamb of God" type. Make me mad, and you've got a wildcat on your hands. I have never run from a fight, whether it's physical or verbal.

I have never cared what people thought of me and have never felt as if I needed to play nice. You may not like what I say, but at least you will never doubt my honesty. Unfortunately, honesty doesn't seem to be a quality that is welcome in all faiths.

There was no way I could tell Bill to go back to church so he could be banned. What the hell should he be put in the ban for, anyway?

In the week that he was out, Bill hadn't done anything that he wasn't doing before he left, including buying some jeans. The only significant difference in his new life was that he had electricity again. He was still the same person, only now he could watch his westerns at home instead of the logging camper.

"I'd just like to get away for a while, somewhere that they can't find me."

I could hear the exhaustion in Bill's voice, "You know that you're welcome to come stay here...but if you don't want to do that, why don't you go to a motel? They wouldn't be able to find you there, especially if we put the room in my name."

There was a pause and then Bill said, "Yeah, let's do that," and he sounded more like his usual self again.

The next morning after chores, I picked him up and drove him to Wautoma to the Super 8, one of only a handful of motels in town. Wautoma has a population of about two thousand people and is the county seat for Waushara County. It's a small town but covers all the basics, from groceries to cars. But for major shopping trips, such as a trip to Wal-Mart and for medical care, most of the people in our area run up to Stevens Point.

Since Bill didn't have a driver's license, I had to sign for the room.

He hadn't brought a bag, so I asked, "Do you need anything? Do you want me to take you anywhere before I go?"

"No, that's okay. I can walk wherever I need to go."

With a grocery store and several restaurants all within a short walking distance, I knew that he could manage.

"Okay...well, call me if you need anything."

It was strange leaving him there. He seemed so out of place...and out of sorts, but I hoped that it would give him a break from all the pressure everyone was putting on him. Even the strongest branch will snap if enough force is applied to it. He had a lot of pressure on him, and I couldn't help but feel that the next time I saw him, Bill would be Amish again.

Ever since Bill left, I had been trying to think of ways that I could help. The best idea that came to me was to track down his sister. Rachel left the Amish several years before I had gotten connected with the community, so I never heard much about her. Even Bill had only mentioned her a few times.

Finding Rachel became my mission. I hoped she would be able to give him the support he needed since she knew what it took to make it in the outside world. But I was also curious about her, ever since Bill had mentioned that she was "some strange religion". What religion would the Amish considered strange, I often wondered. Could there possibly be anything stranger than the Amish?

Rachel had moved to Missouri and fallen in love with an English man, a non-Amish, which was bad enough but what was even worse, according to her family, was that the man was divorced. In the eyes of her community, Rachel committed adultery because the Amish do not permit divorce, or approve it, for anyone.

Knowing her married name and hoping that she still lived in Missouri, a very promising lead turned up in an Internet search almost immediately. I dialed the phone number. *Let this be her*, I thought, hoping that I had found her on the first try. After only a couple rings, an answering machine picked up and feeling a bit deflated but not defeated, I left a message. I may have tried another time as well. No one ever got back to me, but I wasn't going to give up that easily.

One day I dialed the number again.

"Hello?" a male voice answered.

I told him my name and that I was trying to find the sister of William Herschberger.

"Rachel!" he called out to someone, "it's that woman in Wisconsin again!"

Between the surprise of finally reaching a human and the man calling for someone named Rachel, I felt a rush of excitement.

"Hello?" a tentative female voice came on the line.

"Hi, I'm a friend of your brother, William. He's left the Amish, and I thought it might be good for him to get in touch with you."

"He left?" Rachel was clearly shocked at the news. "William left? What about Ruby and the baby?"

"Ruby took Frieda and has moved back home with her parents."

"I can't believe my little brother left. How's he doing?"

Once Rachel understood the circumstances for my call, her initial hesitancy faded, and we chatted easily. I explained to her how Bill and I had become co-workers and friends and everything that had taken place over the last several days. The news that her brother left, especially since he was a church member with a family, took some time to sink in. Her sisterly concern was touching, and I knew that it had been the right thing, for both their sakes, to find her.

We chatted comfortably for a long time, and I didn't want to spoil it, but there was one question that had been nagging me for too long. I had to ask.

"I've been wondering, Rachel, what religion are you now?"

"I'm a Christian."

I couldn't help it, I burst out laughing and quickly had to explain, "Your brother would only say that you were some *strange religion*."

"Well, they would think that, wouldn't they?" Rachel said, sharing my laughter.

As we were saying good-bye, Rachel said something that I'll never forget.

"Watch your back, Karrie."

"What do you mean?" I asked, taken by surprise at her serious tone.

"Be careful. You're helping William, and believe me...I know what I'm talking about. Just watch your back."

Eleven

As charcoal to embers and as wood to fire,
so is a quarrelsome man for kindling strife.
The words of a gossip are like choice morsels;
they go down to a man's inmost parts.
Like a coating of glaze over earthenware
are fervent lips with an evil heart.
Proverbs 26: 21-23, *The Holy Bible*, NIV

Bill

It seemed like a good idea.

Check into a motel for a few days. No one but Karrie will know where I am. No one stopping by. No one trying to get me to go back. Only peace and quiet. Watch cable television. Walk to the store or restaurant. Take it easy. It should have been perfect.

I hated it.

Barely twenty-four hours after Karrie dropped me at the motel, I had enough. I tried watching TV. So many channels, but still nothing to watch. At home, there were all of my John Wayne movies. I walked to the grocery store for some snacks. Took a couple naps. Went to bed early. But I felt trapped. I couldn't take it anymore.

"Hey Karrie, can you come get me?"

"Sure. I can be there in about an hour, if that's okay. We're at Mom's right now and just about to have lunch. I'll come by and get you on our way home."

The next morning, I was already outside waiting when Karrie pulled in the driveway to get me for work. After she had dropped me off the previous day, I was relieved to be home. Going to the motel just didn't work out as I thought it would. While I avoided any unwelcome and unwanted visitors, I felt even more isolated and alone while I was there.

The ride to work was unusually quiet. David didn't say much and barely responded to any of Karrie's teasing. It was odd and when we got to the logging site, we found out why.

"The preachers took me aside yesterday before church," David said as soon as we got settled into the camper for our pre-work smoke. "They wanted to remind me that it's against the *Ordnung* to work with English women."

"What the hell? Since when?" Karrie asked, taking the words right out of my mouth.

"I don't know. I guess since the last church. It wasn't a rule before."

"They're doing this because of me…because I'm helping Bill." It wasn't a question. By now Karrie knew the way things worked with the Amish.

"Of course it is," I agreed. "This is the type of bullshit they pull all the time! Out of the blue, they'll tell you that you're breaking a rule, except it wasn't a rule before. Whenever something comes up that they don't like, they just decide it's against the *Ordnung*. They can't change the *Ordnung* anytime they want! That can only be done at Council church."

Every fall there is a special church service called Council church. It begins at nine o'clock and lasts until about two in the afternoon for non-members and about an hour later for members. During the members-only time, the preacher will read the *Ordnung.* Not the whole thing…just parts of it. If anyone wants to have something added or changed in the *Ordnung*, this is when it has to be done. It is the only time it can be done. When all church members are there to approve it.

The other purpose of Council church is to get church members ready for fall Communion church. Amish receive communion only twice a year, in the spring and fall. In order to get spiritually clean and ready to receive communion at Communion church, members are encouraged to confess any sins they haven't already confessed.

The Amish believe in public confession. Standing before all of the other church members is required. There is no private confession booth with just a priest listening to you. That isn't enough for the Amish. Every church member, your family, your friends, your neighbors, *everyone* gets to hear that you were smoking or drinking or masturbating. Or worse. Everyone knows your sin.

But Council church isn't the only time for public confession. Church members make confessions whenever it's necessary, especially if they've been caught doing something. If it's a regular church Sunday, the non-members will be excused at the end of the service, and all the members will stay to hear the confession. If someone has done something considered a major sin, that person may not be there at church that day. He may already be in the ban. In that case, the bishop will tell the members who sinned, and what the sin was.

It was hard to believe that the church leaders would tell David that he was doing something against the *Ordnung* that he knew wasn't a rule. How could they do that? How could they lie? But I knew it was exactly the type of thing they would do. They were always treating us as if we are children who can't be trusted. They would do whatever it took to protect us from ourselves and from the outside world.

My body felt hot with anger. Then I reminded myself that their rules didn't apply to me anymore.

"I'm so glad that I'm out," I said, glancing at the others. David continued to stare out the steamy window while Karrie nodded with a look that said, *damn straight!*

At our mid-afternoon break, we agreed to quit work early. None of us had been in a very good mood since David told us about the new rule. This change affected all of us. Whether or not we were Amish. It wasn't part of the *Ordnung* yet, but we all knew that it wouldn't be long. There was no doubt about that.

Once I was put in the ban, David and Ferman wouldn't be able to work directly with me. I knew that. I accepted it when I left. But I thought Karrie could still be their driver and could continue to work with them doing the hand-cutting. I might not be able to work at the same site with them, but my crew would be the same. I hoped that things would only have to change a little.

But that would not be permitted. The Amish would soon see to that. At the next Council church, the rule would be added. There would be no working with English women. David and Ferman would be forbidden from working with Karrie. It was unfair to all of us. Especially Karrie.

We decided to go bowling. The way the three of us were feeling, those helpless pins didn't stand a chance! Karrie drove to my house first so I could change.

"I'll be right back," I told them as I got out. It had been one of the few times that I got the front passenger seat instead of David.

As I sat on the edge of the unmade bed to put on my shoes, someone spoke from the bedroom doorway.

"Hello, William."

It was Ruby.
Frieda was with her.

It took a second for me to realize that they were really standing there. My wife and daughter were back! I jumped up and rushed toward them. But before I could take both of them into my arms, Ruby held Frieda out toward me while she stepped back. I hugged my daughter tightly against my chest.

It had only been two weeks since I saw her, but she was bigger and heavier. What else had I missed?

"Are you home?" I asked. Maybe she finally had found out that we could still live together if she was Amish and I was English.

"We're just stopping by," Ruby said, her blue eyes as cool as her tone. "I need to ask you about something. I heard that you and Karrie spent a night at a motel."

"What? That's ridiculous. When?" I knew she wasn't talking about my overnight stay in Wautoma on Saturday. This was something else. This sounded like something that someone was cooking up.

"I don't know...before you left...someone called Karrie's room and said that you answered."

"Well, it's a lie. I never stayed at a motel with Karrie."

Ruby didn't answer, but her thin, pinched lips and narrowed eyes said plenty. How could she believe this nonsense?

"Someone's spreading rumors about me...they're trying to blame Karrie for my leaving, even if they have to make stuff up."

Ruby, of all people, should know better. I was never gone overnight! Why wasn't she defending me against lies? Instead she stood there, staring at me. Her expression that made it all too clear that it was very easy for her to believe the worst. Maybe she wanted it to be true.

"Who told you this crap? Who called the motel?" I couldn't believe she stood there. Glaring at me. As if I was lying. As if I sinned.

She hesitated before answering, "Willard. Willard told me that Karrie's boyfriend told him."

"Just tell me one night when I wasn't home with you? You can't. You know I was never gone. Never. I've been home every night since we've been married! This isn't only ridiculous, but impossible! How can you believe it?"

Ruby didn't answer any of my questions. Instead she said, "Dad brought me over. Do you want to talk to him?"

"No, I don't want to talk to him! I told you that I don't want to talk to anyone!"

Without another word, Ruby took Frieda from me and walked out of the room. I followed her down the hallway and stood at the kitchen door, watching as she stepped up into her father's buggy. After she settled in, her father slapped the reins.

I stood there.
I watched as my wife and daughter left me.
Again.

Twelve

Karrie

Breakfast dishes were piled impatiently next to the sink and too many things hadn't been crossed off my daily to-do list. Soon Kelsey and Clayton would be flying into the kitchen, the glass in the top half of the old, wooden door nearly shattering as they both try to be first to give me a full report of their day, unload several small trees worth of paper into my lap, and then squabble over who got the last of whatever snack had caught their eyes.

It was those last few moments of peace, so quiet that I could hear the raindrops tapping against the kitchen windows, sometimes in perfect rhythm to the melody coming from the radio, with the distant rumble of thunder adding to the bass.

Everything else could wait until I finished my cigarette.

Through the kitchen window's watery streaks, I saw some Amish kids coming up the road. A horse and cart had been going past my house with this same group of kids regularly and I guessed that they were going back and forth to school. Today the cart was nowhere to be seen. One child lead the horse with one of the smaller children riding bareback while the other two walked along behind. With one last inhale, I stubbed out the rest of my cigarette and went to the front door.

"Is everything okay?" I called to them, walking out into the yard.

Four pairs of eyes turned and stared at me as if I was a fox looking into their rabbit warren. A girl of about thirteen, the largest of them, called back, "Something happened to our cart. We're on our way home."

"Do you kids want a ride?"

There was a hesitation and a glancing around among themselves before the girl nodded. She handed the reins to the boy on horseback and said something I couldn't hear. He jabbed his heels into the horse's ribs and continued to the west toward home. The other three kids came into my yard and followed me to the car.

"What happened to your cart?" I asked while pulling out of the driveway.

"I don't know. It broke," the girl, sitting in the passenger seat next to me, answered very softly.

"Is that your house up here?" I turned onto Cottonville, toward what I thought of as the Buchanan farm, even though it had been some years since any Buchanans lived there. The surrounding acreage had been sold off first, several years earlier. Then the house became a rental, and I watched while the old stone and wood frame house quickly went downhill, shriveling up like the lush green canopy of leaves that turn brittle and brown after the first frost.

Then one day it was gone.

The house was completely leveled and in no time, a whole new house had been rebuilt in its place. It didn't seem possible...until I noticed the Amish buggies parked beside the barn.

"Yes, that's our farm," the girl answered.

Even though she only gave me brief answers, I wasn't deterred. I kept right on asking and in the short time that it took me to run them home, I found out their names, ages, and what grade they were in. The oldest, Marietta, did most of the talking that day but in time, they would all open up to me and never seemed to tire of my teasing or making them giggle.

"Thank you so much for bringing them home," their mother, Lizzie Mae, said when I dropped them off that day. She's a slight woman with dishwater blonde hair, at least what could be seen under her cap and behind her big, dated glasses. "Would you be able to take them to school until we get the cart fixed?"

"Sure," I told her.

After the cart was fixed, Lizzie Mae asked me to keep driving because of the bad weather we were having. She would send baked or canned goods with the kids every now and again to compensate me. I appreciated the token payment, but I liked the kids and drove them to be neighborly. That's the way you do things when you live in the country.

That rainy day, when I gave those kids a ride for the first time, took place about the same time that I bought Rex from Amos and Verena. Not long after that, other Amish started to call me when they needed a ride.

And that was how it all began.

I went out one day to help some kids walking in the rain and became an Amish driver.

The distinctive clip-clop and clatter of a horse and buggy could be heard well before I saw it pull into the driveway behind us. Bill had gone into the house only a few moments earlier to change his clothes so we could go bowling.

"This is going to be interesting," I commented, looking into the rearview mirror at David who was sitting directly behind me.

We watched as Ruby went into the house carrying Frieda. She never looked our direction or acknowledged that we were there. In the side mirror, I saw Ruby's father, Ervin Miller, step down from the buggy as well, but instead of going into the house, he came toward the van.

"What the hell does he want?" David muttered, taking the cigarette from his lips. I wondered the same thing.

Ervin is a preacher for East church, so it wasn't hard to imagine what was on his mind. Especially considering the new rule David had told us about earlier.

David opened the van door and the two of them greeted each other in their German dialect.

Germish.

That's what I call it. Not only was it a simple play on their German-Amish language, but I also liked the negative connotation of germs and disease.

Too many times I carted them around while they spoke in their private language to each other. Too many times I sat stewing and getting fed up with their rude behavior. One day I had enough and posted signs in both of my vehicles requesting that they speak English.

Two words: *Speak English.*

That was all I needed to write on my sign, but in Germish. I asked one and then another and then another, but no one could tell me how to spell my message. How could they not know how to spell such a simple phrase? At first I thought it was odd, but then it became seriously troubling.

This was the education the Amish received?

The problem, I would learn, is that Amish children don't learn English until they are six years old and start school. Until that time they speak only Germish. Once they start school, they are taught German, what would be considered proper German, but only on Fridays. Many of them never learn to read and write proper German and while they can all speak Germish, very few of them know how to write it. But eventually someone was able to help me with my sign.

At first I didn't know what David and Ervin were saying. I didn't really care. I knew David would fill me in later...if there was anything worth sharing. But then David said something that I had no trouble understanding at all.

"Well, then, I guess you can tell my parents that I'm not coming home."

Ervin responded in Germish, but David cut him off, "I'm not going home. So if you don't tell them, then I guess they won't know."

I saw a puff of smoke, and David shut the van door.

"That's something that I've always wanted to do."

"What's that?" I asked, watching Ruby's father trudge back to his buggy.

"Blow smoke in a preacher's face."

"Give me a haircut, Karrie," David said when we got back to my house later. He was desperate for a trim, so I got out my scissors and had him sit down.

The Amish have strict rules on hair for both males and females. Girls can't ever cut their hair and while they're young, they wear it tightly braided. When they are older, it is pulled into a very tight and secure bun. Hair must never be worn loose. Women are not permitted to shave their underarms or legs, pluck their eyebrows or even a stray whisker from their chin. There is a joke that some Amish women have better beards than the men.

All Wautoma Community Amish males receive the same haircut as soon as it's necessary and for the rest of their lives. No matter how much or how little hair a fellow has, he gets a bowl cut. There is no crew cut or mullet or comb-over in the Amish world. The cut can vary slightly among communities, such as how much of the ears are allowed to show, and those guidelines are set in their *Ordnung*.

I've given a lot of haircuts over the years. My son doesn't trust anyone else and before long, a lot of his friends started coming to me as well. But even before I had a son, there had been countless others...of the four-legged variety. Grooming dogs exposed to me to a wide range of breeds, with all types of hair, and each with its own specific grooming requirements.

"How do you want it cut?" I asked, running my fingers through David's thick, curly hair. Poodle hair. Unruly and out-grown poodle hair. Poor David, he really needed a trim.

"I don't care...just cut it shorter so there aren't so many damn curls."

My scissors snipped away, and his dark locks quickly littered my kitchen floor.

When I finished, David rushed to the bathroom to look at himself in the mirror. He let out a whoop of pleasure that made me smile as well. It's hard to imagine that such a simple thing could make someone so happy, but then we take haircuts for granted in our world.

David got the trim he wanted and needed, but there was more to his haircut. His haircut was an act of rebellion. It was his own declaration of independence.

The memory of those shy Amish kids that I gave a ride home that rainy day came back to me again the next morning as I drove the three of us to work. Those kids were the main reason that I became an Amish driver. And here I was, still driving around the Amish.

A lot had changed, though. Technically my current passengers weren't Amish, since they had both left, and they weren't children. But even so, Bill and David seemed to need my help as much or even more. Somehow I went from helping some kids get home in a storm to providing a safe-house for Amish refugees.

Truth be told, I had been giving shelter to the Amish for some time, it just wasn't initially for people.

After I got to know many of the Amish in the Wautoma Community, some of the young folks asked if they could hide their contraband in my barn. Mainly it was televisions, VCRs, and radios. There was even one teenager who called and wanted me to provide a pick-up service as well!

"Karrie, I had to hide my TV. Can you go get it?"

"You bet. Where is it?"

"It's in the ditch," he said relieved and told me how to find it.

I just laughed...all the way there and all the way home. I've always been a rebel, especially against people or things that I didn't respect. To me, it's part of the teenage experience to act out and break the rules, whether it's an Amish teen with a forbidden radio or some of the stuff I did at that age.

I'll never forget the time I showed up at the roller-skating rink in Plainfield, about fifteen miles from my home. My friend had called earlier asking me to meet her. My parents were gone for the night, but I didn't let that stop me.

"How did you get here?" My friend asked a little later, looking up at me from the seat where she was lacing up the dirty, white rental skates.

I didn't say anything. I just held out my mom's key chain and let it swing meaningfully from my finger.

I was twelve years old.

Some Amish communities allow their youth to have *rumspringa*, a time when the rules are relaxed for a bit. In some communities, the youth might be allowed to dress English or own electronic equipment.

There is no *rumspringa* in the Wautoma Community, at least not in that sense. At sixteen and a half, the youth are allowed to begin dating. That's it. That's their *rumspringa*. So when a teen needed me to get his TV, or to hide his radio, why shouldn't I help them have a little fun? Why not help them have a little freedom. What was it hurting?

Allowing teenagers to hide their contraband on my property would probably have been overlooked within the community as long as I was still serving a purpose, particularly as a driver. Helping and sheltering Bill and

David was completely different. It could not be overlooked. There would be consequences. There would most definitely be consequences.

My relationships with many in the Wautoma Community would be forever damaged. I knew that. Many relationships would be completely severed. That was was the price I would pay for helping my friends.

It was regrettable, but unavoidable. I accepted that.

But what I didn't know, and what I didn't expect, was how malicious and violent the so-called peaceful people could be. I wasn't prepared. Not even with the warning Rachel gave me.

Thirteen

Karrie

Wednesday, February 19, began just the same as many other days. There was the mad rush of morning: making breakfasts, packing lunches, and getting Kelsey and Clayton off to school. Then there was a brief lull before I drove Bill out to the work-site and left him there.

Alone.

The hand-cutting at the site was complete, so my plans for the day were to run some errands, do some household chores, and to make a birthday cake for my daughter. Bill had to finish up the skidding before we would be ready to move on to the next job. Typically David would have also been with Bill doing the skidding, but he wouldn't be working with us anymore.

David had gone back to the Amish the night before.

From the moment the previous week when David left the Amish, I never thought that he would stay out...that he would remain English. He had taken great pleasure in blowing smoke in a preacher's face and getting a haircut, but David's leaving didn't seem to be about making a new life. His leaving seemed to be about protest, specifically protest something... something he knew was not in the *Ordnung*.

Both David and Bill stayed at my house after David left. One day during the week, Bill called his sister Rachel and talked to her for the first time in nearly twelve years. He seemed to appreciate that I had tracked her down, although he never said anything about it.

Bill had another milestone that week. On Wednesday I took him to Wautoma to take his written driver's license exam. He passed and could now legally drive, as long as he had a licensed adult in the vehicle with him. He had to wait at least two weeks before he could take the driving exam and if he passed, he would get his permanent license.

Just as with David's haircut, getting a driver's license is another declaration of independence for someone leaving the Amish, but it is one that can be much more difficult. Many Amish are in such a hurry to leave that they don't remember to take their birth certificate or Social Security card. Even though the Amish don't participate in Social Security, many of them have a card.

Contrary to what some people believe, Amish pay taxes. Sales tax, property tax, federal and state taxes. But they don't pay into Social Security. Social Security was implemented as social insurance. The Amish don't believe in insurance in any form. They believe that it is the responsibility of the family and the community to care for one another, not the responsibility of the government. Since they don't intend to ever collect Social Security and because it goes against their faith, they and a few other religious groups were exempted in 1965, and it became law.

Bill was lucky because he had his birth certificate and in no time, his brand new learner's permit was tucked neatly inside his wallet. As soon as we got out of town, I pulled over.

"You drive," I told him and switched places with him.

It was strange being a passenger in my own car. But I reminded myself that Kelsey would be turning fifteen in another year and then she would be old enough to get her permit. And just a year after that, it would be Clayton's turn. This was only the beginning for me. With a sigh of resignation, I settled myself mentally and physically into the passenger seat.

David was curious about Bill starting to drive, but he never said anything about getting his own learner's permit. The first Sunday afternoon after he left, David's sister, Ruby Hochstetler, stopped by my house to invite him to supper on Tuesday.

"If you go over there, David, you know you'll go back," I warned him.

He shrugged but didn't look at me, "It's okay, I want to go."

It wasn't that I didn't want David to go back to the Amish. It was his life and his choice. As his friend, I wanted to make sure that he knew what he was getting himself into by going to his sister's for supper. I didn't want him doing anything that he didn't want to because of family pressure. If there was anything that I was certain of, it was that there would be pressure.

When I pulled into his sister's driveway on Tuesday night, I told David, "Just call me when you want me to come get you, okay?"

"Okay," he said quickly, getting out of my car like a kid being dropped at a friend's house for a play-date and ready to be rid of his mother. I watched as he walked to the house. He was wearing his English clothes, but it was so obvious; underneath, he was still Amish.

From my kitchen, sitting at the red and chrome retro 1950s table, I can see everything. My kitchen is laid out in an "L" with the dishwasher, sink, stove, cabinets, and refrigerator all packed galley-style into the small, horizontal part while the rest of the room is open space, filled only with the table and various chairs along the outer wall, and a large antique wood cook stove anchoring the upper, inside corner. Next to the antique stove, on one side, is a wood and glassed built-in hutch that is filled with an array of dishes and untold treasures, such as the elaborate clay haunted house I made back in grade school.

Behind the stove in the stained-wood wainscoting, is an angled door to a small storage area under the stairs. Anyone coming down the stairs is deposited onto the upper edge of kitchen, in an area that also serves as the passageway into the living room. The entire front half of the house is one large living area, with the television in the furthest corner from the kitchen. Continuing clock-wise from the TV area, back toward the kitchen, is a room that typically would serve as a dining room, but I use it as an office. The doorway to the downstairs bathroom is in the office. There are no hallways on the main floor, one room simply leads into the next and much to the delight of children and pets, it is possible to run a circle around the entire ground floor.

Next to the kitchen table, there are two tall, wide-set windows that offer an expansive view of the outside world. I can see most of the driveway running along that side of the house, and across the road to where the earth drops away, down to the Mecan River. Looking out toward the east, I have advance notice of anyone coming from that direction before they even turn into my driveway. Glancing through the office doorway to the west, I can see out the large windows on that side of the house and spot anyone coming from that direction.

The front door is in the living room, but no one visiting would ever use it. Everyone comes to the kitchen door since the driveway circles around the back of the house. After climbing a couple steps and crossing the wooden deck, there are two doors into the kitchen with the first opening into the mudroom. Both kitchen doors are glassed on the upper half, so visitors are instantly visible.

I can see everything from my kitchen table. As any skilled hunter, I know about sight lines and naturally position my chair for the best possible view. The world inside and out can easily be monitored from my kitchen. It is the heart of my home, the circulatory system that pumps everyone in and out and all around.

While tapping the ash from my cigarette, I heard a horse and buggy coming down the road, then the sound changed as it left the road and turned into my gravel driveway.

It was David.

He's gone back.

I knew it in that instant.

A few moments later, footsteps clomped across the porch. Our eyes met just as he began to open the inner kitchen door.

"They got you to come back," I said with certainty, and he looked sheepishly down at the narrow, well-worn, wooden planks of my kitchen floor. "As long as it's what you want, David…" I said quickly, regretting any harshness or disapproval he might have heard in my words.

"Yeah…I've gone back. I think I made my point…that they can't just change things. That's not right…and it sounds like they've backed off on that now."

The Amish were never really in any danger of losing David. He's very close to his family. His leaving was meant to make a statement. David had complained about certain things, just as Bill and others had. But unlike Bill, it was never with the same vehemence or frustration. David's complaints seemed to be the typical venting that everyone does from time to time.

In the short time that he stayed with me, David never made plans to stay English. He was intrigued with the process that Bill was going through, but David never talked about getting a driver's license. The most drastic thing David did was to have me cut his hair, and he would suffer that for some time after he returned. He was put in the ban until his hair grew out, having to miss at least one wedding…a major event for the Amish.

After David returned, we worked out a compromise of sorts for work. David and some other Amish guys would work a site doing the hand-cutting, using a different driver to get to and from work, and then Bill would go skid after they finished. I continued to work with Bill, driving and doing whatever else needed to be done at the site. Technically, David still worked on Bill's crew, but we no longer worked *together*.

The Amish had prevailed.

After dropping Bill at the site that morning, the first time without David, I headed toward Wautoma to get groceries and everything I needed to make Kelsey's birthday cake. I hadn't gone but a few miles when my cell phone rang.

It was Bill.

"Everything okay? Did the skidder break down?" I asked, mentally crossing my fingers. I had too much to do today without dealing with that machine again.

"No, it's fine," he said. The machine might be fine, but I could tell that Bill wasn't. It was too quiet out at the site and he wanted to talk to someone, especially now that David was Amish again.

"I'm at the grocery store, anything you need?" I asked.

"No, but if you get a chance, can you stop by my house and get my mail?"

"Sure," I replied and had no idea that such a simple act would drastically alter the rest of the plans that I had for that day.

Fourteen

Karrie

"Hey, Bill, it looks like you got a letter from your dad."

The return address on one of the letters immediately caught my eye when I'd pulled everything from Bill's mailbox. Everything else had been tossed on the table when I walked through the kitchen to the office.

"Do you want me to open it?"

"Sure, go ahead," he mumbled without any enthusiasm. After all the visits and calls that had already come, we both knew that the letter would just be more of the same. But that didn't stop me from being curious. I wanted to see for myself what the crotchety old goat had to say for himself.

As I ripped open the envelope, the image of Chris Herschberger came into my mind. I could still see exactly the way he looked in my rearview mirror the first time we met. He sat there, directly behind me, with his arms crossed over his chest, his eyes vengefully glaring back at me, and a scowl so severe that I was certain that his mouth might slide right off his face and onto his chest.

Ole Chris and I did not hit it off from day one.

About the time Jerry asked me to become Bill's driver, I was hired to drive Bill's parents, his brothers Toby, Monroe, Adlai, and the wives, as well as some of the kids, to a funeral in Bonduel, a town up near Green Bay. I don't remember exactly when it was, but it was after I had been driving the Amish long enough to have become fed up with their rude behavior speaking Germish.

My "Schwetz English!" sign hung prominently from the passenger visor. No one ever seemed bothered by my simple request. Everyone spoke English in my vehicles without any complaint. That is, until the day Chris Herschberger got in my van.

My first stop was at Toby and Millie's farm. Toby got in front and directed me to the other two or three stops to pick up the rest of the family. We hadn't been on the road very long when I heard someone speaking Germish behind me. I looked in the rearview mirror and dark eyes locked with mine.

Without breaking eye contact, I purposefully pointed to the sign. Chris' eyes followed my finger, and I watched as those eyes narrowed and the corners of his lips sunk so low they seemed to disappear into his beard. He pushed back into his seat and crossed his arms over his chest. That was how he stayed for the rest of the trip, two hours each direction, like a pouting toddler. He spoke very little and only in response to direct questions, no matter how many ways the others tried to draw him out. The rare instance when he did speak, it was with such extreme exasperation, as if speaking English was a great burden for him.

The only time he quit sulking was when I lit my cigarette. Smoking is a terrible addiction that I have tried to quit. If I light a cigarette in a car, I always crack the window in consideration of others. That day, before I even got the chance, Bill's dad reacted with such an exaggerated coughing fit that if it hadn't already pissed me off, I would have burst out laughing. It was obvious that he was only being spiteful because of my "Speak English" rule.

Fine by me, I thought, if that's the way you want it! I put my hand back on the steering wheel without cracking the window, and chain-smoked the entire trip.

That first meeting would forever set the tone of my relationship with Chris Herschberger. Of course, he had his mind made up about me even before he was forbidden from speaking Germish in my van. He judged me because of the way I dressed or for being divorced. There were plenty of things about me that his Amish morality would have found wicked. Or he may have made up his mind the time he happened to be in the car when I chewed out Lester, another Amish driver.

Back when I was driving Lizzie Mae's kids, we used to get to school early so we could play volleyball. One day Lester pulled into the school just ahead of me with his carload of kids. I watched in disbelief as he swerved his car intentionally so he would run over a volleyball that had been left lying in the driveway.

"Sorry kids, I guess you'll need a new ball," I told them as they got out, hating to see their sad faces.

It was a shitty thing for Lester to do, but I didn't think much about it until it got back to me that he was telling folks that I was the one who ran over that ball.

There was no way I was going to stand for it. No way in hell.

The next time I saw Lester, which happened to be again at the school when we were both dropping off kids, I stormed over to his car.

"You son of a bitch! Who the hell do you think you are telling lies about me? I saw you run over that volleyball the other day! Now you're saying that I did it?"

"I was only kidding," he grumbled.

"Like hell you were!" I snapped at him and continued to tear into him with a wide variety of cuss words, although the one beginning with 'f' is always a favorite of mine. At some point I realized that there were two older Amish men sitting in the back seat and one of them, I found out later, was Chris.

Lester admitted that he lied and that he ran over the ball, but I was the one who bought the kids a new volleyball set. I knew Lester would never get around to it, but I'm sure none of that swayed Chris Herschberger's opinion of me. He judged me before we ever met.

All of those things paled, however, once I became the Englishwoman who helped his son leave.

Reaching into the envelope, I pulled out a single sheet of paper with writing on one side only, unfolded it, and began to read to Bill:

William you Shall read this message and take it to heart.
Feb. 17-03
Dear Son,
Greetings in Jesus Name.
I'll try to make this message short.
From what David Hochstetlers say you and David Wm. are there or were anyhow with Kerry on Sunday.
Well as we all know humane natur and lust is probaly taking it's course.
All I want to warn you if a Child is conceived someone has to pay support. Yes I know of birth control but we also know of several cases just like this where this is a way to trap you poor guys.
Dan A Miller was a boy doing pretty much like this and did wind up with child support and of course She left Him and He came home crying! poor boy! Then later Cancer set in and the poor Man died like that.
several years ago one done this but even turning around now He still has I think it's 3 or 4 to support outside of his own Family. Yes if He is truly repented am sure it can be forgiven, but this still saps Him.
as can be and has been said it don't sound very nice (but they'd better enjoy it if they think that's what it is) because it don't last long the grave is not far off for any of us compared to eternity.
Out of Love,
Dad and Mom
We are praying and crying for you!

Rarely, very rarely, am I at a loss for words. I can usually muster some type of retort, even if it's only a "fuck you" or giving someone the middle-finger salute. After I finished reading the letter, there was a long pause when there were no words, only great, towering black storm clouds of pure emotion rising up inside of me.

When the ability to form words finally returned, I opened my mouth, and it was as if the gates of profanity hell had been ripped off their hinges. The words came, boiling up from my core, spewing out of me like magnificent eruptions of searing lava.

The letter had offended me in so many ways, but the worst was having Bill's father insinuate that not only was I supposedly sleeping with both Bill and David, but that I was going to trap them by getting pregnant! Un-fucking-believable!

"That's it. I'm going over there," I stated after the inferno of obscenities had eventually subsided. "Who the hell is he to spout shit like this! I'm going to pay Mr. Herschberger a little visit. We're going to have a nice long chat!"

"Be careful," Bill warned. He didn't seem surprised or even upset, but then I was livid enough for both of us, with plenty of pissed-off left over.

After Bill and I hung up, I called his sister Rachel. As I re-read the letter to her, I noticed other things in it that flamed my simmering anger back to a boil, particularly the tragic morality tale of the "poor boy" Dan Miller, who was "doing pretty much like this."

"So this 'poor Dan' returns home, crying after being dumped by an Englishwoman he obviously had a kid or two with, which saddled him with child support payments, and then he got cancer and died. What? Like he wouldn't have got cancer if he hadn't left the Amish? Can you believe it?" I asked her, "It seems like your dad is wishing all that bad shit will happen to your brother if he doesn't go back!"

"In Dad's mind, William...sorry...Bill as he likes to be called now...is going to hell if he doesn't go back...and *nothing* is worse than that. Dad will say whatever it takes to get him back."

"Well, I'm going to go over and have a little talk with your dad. He can't write shit like this and not expect me to have something to say about it!"

"Don't go over there, Karrie!"

"I'm going! I'm not afraid of him."

"You're really going to go?"

"Damn right, I am!" I told her, "Your father doesn't scare me."

"You've got more guts than anyone I know if you go over there."

"Hell yes, I'm going! I'm going right now, I'll call you back."

"Be careful!" Rachel warned me once again. In her voice was both the disbelief and awe that someone was finally going to stand up to her father.

When I got to the Herschberger farm, Bill's brothers, Adlai and Monroe, were at the back of the driveway working on some of their machinery.

"Is your dad here?" I asked, slamming the car door as if it were an exclamation point. My question carried with it all the anger that was coiling up inside me, like a rattlesnake getting ready to strike. If they knew what was good for them, they would find their father in a hurry and stay out of my way.

"No, he's not. What do you want with him?" Adlai asked.

"I want to talk to him about this letter he wrote Bill," I waved the letter that was clutched in my hand. I brought it along intentionally since I didn't want Chris to suddenly develop a typical case of Amish amnesia and forget the vile crap that he had written. "He needs to knock off the libel and slander. I'll sue his fucking ass!"

"He's not here, he'll be back about eight o'clock tonight. I'm sure he'll see you then," Adlai told me calmly.

"Dad's just worried about William," Monroe spoke up with an attitude. He may not have read the letter, but there was no doubt that they all knew what was in it.

"And that makes it okay for him to accuse me of sleeping with two guys and trying trap them by getting pregnant? I thought you were such good Christians! That sure as hell doesn't sound like a very Christian thing to say about someone!"

"We don't know what trouble William might be getting into since he left…" Monroe said as he walked toward me, leading with his chest, in some type of primeval show of aggression.

"Maybe he's not getting into any trouble at all! Maybe he's happy! Maybe for the first time in his life, he's happy!"

"You think you know William better than anyone, huh?" Monroe had come to within an arm's length of me, his cheeks flushed red to match his hair.

"I do know Bill better than any of you, since I'm the only one who's ever listened to him…really listened to him!" I wasn't about to back down. If he got his ugly face any closer to mine, I was going to deck him.

But Adlai, always the peace-keeper, stepped in before anything could happen, "Dad should be home by eight, if you want, you can come back then."

I turned and got back in my car, angrier than when I first got there. How convenient that Chris wasn't around to see me. Now he would have plenty of time to prepare for my next visit. Or maybe they didn't think I was brave enough to come back again later. They didn't know me very well if they thought there was a chance in hell of that! I would see Chris Herschberger and tell him exactly what I thought of him and his lies.

It was slightly after eight o'clock when I went back and immediately spotted Chris Herschberger out in his workshop. While there was no question that he knew I was there, he made no move to come out or even to greet me. He had several hours to prepare for my return visit, thanks to his sons. A decent person would have at least acknowledged me, but not Chris. He kept puttering around, pretending that I wasn't there, until I spoke.

"I want to talk to you about this letter you sent Bill."

"That is a letter sent to William, not you," he answered calmly, still not looking at me or even in my direction.

"Bill told me that I could read it, and since you say all kinds of shit about me, I'm glad I did! Who the hell do you think you are? What gives you the right to spout shit like this?"

"I'm a father who's worried about my son."

"That's no reason for you to say what you did about me! You'd better knock it off!"

"It's a sure way to hell, the way William is going."

He had an answer for everything, and it all sounded so lofty and innocent, but why wouldn't he have answers? There had been plenty of time for him to come up with perfect responses.

"Well, it will be a cold day in hell before you can get up on a pedestal and accuse me of sleeping with two Amish guys! Where do you get off saying that I'm trying to get pregnant to trap them? That's called libel and slander. I could sue your fucking ass!"

"I'm protecting my son. It might be true, for all I know. You're taking my son to hell."

"I'm not taking your son anywhere and YOU CANNOT DO THIS SHIT!" I screamed and my hands itched to pick up something and smack him with it until I got some sense through that granite skull.

"I've lost my boy!" a new voice came from behind me. It was Bill's mother, Fannie, sobbing in the doorway. Her plump figure somber in a navy dress with the ever-present white cap on her head, and the tears rolling down her cheeks. "I've lost my boy! You're a mother...how would you feel if you lost your child?"

Fannie always seemed to be a very kind person and under different circumstances, I might have felt sympathy for her. But not today. Today I had it with *all* of them. How dare they accuse me of such things! How dare they treat Bill this way!

"You haven't lost your son!" I snapped at her with disgust, "Your son is alive. You act like he's dead, but he's not! He's alive and happy. Isn't that what a mother should want for her son? So what if he isn't Amish? He's alive!"

I stomped back to my car and drove away as fast as possible, but the image of them stayed in my head, the way their smell used to linger in my car. Who the hell do they think they are? What gives them the right to say that I'm some conniving whore set out to trap wayward Amish boys? How could Bill's weepy mother prefer to think of him as dead than English? How could a mother forsake her child?

The worst part was that they really would have preferred it if Bill had died. If Bill had died, he would have been Amish. It was better to be a dead Amish than a living ex-Amish.

How could anyone think that way? It was unbelievable and inconceivable to me...especially for parents to think that about their own child! I would be worried and upset if my kids got involved in something that was harmful or illegal, but there is nothing...*not one thing*...that either of my kids could ever do that could make me prefer for them to be dead.

But that's not how the Amish think.

Bill's family would have been happier if he had died.

Damn them all and their twisted reasoning!

Fifteen

Therefore, rid yourselves of all malice and all deceit,
hypocrisy, envy, and slander of every kind.
Like newborn babies, crave pure spiritual milk,
so that by it you may grow up in your salvation,
But you are a chosen people, a royal priesthood,
a holy nation, a people belonging to God,
that you may declare the praises of him who called you
out of darkness into his wonderful light.
1 Peter 2: 1-2, & 9, *The Holy Bible*, NIV

Bill

I knew I had to leave the Amish.

I had known it for years.

For far too long, I felt like a salmon swimming upstream, always struggling against the current. There were times when I grew weary of the battle. Times when I didn't have the strength. Times when I gave in to the unyielding pressure.

How easy everything was when I stopped fighting. How much simpler it was to let myself be led. Just like the Sunday morning when I was seventeen and my mother came to wake me up.

"Do you think you'll talk to the bishop today about becoming a member, William?" she asked, standing in my bedroom doorway.

Everything was too loud and too bright. I had only gotten home from Johann's a few hours earlier.

I was hung-over.

It was church Sunday.

I hated church Sunday.

I hated wasting my time there. I hated sitting on the unpadded wooden bench for hours. It's hard to sit still that long, especially when you're a child. But you either learn to sit quietly or you get taken outside for a spanking. At least I was too old now for spanking. I had also learned how to sleep sitting up. It was a good skill to have. It was the only way I could get through the services.

Some people enjoy seeing their friends and family at church. They look forward to the socializing. Not me. Too many years there hadn't been any kids my age. Maybe some people got something from the sermons. I never did. Instead I tried my best to get out of going. If there was even the slightest chance, I gave it my best shot.

Sometimes I pretended to be sick. After everyone else left the house, I would sneak out and go fishing or hunting. I had to be careful not to get caught, but it was worth it. It never seemed right that I had to waste so many perfectly good hours doing something that I didn't want to do.

As soon as I became a Young Folk at sixteen and a half, I started to get pressured to become a church member. Every two weeks, my parents would ask me if I was planning to talk to the bishop about joining.

I would stall.
I would tell them that I was thinking about it.
I would say whatever I could to put them off just a little longer.

But then two weeks would pass, and they would ask again. Each time they pushed a little harder. I began to dread church Sunday even more. Eventually, I knew they would wear me down. It was only a matter of time.

"If you wait any longer it's going to be too late for you to join at fall Communion church," my mother said. Standing there in the doorway. Waiting for my response.

To become a church member, you are required to attend special lessons with the bishop. The lessons take place every other week during the first part of the church service. It would be nine meetings. Nine long meetings. Just me with the bishop, preachers, and deacon. None of the other Young Folks in the community were eligible to join. Only me.

If there had been someone else my age to become a member with me, maybe I wouldn't have kept stalling. Maybe I wouldn't have dreaded it so much.

Maybe. But I doubt it.

In my heart, I knew that I didn't want to become a church member.

I have always known.

"We've talked to the bishop already...your father and me...Do you think that you'll speak to him today?"

There I was, in a weakened condition. Tired and hung over.

My mother standing there. Waiting.

Holding the hot breakfast that she had just cooked for me.

Worrying about my soul.

The guilt was too much.

I was too weak to fight any longer.

"I guess," I mumbled.

Surrendering.
Letting myself be carried away by the ceaseless and invincible current.

On August 10th, 1996, I became a member of the Amish church. It was a day that I will never forget. It was also my eighteenth birthday.

That morning, while the congregation sang several hymns, I joined the deacon, preachers, and bishop for their meeting to discuss the service. The nine private lessons were behind me. Today I would become a member.

As the congregation finished the last hymn, I entered behind the bishop, the preachers, and the deacon. I took my place alone at the front of the church. Between the men's side and the women's side. On the bench reserved just for me.

One of the preachers said a prayer, and then the sermon began as it did every time someone was going to become a member.

First it was Genesis and the beginning of all things. The bishop hit all the main events of the Old Testament and then moved into the New. Sitting on that bench by myself meant that I couldn't sneak in the nap that I normally would. I had to keep shifting around to keep from falling asleep.

Amish, like some other Christian faiths, believe that baptism should not be given until the person is older. The Amish believe that someone should be old enough to understand the commitment he or she is making to the church and the community. Amish baptism marks membership in the church.

After the bishop got to the story of John the Baptist and the baptism of Jesus, the focus shifted to me. I was told that if I still wished to be baptized and to become a church member, that I should come forward and kneel. After I did so, the preachers, deacon, and bishop all gathered around me. The bishop said a prayer that seemed to go on forever. In his hands, the deacon held a small tin cup, about the size of a shot glass, filled with water.

My knees were aching by the time the prayer finally ended. I remained kneeling while the bishop asked me the three questions. All of this had been explained to me beforehand. All I had to do was answer yes each time.

"Do you promise to live your life according to Amish beliefs?" the bishop asked in our Amish-German language.

"Yes."

"Is it your desire to set yourself aside from this world, to seek peace with God and the church, and to ask the church to pray for you?"

"Yes."

"Do you believe that Jesus Christ is God's son?" It was the final question.

"Yes," I answered for the last time.

At that point, the bishop dipped his fingers into the tin cup that the deacon was holding for him and sprinkled three drops on top of my head.

One for the Father.
One for the Son.
One for the Holy Ghost.

There was only one thing left.
The Holy Kiss.

The Holy Kiss is from the Bible: *Greet ye one another with a holy kiss.* In the Wautoma Community, the Holy Kiss is given to all new members when they join and to all members at Communion church. It is just a quick peck on the cheek with the bishop giving the Holy Kiss to men, and the bishop's wife giving the Holy Kiss to women.

Many of the Elders will greet each other with a Holy Kiss and a handshake every church Sunday but most of the time, men in our community only shake hands. One time, when I was in Montana, I attended church and was surprised to see everyone greeting each other with the Holy Kiss.

Shaking hands is one thing. I'm fine with that. No way was I about to Holy Kiss with everyone. When the first man leaned in toward me to Holy Kiss me, I leaned back without even thinking. After that, I made a point of quickly extending my hand before anyone could get near my cheek.

After sprinkling the baptism water on me, the bishop motioned for me to stand. It was a relief to stand at last, but I rose slowly since my knees were stiff and numb. In front of the congregation, the bishop gave me the Holy Kiss. It was my welcome. I was the newest member of the Wautoma Community Old Order Amish.

On either side of the room, my parents were beaming with happiness. Both had tears in their eyes. My mother dabbed at hers with a tissue. Their youngest child was now a member. Their world was perfectly aligned.

I had answered the questions.
I had been baptized.
I was now a church member.
I stood in front of the entire congregation as a proper Amish.
Except that I wasn't.
No one could see the pack of cigarettes in my jacket pocket.

Sixteen

Do not be yoked together with unbelievers.
For what do righteousness and wickedness have in common?
Or what fellowship can light have with darkness?
"Therefore come out from them and be separate, says the Lord.
Touch no unclean thing, and I will receive you."
II Corinthians 6: 14 & 17, *The Holy Bible*, NIV

Bill

Looking back, it's pretty obvious that I didn't become a church member for the right reasons. I joined because of the never-ending pressure my parents put on me. I joined because of guilt. I joined because my mother caught me at a weak moment when I was hung-over. But none of that really mattered. I joined because it was expected of me. Joining had always been inevitable, just like the sun rising, and the geese flying south for the winter. I was Amish. Eventually, all Amish become church members.

When you're born Amish, you grow up knowing that your life will consist of certain milestones. Going off to school at six. Becoming a Young Folk as a teenager. Joining the church. Getting married. Having a family. Dying. Through it all there is the constant and endless work.

Day in and day out.
Week after week.
Year after year.
There is always work.

Amish children quickly learn that everyone contributes to the family. When I was about five or six, I was old enough to have a chore. My first chore was to milk two cows twice a day, every day. Before I went to school, and after I got home, my brother Monroe and I milked our cows.

As I got older, and as my older brothers and sisters moved out, I was given other chores to do. There's always plenty to do when you live on a farm. Amish children finish school after eighth grade. After that, a girl will nearly always stay at home and help her mother and a boy will begin working full-time on the farm or elsewhere.

When I was fourteen, I started working for my sister Millie's husband, Toby. We did a lot of masonry work, mostly basements and pouring slabs. We also built fireplaces, ditch culverts, and some other odd jobs.

"You're learning good skills, William," my father always assured me.

Until I was sixteen, I worked at the sawmill during the winter. I liked the mill. I liked the smell of it. I didn't mind the noise. After I turned sixteen, I was asked to join a logging crew. I did that during the winter and then went back to working for Toby during the summer. For about two years, I did logging and masonry, and then decided to log full-time.

Life becomes routine.
You know what to expect each day.
Change is the enemy of the Amish.
It's something they resist.
At any cost.

As a proper Amish, you are expected to find your place and settle in, like the teeth of a gear when they lock into place with the teeth of the other gears. That is your role. You learn not to have any other dreams or ambitions. You become part of the Amish machinery. Endlessly turning. Endlessly grinding.

After I moved out on my own, I wanted to set up my own sawmill. The mill I wanted to get used hydraulics. It would have increased my production, which was important since I would be working alone.

When I mentioned my plan to my father, he agreed that it would be a good idea for me to get my own mill going. But then he reminded me that the use of hydraulics was forbidden.

Once again my dreams were stubbed out faster than a stale cigarette.

Karrie and I went to Wautoma on February 24th so I could buy a truck. The one I bought was a purple, 1998 Dodge Ram. As I drove us off the lot, it was hard to believe that I owned my own pick-up. I didn't even have my driver's license yet. But I would soon. Then I would be able to drive myself anywhere, anytime. My new English life was coming together, but my link to the Amish had not been severed completely.

The visits and phone calls began as soon as I left. I knew it wouldn't be long before the letters started coming as well. My father's was first. His letter made Karrie angrier than I had ever seen her. She isn't someone to take injustice quietly. It didn't surprise me that she confronted him.

Someone needed to. My father is a bully. It had been too long since someone stood up to him.

I understood Karrie's anger, but I didn't share it. To me, it was just more of their bullshit. They will do anything. They will say anything. Whatever it takes to get me back in line. I had seen it all before. I knew there wasn't anything Karrie could do to stop it. It wouldn't matter how mad she got or how much she argued. They would never stop trying to get me back.

The next letter came about the time I got my truck. This one was sent anonymously.

Fri. aft.
Dear Friend William,
Greetings of Love in Jesus' Name. The one who gave his life on that we may find happiness.
It's a beautiful day again – feels like Spring, but we don't really expect that it's here to stay yet. A wonderful day for working tho, so let's enjoy it! I hope you had a good day today, although it seems we need some not-so-good days too. I think God sends us those to help us remember who is in charge & so we don't forget to be thankful when things go better again.
William, I know that you must be hurting deeply with the way things are & I just wanted you to know that we are hurting with you. It sounds like David has found peace again & we praise God for that. But William, God loves you too, just as much as He loves David, so I'm sure He is hurting even more than you are. And He would be so happy to help you find happiness too.
It really doesn't matter how many terrible things we have done in our lives – He will always keep loving us & hoping to help us. But He won't push himself onto us – He wants to be asked.
But William, I don't need to preach at you & I don't want to. Just wanted you to know that someone cares.
And if you were angry about some of the gossip, I am very sorry for any part I may have had in it. But you can take comfort in the fact that it's only the truth that needs to hurt us. The rest is just like water – it can slide right off & do no harm.
May God Bless You from here on. And don't forget – there are folks who care & so does God!
Only a Friend

After that letter came another, from a Wautoma Community Amish store owner in my district.

Feb 27, 2003
Dear brother in Christ,
Greetings of cheer and patiance from us in the name of our Lord Jesus. I am writing this with a heavy heart. It was a real shock to us to hear how you are going on. I thought it looked like you were trying to be gehorsum.
Please look into the futcher. How things will be after this time "evichkeit" Heaven or Hell!
Think how terribel tireless the hell must be and how glorious heaven will be. Please read Chapter 5, 6, 7 of Mathäi study it! The ten commedments teach us to honer your father and Mother your life long that means to do as they do and what they teach you.
Think of your dear wife! What she has to go through. She can never be married to anyone but you, as long as you live. Think the lonely life she has to face, and who is going to support her? Our granddaughter Rose Anna was als shocked and saddened to hear about your doings. She als thought of it Jake and she would come together they would have close, good neighbors! Please turn around repent and set things straight with God and tell off the worldly things and that also means Carrie! Get another job if you need to.
Now if this makes you mad or so and you can teare it up, take it down and stump on it. Gods Word Still Stands. So please think sirius about this all and repent, come back and make peace with God, church, your wife and folks. And pray to God for forgiveness.
Your saddened brother in Christ,
Menno J Mast
P.S. I am also weak by myself and do things I shouldn't. But I pray for forgiveness.

The letters irritated me. Most of the time, I didn't even want to open them. Why bother? I already knew what they would say.

Every letter that came was the same. The same plea for me to come back where I belonged. They could keep begging. None of them could give me a reason to want to go back. I wasn't interested in setting things right. I resented that they blamed Karrie. Was it really so hard to believe that I made my own choices? Was it easier to have a scapegoat than to consider that I had enough backbone or intelligence to make up my own mind?

But part of me appreciated their concern. It's always nice to know someone is thinking of you.

There was one person in particular that I hoped was thinking of me.
The one person who might have gotten me to go back.
My wife.

Ruby called every day. She would ask if I was coming back. I would ask if she was coming home. Sometimes we might chat a little about how my work was going, or she might give me some news from the community. I missed her and Frieda. I still believed we could find a way to be a family if I was English and they were Amish. She never said much about the house that had been moved for her. I never asked. It would be several months before it would be fixed up enough so she could live in it. In the meantime, something much more important came up.

"I'm pregnant."

Right after I left, Ruby had mentioned to me that her period was late. She hadn't made a big deal about it. It was possible that she was only saying it so I would come back. After she didn't mention it for a while, I figured that it might have been a trick. She might have gotten her period and just didn't bother to tell me.

"William...I'm pregnant," she repeated.

"Are you sure?"

"Yes. I'm sure."

"You should come home."

"Will you come back?"

"No. You were supposed to find out if we can get permission to live together if I'm English. Haven't you heard anything yet?"

"Well, your parents said it would be okay, but my dad isn't sure. He thinks we split up pretty fast and that we should give it some time..."

"Give it some time? For what?"

"I don't know! Time for us to think about what we're doing, I guess."

More likely it was to give me time to get my head on straight and come running back. I knew it was his plan, but I didn't say that to Ruby. It would only make her mad. She wouldn't like me saying anything against her father.

"Do you need anything? Should I drop off some money?"

"No, I don't need anything."

I hadn't seen her and Frieda for weeks. It might even be a month now. Was that possible? Had a month gone by since I last saw my wife and daughter? Work had kept us so busy that the days had slipped by without

92

me realizing. And it wasn't as if I hadn't tried to see them. Anytime I tried, she always put me off.

Maybe she didn't like it that I was spending so much time with Karrie. When David left the Amish, we both stayed at Karrie's house. After David went back, I stayed. It was simpler, at least until I had my license and could drive myself. It was nice not being alone. It was nice to be part of a family again.

If Ruby had ever told me to come home, I would have gone. Had she ever said that that she would be there waiting for me, I would have gone. Without her and Frieda, I had no reason to go home. It hurt that she seemed to be happier now that she was living at her parent's house again.

A letter arrived from my mother at the beginning of March. My brother Lewis was moving. Lewis wanted to move to a different community before his kids got old enough to join the Young Folks. He felt that the Wautoma Young Folks had gotten out of control.

3/3/03
Dear Son,
Greetings of Love in Jesus Name. Do hope this finds you well & on the go. We are a going. My ear infection is Better except I can't hear very good out of that ear so I hope to get that all Back with time. Lydia Ann did my washing today with her's so I took care of Larry but he slept most of the time. Doesn't seem possible but in a few days he will be 11 mo. old. He has 4 teeth already. Just a short note to let you Know that we are thinking and praying for you. Guess Lord willing Dad will go to Mo. in the morn. with Lewis's & I will stay with the children while they are gone prob. 3 days. They are looking in Northern part of MO & Toby's in south part I guess. So take care.
Lots of love,
Dads & Elvie

My brother Elvie is the oldest of all of us kids. I'm the youngest. There is a seventeen-year age difference between the two of us. He should be married with a family of his own, but that will never happen. He will always live with my parents. I've never been exactly sure what happened, except that Elvie got sick when he was a baby and had a high fever. I don't know if they didn't take him to the doctor in time or if he got sick again but whatever it was, he became brain damaged. Elvie was sent away to a special home for a while, but then my parents brought him back home to live with them. Elvie can take care of only his very basic needs, like a toddler. He can't speak, not even to say names.

On March 5th, I took the driving test for my license. It was the last hurdle before I would finally be able to drive myself. Once I passed, I would feel completely English. I would believe that it was all meant to be.

Technically, I could have taken the driving test two weeks earlier, but Karrie talked me out of it.

"You're not ready, Bill."

"What do you mean? I've been driving tractors and skidders for years. How much harder is a truck?"

"I've never seen you parallel park a skidder on Main Street!"

She was right. Even worse, she knew she was right. I argued with her a bit more just to defend myself but in the end, I waited the extra two weeks.

Two weeks can be a long time. Two weeks can feel like forever. But then it was finally testing time again. Karrie and I drove to Wautoma first thing that morning. I went out to the truck with the examiner. And in no time, it was over.

"A lot of people fail the first time," Karrie said, trying to cheer me up. She sat in the passenger seat. She was still my mandatory licensed driver and not just a passenger. "Especially guys. They want to make sure you don't get all cocky and get in a wreck. I bet when you try again in two weeks, you'll pass."

"Yeah, sure," I was disappointed. I had my own truck but couldn't drive it by myself. What's the point in that? I was twenty-four, not sixteen! I hadn't expected it to be this hard. Was it worth it? I failed. Was it a sign?

"Well...I guess if I go back to the Amish, you can have my truck," I said.

Karrie laughed.

It was meant to be a joke when I said it, but there was something else there. Some bit of truth. Was I meant to go back?

There were times when I really wondered if I should go back. I had a truck that I couldn't legally drive by myself. I owned a house but slept on a spare bed at Karrie's most of the time. My wife was pregnant with another child.

Like salmon returning to their original freshwater home, I felt myself being pulled back to my origins as well.

Back to the Amish.

Seventeen

The LORD is righteous in all his ways
and loving toward all he has made.
The LORD is near to all who call on him,
to all who call on him in truth.
He fulfills the desires of those who fear him;
he hears their cry and saves them.
The LORD watches over all who love him,
but all the wicked he will destroy.
Psalms 145: 17-20, *The Holy Bible*, NIV

Bill

After failing my driver's test at the beginning of March, I was pretty discouraged. Getting my license was more than just being able to drive myself. It was proof that I could be English. It was proof that I *was* English.

I accepted the first failure.

Maybe I wasn't ready. Maybe it was just bad luck.

But failing a second time could be a sign. It could be a sign that I wasn't meant to be English. A lot was at stake when I went to back on March 26th.

This time I passed.

It was a good sign.

As I slipped my new driver's license into my wallet, I thought about how many Amish rules I was breaking. No more traveling by horse and buggy. I could now legally drive myself, in my own vehicle. No more being separate from the world. I was in the system. I had a government-issued, Wisconsin state driver's license, with a photograph. Amish don't allow themselves to be photographed. They believe it breaks the Second Commandment forbidding graven images. They believe it doesn't show the proper humility. They believe that it causes vanity. It's hard to imagine that such a little piece of plastic could break so many rules. It wasn't even a good picture.

For the next few weeks, I enjoyed my new freedom. Having a driver's license made everything so much easier! I could leave when I was ready to go to work in the morning. No more waiting for a driver. No more wondering what to do if the driver didn't show up or was running late. It was such a stupid Amish rule! Why was it that I could drive a skidder, using diesel gasoline, but not a pick-up truck? What if my pick-up truck ran on diesel? What was the difference? Why did the Amish have to work so hard, with so many rules, to keep our lives simple?

Around the time I got my license, my English friend Ron stopped by for a visit. We first met when he would drive for the Amish. It was a nice change of pace to have someone come to visit who wasn't there wanting something from me. Someone who didn't come to try to talk me into going back.

"Ruby sure looks like crap," he said out of the blue.

"What do you mean?"

"I saw her the other day. She looks like she's sick or something."

I waited for him to say something else. Did he suspect that she was pregnant? Was she showing? But he changed the subject. He didn't say anything else about Ruby, but it made me wonder.

When Ruby was pregnant with Frieda, she had morning sickness pretty bad. Ruby must really be pregnant. Not that I thought she was lying, not even the first time she mentioned it....but I wouldn't have put it past her. I wouldn't put it past any of them to tell me anything if they thought it would get me back.

Thinking about Ruby and Frieda always brought me down. Soon Ruby and I would have another child. Was it a boy or a girl? Would Frieda have a brother or sister? It would be nice to have a boy. One of each. But more than anything else, I hoped the baby was healthy and that everything would go okay.

How could Ruby not come home? Why didn't her father tell her that. Why didn't he command her to go home to her husband? Why was he building her a house next to his? Why weren't others in the community asking this question?

Not long after Ron's visit, I received another letter.

Dear William,
Greetings of Love in Jesus Holy Name.
Will mol try & write a few lines your way this eve I've been wanting to for quite a while, but just didn't get to. We worked in the Shop until 8:15 or so now have had supper & will soon be bedtime. We got word this afternoon that Maklou Mullett Lizzie Mae in Clare Mi passed away, but guess we won't go for the funeral. So now her life here on earth has ended & some day it will be our turn.

I would very much like to talk with you a bit, but didn't know when to find you at home, so will do next best & write. I've got something on my mind, I would very much like to know if I ever said or did anything that caused you to take the step you did? I sure didn't want to if I did but I make lots of mistakes. I am going to send along a self addressed envelope so <u>Please</u> do this for me, let me know either yes or no. I don't want something against me, we never know when our End might come. If you have something against me, don't be afraid, say so, tell me what & I will try to make it right if possible. Hope you can understand what I am trying to say. So <u>Please</u> answer.

Lydia Mae fell asleep, so I better quit & go to bed. So will close with Love & Prayers. We think of you every day.

Sincerely & With Love,
Levi & Lydia Mae

Enclosed in the letter from my Uncle Levi was a piece of paper with "Yes" and "No" written on it and the self-addressed envelope he mentioned. This letter was probably the toughest of any that I would receive. I didn't have the heart to circle the "Yes" knowing how much it would upset him. He's too good of a person. I would never want to hurt him.

On the other hand, I couldn't lie. I couldn't circle the "No" either. Not even to give him piece of mind. Although I was tempted. There was no denying that his sermon that day, the "How do we know?" one, had played a part in my decision. But my leaving had always been inevitable. It had been destined to happen. Uncle Levi's sermon was just that final nudge. Like the chainsaw cutting through that last bit of bark before the tree fell.

I didn't have the heart to tell Uncle Levi any of that. I didn't want to hurt him. I didn't want to lie. So I did nothing at all.

Another day a letter arrived from my aunt, my father's sister, along with a "Thinking of You" card.

In the card was written:

Dear William,
With Love & Best Wishes
Andy and Irma Schrock

Inside was the letter:

4-18-03

Dear William,

Greetings in Our Dear Saviours Name who died on the cross to <u>save</u> us poor sinners from eternal punishment. Today is the day (GOOD FRIDAY) that we keep in memory as the day he was crucified.

It is rather chilly today. Rained just a little bit several different times today already but sun also shone at times so seems like a typical April shower day.

We were just at home in a.m. then went visiting at several different places in p.m. so now we are back at home and have had supper. Seems sort of quiet around here this evening as Irma & I are here all to ourselves. We are boarding a school teacher here this school term but she went home yesterday p.m. and won't be back until Mon. morning school time. She is from Kalona, Iowa. Her name is Heidi Miller, daughter of Sanford Miller. School will let out here in May 1ˢᵗ according to schedule. We have plans to take dinner along over to where and when Lewises' move and hope it's not the same day that school lets out, although it could be. It is sad to know how things are going in Wautoma area. Can't say that I blame Lewises' for moving, although that isn't always an easy thing to do but feel that is better than to stay there among those questionable attitudes. Thank goodness not all Amish people are living such lives.

Often wonder how you are making out by now? Was a shock when we first heard about your decision to not want to stay Amish but from what little I really know about your growing up years and know how the church there operates it does seem some what fit together and to say the least we do feel sorry for you. As I remember, you never did talk a lot so probably didn't discuss problems openly with anyone so with problems in the church it caused bottled up feelings & discouragement. Now this is just my thinking maybe I'm wrong but surely you must feel confused. It is not God's will that even one person should perish (miss heaven) so John 3-16 says that "God so loved the world that he gave his only son that who ever believes on him should not perish (be lost) but have ever lasting live" (in heaven). God wants our obediance but doesn't expect us to be perfect. He knows our human nature and I do believe he allows for that some what. Although we need to let our words and actions be guided by God's Holy Spirit. Now if we resist the pleas of our parents & the church can we expect to receive the help of the Holy Spirit to guide us through life? In John 5 - 24 we read "Wer mein wort hört, und glaubet dem der mich gesandt had der had das ewege leben". So we can see that we need to believe in Jesus Christ & to really believe is to do his will which might be some what confusing when living in a community where we don't really feel confident in some of the leadership.

The Bible tells us that Satan can come as a rearing lion and seeks to devour us. He is the author of confusion and the truth is not in him. So to me it appears that when there is disunity in the church it can cause doubts to arise in individuals as to the value of belonging to such a group and if not careful can lead a person out into the world.

Now in your case you have chosen to do without your wife and child rather than stay within the church. If you really love your wife like I have no reason to believe otherwise then it makes you feel bitter towards the church and makes you want to look for something else. Now if you read Ephesians Chapter 5 it can give a person a lot of food for thought. We husbands are to love our wives even as Christ loved the church and gave himself for it. We wouldn't expect Christ to do anything to hurt the Church so we husbands shouldn't do anything to hurt our wives. What I'm trying to say is that the Devil is happy to have you discouraged so far as to leave the church and also cause a difference in thinking between you and your wife so much so that it is difficult for youns to live together. How Sad. I do hope & pray that you will seek help before it is too late. I do feel confident that deep down you do want what is right but surely you realize that if you choose to live without any church guidance and in a way that even your wife is afraid of, you are on dangerous ground. I believe the devil likes that.

We are here on earth to help each other so may advice would be, don't be too quick to think the Amish church is all bad. Not all communities operate the same. I think you could be a lot happier than you are now if you would come back and make things right with the church there then take your wife & child and move to some other community that has a good reputation. You'd be surprised how much more life would mean to you and your wife also. I know of a boy that was dissatisified in his home community because of circumstances he felt were not right and said he isn't going to stay Amish. His parents talked to him about going to another settlement to some of their relations maybe he'd feel some what different. He finally said he'd try it but still said he wasn't going to be Amish. In this new settlement he felt a different atmosphere and after a time he seemed to lose the bitterness he had for the home community and now he is a Amish church member and as far as I know he is a satisified person. Thank God. I hope you understand why I'm writing. I'm not trying to just criticize you for what you are doing but want to let you know that we feel sorry for you and would like to be an instrument in God's hand to help guide you to a better life here on earth and in eternity. Eternity is never ending and we can't afford to miss heaven by bending to the wishes of Satan.

The boy I mentioned above made the remark that the new community was so different from his home community. He just didn't realize it could be so much better. So my advice would be, don't give up to Satan and just go on living on your own day by day as you will never find true happiness that way. Being together again with your wife (as you promised on your wedding day) and living in harmony with God's word & the Church can bring true happiness. I would suggest that you seek help for some of the doubts your probably have about the Amish Church. There are some answers available if you really want to be helped. I could make some suggestions as to help and also to communities to move to but hesitate to do so unless you really want to know. Any way I know that some people that lived in some what confused conditions have been helped and have a different out look in life God has the answers so really there is no need to live in a state of confusion so great that we put our marriage in danger by not living together, but can you blame her is she had a fear of being led astray. Husband & wife need each other. It is hard to stand alone.

I wasn't going to write this much when I started out but do have a feeling for you and Ruby and just had a desire to share some of my thoughts so if I wrote something that is offending to you please forgive me for doing so it was not my aim. Just meant it all good.

So my plea again seek help (talk to some one) don't bottle it up to yourself. Your own family could probably give you some good advice but some times others not related might get it across to make it more meaningful if not having been involved before. If interested in more information please let us know. Would be glad to help. Will be praying for you and Ruby.

Aus Liebe,
Andy Schrock

Move to another community.

My brother-in-law Toby suggested the same thing that night when Karrie and I tried to go bowling. The night Toby and my brothers had been waiting for me.

When Toby first suggested it, I shrugged it off. I wasn't interested in moving to another community. At that time, I thought Ruby would be back soon. I believed that within a few days, she and Frieda would come home. But that hadn't happened.

Weeks had passed.

Ruby had a house moved for her. Ruby was carrying my child.

Move to another community.

Maybe it was something to consider. If it would bring my wife and child home, I'd move. At that point, I was willing to find a way to have my family back.

But the times when I mentioned it to Ruby, she always gave me the same answer.

"I don't want to move. I don't want to leave my family."

"I'm your husband. You'll leave me, but you won't leave them?"

"You left the Amish. I'm afraid to go with you. I'm afraid that if I go with you, I'll leave, too."

I didn't know what to say to that. I felt a tiny spark of hope.

Maybe she would leave. Maybe we could be a family again. Maybe she was coming around and would honor her vows and follow my leadership of our family.

Maybe there was reason to hope.

Give it time.

That's what her father had suggested.

Give it time.

I was willing to do that.

Let them see that I was serious about not going back. My offer to move to another community seemed to be a reasonable compromise, but it didn't seem to be good enough for them, at least not yet.

Give it time.

Eventually Ruby, and her father, will see that she can't have everything her way.

Another time when I talked to Ruby, I asked her to meet me somewhere. Anywhere. Alone. Just to see her. I wanted to talk to her. I wanted to hold my wife and daughter.

"I don't want to meet you anywhere, not alone," she answered.

"Why not?"

"I'm afraid you'll kidnap me."

"What?" I asked, stunned.

"I'm afraid that if I meet you alone, you'll kidnap me and Frieda."

"Where would I take you?"

"I don't know. I'm not going to meet you by myself. That's all there is to it!"

I couldn't believe it. One time she tells me that she's afraid she'll leave the Amish if she meets me, and the next time she's accusing me of planning to kidnap her! I didn't know what to say to such irrational fear. Did she really believe that I was capable of such a thing? Or was it because I was English now? Amish are taught that English are liars and can't be trusted.

Give it time.
That's all I could do.
Just a few more weeks, I told myself.

Give it more time for them to see that I'm not going back. Maybe then she'll agree to live with me and let me be English. The community had already approved it. Maybe she would consider moving to another Amish community with me.

I wasn't going to give in.
I wasn't going to give up.
I would give it more time.

Eighteen

Karrie

Spring arrived.

After the cold, dark of winter, it usually only takes a few warm days for people to put away their parkas, flannel shirts, and thermal underwear and start pulling out their shorts and t-shirts. They are ready to burst free from the cocoon of winter clothing. The thermometer may not have risen to a level that many people, especially those in other areas of the country, would consider warm. After the sub-zero Wisconsin winter temperatures, sometimes 30°F can feel like a heat wave.

Officially spring arrived on March 21, 2003, and that date seemed to work for Mother Nature as well. As soon as the snow began to melt, I made my way down to the Mecan. No matter how old I get, I'll never outgrow the need to play in the water. As long as I'm able, I'll pull on my muck boots and tromp around, smashing the melting ice sheets and making dams.

Spring is the best time of the year at the Mecan, before all the reeds and brush grow too thick and dense. Flocks of Canada geese would soon arrive, some merely passing by on their way further north and some sticking around and making nests, but it was another bird that we were waiting to see. Clayton was the first to spot it that year. Regardless of the temperature or the calendar, spring doesn't truly begin until the robins return.

One morning in early April, Bill left to skid a job in the Kettle Moraine, an area to the east of us, toward Lake Michigan. I was skidding another job closer to home and had gotten all the way out to the site only to realize that I didn't have the keys for the skidder.

"Go get the keys from the other skidder," Bill told me when I called him. There was a third skidder sitting in my yard that we were cleaning up so it could be sold.

"Shit! I can't believe I've got to drive back home," I said with frustration, "Yeah, okay. I'll call you later."

It was a chilly morning with a heavy frost on the ground. The skidder was parked on the east yard in a large grassy area. I tucked my hands into the pocket of the hoodie after I got out of the car to warm them before I grabbed the cold metal of the machine. Anxious to get back into the warmth of my car, I quickly climbed up two of the steps and opened the cab door, leaning in from the top step. The keys were there, hanging from the ignition. I reached my arm toward the keys, my fingers just about to close over the keychain, when my world shifted.

It's strange how your life can shift from normal to something completely different in a flash, and this alternate reality has a completely different set of rules. Time passes in slow motion and somehow, at the same time, it is also sped up, faster than your mind can process. It's like watching a spinning merry-go-round: you can see the individual handles, but it all becomes a blur.

My fingertips had been about to touch the keys that I needed to get on with the day I had planned: my day of work. Instead I watched as those keys got further away. There was an intense pressure across my throat. I felt myself falling, and it seemed to last forever as I was pulled back from the skidder into nothingness. The only thought that came into my head was that I was in great danger.

As I fell backwards, I made contact with another body. Where had he come from? Grabbing me by the hood of my sweatshirt, he pulled me back from where I stood on the skidder steps and spun me so I couldn't get my footing. By the time my brain processed what was happening, I was lying flat on my back in the crunching, frozen, brown grass.

The air was knocked from my lungs but before I could get a breath, there was a sudden pressure on my chest. Then my face exploded with pain, first on one side and then the other.

This wasn't possible! This was not happening to me!

Finally, my survival instincts kicked in. My arms came up to cover my face preventing any more direct punches.

"If you know what's good for you," the man hissed as he hit me again and again, "you'll tell William to go back." His punches made contact with my arms. It was still painful, but not as bad as when he struck my bare face. "If you don't get him to go back, we'll come back every week...it'll only get worse for you."

Before my brain could even form a response, he grabbed my wrists and pinned both arms down to the side of my body. He leaned forward and shifted his weight so that he was completely on top of me, his body covering mine. I wriggled and squirmed beneath him, but I was caught. Trapped. Every cell of my body was screaming, but no sound came.

My brain processed only flashes of information, like a strobe light going off in a dark room, freezing images into single snapshots. Standing only a few feet away, I realized, was a second man. Another man. Another man standing there watching while his friend beat me.

The man attacking me leaned down so that his lips were next to my ear, and that's when I knew. A bristly beard scratched my burning cheek and my nostrils were filled with an all too familiar smell that made my stomach turn.

He was Amish.

"Is this what you're getting from William?" He whispered while rubbing himself against me. "I can give it to you too, if that's what you want..." He pressed his groin into me and I could feel him. Disgust and fear coursed through my body.

He was going to rape me. Right here in my yard.

The reality of the situation hit me and snapped me back like a yo-yo after its free-falling drop. My fighter instincts, enhanced with primal fear, took over with a vengeance.

This was not going to happen.

Not today.

Not to me.

With every adrenaline-enhanced muscle in my body, I fought him. Fought like a wild cat. Then we both heard it. For an instant, we both froze. In the distance and growing louder was the sound of a car coming down the road.

The approaching car got his attention and in a heartbeat, he was off me and running. I was free. As I scrambled to my feet, I saw that he was heading toward a truck that was parked on the side of the road. The other Amish man who stood nearby already had a head start and was about to get in the truck.

But the fight wasn't over, not if I could help it. I glanced around frantically for something...anything I could find...anything I could get my hands on...to stop him...or hurt him.

There on the ground and only a few steps away was a splitting maul. I grabbed it by the handle and flung it at my attacker with everything I had.

Contact!

The maul struck him in the low back, knocking him to his knees. He struggled back to his feet and started running again, limping and not as fast. I looked around again, searching and hoping, but there was nothing else for me to throw. When I looked up again, my attacker was in the truck. As the English driver pulled away, I rushed to the road to try to get a license plate number, but there wasn't one. It had been intentionally removed before they came over.

And then they were gone.

I stood there at the side of the road, battered and shaking. None of it seemed real, but my aching body was proof that it was. My face felt puffy, and I could taste blood at the corner of my mouth.

Rachel's voice came into my head as I walked to the house to call the police and to get some ice for my throbbing and swelling face.

"Watch your back, Karrie," she had warned me months ago.

They blindsided me. My hunter instincts are usually well in tune, but this caught me totally off-guard. I never imagined that they were capable of this. To violently attack me. And if that car hadn't come down the road, it would have been worse. He would have raped me.

"Watch your back, Karrie." Rachel's voice echoed once again inside my head.

"They'll never do anything like that to me ever again," I vowed.

Nineteen

Let the heads of those who surround me
be covered with the trouble their lips have caused.
Let burning coals fall upon them;
may they be thrown into the fire, into miry pits, never to rise.
Let slanderers not be established in the land;
may disaster hunt down men of violence.
Psalm 140: 9-11, *The Holy Bible*, NIV

Bill

"I just got attacked."

"What?"

"Two Amish guys were here. They attacked me. One yanked me out of the skidder and started beating on me. He had me pinned down on the ground. He said he was going to rape me...and he would have tried if a car hadn't come down the road."

"When?"

"Just now! Right after I hung up the phone from you."

"Are you okay?"

"I've got an ice pack on my face. I've got some scratches and swelling, but that's the worst of it. The sheriff is on his way out here."

"Do you want me to turn around? I can be back there in an hour."

"No, it's okay, go on and get the skidder moved."

"Do you know who it was?"

"I didn't recognize them. It was a green Dodge pickup, but there was no license plate on the back. They must have taken it off so I wouldn't see it. He said that if I didn't quit helping you, they'd be back..."

A rush of ice and fire coursed through my body. The cold came because of the guilt and shame that Karrie had been attacked because of me. Right behind was the searing anger at the attackers and every one of the goddamn Amish.

How dare they? Who the hell did they think they were, beating up someone for being my friend? Such fucking hypocrites! How many sermons had I heard about turning the other cheek? How many times had someone mentioned those violent English and told us how that is not our way. The Amish have the world convinced that they are peaceful people. They have the world convinced that they are better.

Bullshit.

Bullshit and lies.

When I left the Amish, I expected backlash. I knew there would be plenty of visits and phone calls and letters. There would be pleading and tears and lectures. They would try their best to get me to return. They had done all those things. They had tried so many ways. Except one. There was one thing they hadn't done. There was one thing that would have guaranteed their success. But it went unused. Why?

Why hadn't they used Ruby and Frieda to get me to come back?

How many times had I asked Ruby to come home. How many times did I tell her that I would come home if she and Frieda would be there? How many times had I offered to move to another community? If Ruby would have come home, I would have gone back.

But she never did.

They never played their ace.

Instead there was the daily phone call she made to me. But even that felt as if it was only out of obligation. It never seemed that she called because she missed me. She never acted as if she missed our life together.

Rather than send my wife home to get me back, they sent thugs. You don't expect the people who claim to love you, and who supposedly care so much about you, to hurt you. Not even if you've done the unthinkable.

When my brothers came over that night, Karrie thought they were there to beat me up. I laughed at her. The Amish wouldn't get violent. I was so certain. Begging and pleading and pressure, that was their style.

But Karrie had seen the possibility. And now she had been threatened and beaten and nearly raped. How could my family, my friends, my community do such a thing? Was the fear of losing one of their own so great that they could justify attacking someone who is helping me?

How the hell did they think that would get me back? If this is how they treat my friends, with violence and threats of greater violence, why would I want to be a part of them? What sort of sick mind tries to get someone to do something by threatening his friend?

They were desperate and in their desperation, I saw the true Amish.

Hypocrites.

They were hypocrites.

They are not the peaceful people they claim to be. They are just another cult. They use whatever means necessary to bring back someone who has escaped.

Several times on the way to the worksite, I slowed down and almost turned the truck around to go back, even though Karrie said she was okay. The sheriff was probably there by now. Karrie told me to go on to work, but it was a struggle.

When I thought about her being attacked, I wanted to find those bastards. I wanted to make them sorry for what they did. They should have come after me. Not Karrie.

Someone put them up to it. Someone arranged the attack. Someone got those guys to make Karrie sorry that she got involved. Someone set it all in motion. Someone who wanted me back.

Someone who couldn't stand to have another of his children leave.

Someone who had done something like this before.

Twenty

Karrie

"Watch your back."

Rachel warned me months ago. She never gave me any specific details for her ominous warning, only the cryptic reply, "Just believe me...I know what I'm talking about."

Immediately after the attack, I called the police, then Bill, and then I called Rachel.

"Oh, Karrie! How terrible! I was afraid they might do something to you, but I hoped they wouldn't."

"The asshole who attacked me made it clear that they don't like me helping your brother, but I'm not afraid of them. They'll be sorry if they ever try something like that again."

Unfortunately, physical violence was something I was familiar with. I grew up with it. My brother could do no wrong while I never seemed to be able to do anything right. There was always hell to pay for something. I got hit once because some Dentyne gum was missing from my mother's purse. It didn't matter that I don't like anything spicy or hot. There was no way I would have snitched cinnamon gum.

Another time when a Tupperware bowl went missing, I was the one who took all the blame and got the beating. Years later, after I bought the house from my parents, I found the bowl, filthy and faded, outside in some bushes under my brother's window where he had obviously thrown it all those years before.

I vowed, before I became a mother, that I would never strike my children. Never. I would break the cycle. I have never broken that pledge.

When you grow up with violence, it's a hard to keep it from roaring out of you. In my marriage and some other relationships, there were times when fights turned physical. I always gave as good as I got. Why not? I had been well-trained.

One time, during an argument with a boyfriend, he pointed a gun at me. After I got the gun away from him, I told him that he better not ever fuck with me again or the next time I would pull the trigger. Never before in my life have I ever pointed a gun at someone. I hope that I won't ever have to, but I knew that if my attackers came back, I wouldn't hesitate to get my gun. And use it.

For as long as I could remember, there had been violence in my life. But the attack by the Amish guys left me more shaken than anything I had ever experienced. There had been plenty of fights over the years, and I was not the type to ever run away, but in all those other instances, there had been some type of warning. This attack was an ambush. They caught me completely by surprise. But it sure as hell would not happen again.

"I didn't see it coming, Rachel. I don't think I really believed they were capable of this. It was one thing to have your dad and the others spreading lies about me, saying that I was sleeping with your brother and David. That pissed me off. And it was bad enough. But I sure as hell never expected them to come try to beat the crap out of me or to say they're going to rape me!"

"You're the one helping William. They figure if they can get you out of the way, he'll go back to them. They will do whatever it takes, Karrie. I should know. My dad and brothers beat up James before we were married. They kidnapped me...just to try to get me to go back."

Rachel sighed and told me the rest of the story.

When she was a teenager, Rachel had some problems and went to live with her sister and brother-in-law, Amanda and Chester, who lived in the Wautoma Community at that time. After awhile, Amanda arranged for Rachel to go stay with Chester's family in Missouri. A great-uncle of Chester's was known as someone who helped troubled teens. Rachel was happy to get away and quickly settled in.

Back in the Wautoma Community, Bill heard rumors about an older man who was trying to start his own sect. This man was supposedly targeting some of the young girls and had some strange idea of cleansing sins by staying in a room with them. Was the man really doing something wrong, or were some people talking about him because he helped teens who weren't sure that they wanted to be Amish. Bill never did find out the truth.

Life in Missouri was good for Rachel, and she even started taking the classes to become a church member. About halfway through, she realized that she didn't want to continue the class. She didn't want to be baptized or become a church member. She didn't want to be Amish.

Rachel decided to leave.

After she left, Rachel met James. They started dating and before long, they became engaged. Since she left before becoming a member, it wasn't required that Rachel be shunned or excommunicated, although anyone who leaves is always treated differently and kept at a distance. In the Wautoma Community, those leaving before joining the church aren't forbidden from visiting, but they aren't necessarily encouraged or invited...except of course, as part of the continuing effort to get them back to the Amish. The Amish never give up hope that the wayward will return.

Even though Rachel wasn't a church member, her future husband was considered unacceptable because James was English and even worse, he was divorced.

In the spring of 1993, when Bill was about fourteen, the family hired a driver and went to Missouri to visit Bill's sister Amanda and her family. Chester and Amanda had moved there not long after Rachel. While they were in Missouri, the family made plans to visit Rachel as well. At least that was their cover story. The real plan was something completely different.

The family picked up Rachel and James in the hired van one sunny day to go for a drive and see the countryside. Besides the English driver, there was: Bill; his mother, Fanny; sister Millie and her husband, Toby; two brothers, Lewis and Monroe; and Rachel and James. Chris Herschberger decided to stay back at the house.

They traveled down twisting, back country roads, enjoying the scenery and commenting on the farms as they passed. Everything seemed normal, even when they turned onto a secluded gravel lane.

The van stopped in a heavily wooded area with no homes in sight because Lewis and Toby said something was wrong with the door. But it was only an excuse. They both got out and then opened the front door where James was sitting in the passenger seat and taking him by surprise, pulled him out. Lewis and Toby threw him down to the ground, pinning him, and began to beat James. Monroe also got out and stood nearby as back-up.

As soon as she realized what was happening, Rachel went crazy screaming and trying to get out, but her mother and sister held her back, ripping the back pocket of her jeans.

In no time, Lewis, Toby, and Monroe climbed back into the van. They yelled for the driver to go, leaving James behind. Through her tears, Rachel looked out the back windows and saw James clambering up the embankment, his face bloody. She watched him throw a handful of gravel at the van before he disappeared from sight.

After a short drive, the van stopped again behind another vehicle. Rachel and one of her siblings were transferred to the waiting minivan and taken to an Amish counselor while the rest of the family went to get Chris and then drove back to the house where Rachel was being deprogrammed.

The so-called counselor worked with Rachel for several hours, trying to convince her that she belonged with her family, with her community, with the Amish. But there was no way she would ever go back, especially after witnessing her family assaulting her fiancé. The deprogrammer finally told the family that it was no use. He told them to let her go.

About a month later, authorities in Wisconsin served a subpoena for the state of Missouri. Lewis, Toby, and Monroe, as well as Chris, who had been the ringleader, were all required to return to Missouri. They were arrested and fingerprinted. Monroe's charges were dismissed due to his age and because he had only watched the assault and hadn't actively participated. The sentencing of others was reduced to probation and they were allowed to serve their time in their home county.

The more Rachel opened up to me and shared about their family and the Amish, the more resolved I became. I vowed to do whatever I could to help Bill, and anyone else, leave the Amish cult.

Twenty-one

Brothers, do not slander one another.
Anyone who speaks against his brother or judges him
speaks against the law and judges it.
When you judge the law, you are not keeping it,
but sitting in judgment on it.
There is only one Lawgiver and Judge,
the one who is able to save and destroy.
But you—who are you to judge your neighbor?
James 4: 11-12, *The Holy Bible*, NIV

Bill

Another letter from my mother. It has a "Thinking of You" sticker on it.

Thurs 4/24/03
Dear William,
Greetings of Love and in Jesus Name. Once again I want to write a few lines to you, if we can't seem to be able to contact you in person. Hope you are in good health. We are on the go and thankful for that.

Today as of now its quiet around here as Dad went to help at Lewis's again. Today in a week they are planning to load the rest of there belongings and start for MO. Hope they can get everything done that needs to be done B-4 then and one thing is that Lewis and Ester want to see you yet before they go if it is possible?? Hope so!

Monroe went to help Adlai haul manure out of the shed and Lydia Ann & kids also went to help w/ dinner and spend time with Rosanna (seems she still isn't as strong as we'd like to see). But being there and doing the house work & fixing the meals & etc. is worth a Big Part of being a family. So we thank God for that.

The Boys have the oats in now and will start planting soon for corn. It's about that time of year again. Wonder what you will do with your corn plot this year. Hope something. Dad could do it but knows he doesn't have time before Lewis' move. So let him know if you want help.

Of course you found out that you had company Sun. p.m. and were not at home. Which they were sad about that as everyone has a longing to mol *vedar visit with you. Yesterday Dad went to the frolic at Firman's they got quite a Bit done on it...the house. Mark's crew is also building the shed as of now and prob. done soon too. So maybe B-4 long they can move over to there on house. Our communion is at Melvin Bylers on Sat. as it's our turn (East ch.) for weekday then West is on Sun at Allen Bylers. We <u>will</u> miss you there!*

Tue. us women went at Lewis' to help and Ruby & Frieda Baby (is so sweet!) were there too. I feel sorry for them as she is so sad & we all are missing you tremendously and its not just the family there are lot of other people concerned and praying for you, like when we were to Clare, Mi. for Lizzie Mae Mulletts funeral I found out that Willard Beechy just can't get it over himself that you could do this. He just again & again talks how unreal it seems to him. So lets be ever so thankful that we have friends that care. Lloyd Mullett (Clair, Mi.) also is grieving. Its hard to see to write with tears in my eyes!

I guess I have this song in my mind so much this morning so I'll share it with you.

(1) My ways are not your ways -
Oft the way to the good seems so weary and long,
Trials almost take away our song.
Then we sign and we cry, and we ask "Father why,
Does this life my wishes all deny?"
Cho: My ways, my child are not your ways,
My thoughts are higher then thine. Let me lead you
Each step of this long, weary day, Let me clasp thy
trembling hand in mine.
(3) So I'll leave all to Him, He had promised to Share
and my load and every care to bear.
There is joy in my heart, and on my lips a song.
Even though, Lord, I don't understand. (Chorus)

Am sure you remember this chorus as you'd sing it on 227 at the singings "Nun sich der Tag geendent hast"

Well I expect I should get to work again as I'm hoping to get the yard cleaning all done for the time being, we had a rack wagon load of pine cones & sticks again, so I'm glad for all thats done. Have some bread dough nearly ready to put in the pans to bake too.

So really and truly its your turn to write us a letter and you could just a well. !

Will close with a prayer in my heart for you. And God Be with us all till we meet Again!

P.S. Can you stay at home all day Sunday in case Someone will go over?? Let us Know if you can not.

Following close behind that letter was one from Ruby's aunt, a bishop's wife:

Dear William,

My thoughts and prayers have been so much with you. Its hard to go on with life if you are not included in our circle. We've had great news last night when Elmer & Darlene were blessed with a baby girl Lisa Mae 6# 14 oz and 21 inches long. It was almost on my birthday so did get my middle name. Our hearts try and rejoice but like I said your leaving still holds sad hearts.

I am writing and hoping if we did or said anything that made you leave please come tell us. I just can't bear going thru life if I know someone fells bad about me of things we did or said. We hear there are alot of rumors out about us. But we'll forgive. God knows whats true. We don't have to be judged for that. We feel while you were in our circle we did not neighbor like we should of. And do apoligize for it.

I just don't know where to begin it just hurts so. Today in die gros gma at Allens it was just so hard to now Ruby is there to take part, and oh if only you could of also been. Tears fell for you both I just could not help it. Its so hard to see Rubys great sadness. She's always been my favorite niece, because she was a person who was, always happy, always willing & it seemed always doing more than her share. But it so hurts to see her. As her happiness is gone. The sad looks in her eyes. But yet she is still trying so hard to support herself & Frieda. And I know right now that's awhard for her in her condition. We hear you still think you could be Eng. & she Amish & live together. I am wondering what you would expect to tell your children then when they grow up? Wouldn't they have to live a very mixed up life? Oh, please William don't think we're putting you down. We all still love you. During the day so often its hard to go on my thot's are with you... with Ruby. I am wondering if you can say you really are happy? If you can't honestly say yes to this please repent. One soul is worth more than all the world & its treasures.

Just start over put everything away, make peace with the church. And you can be happy again. Satan has lead many a man astray. But you know with Almighty God All Things are Possible. Don't think we look down on you. We don't you're just a person who got on the wrong track. Which we

116

are all bound to fail. There is no person so bad that there's no some good in him. And no person so good theres not some bad in him.

Why don't you come back & you & Ruby run the store & stay home & work side by side. Im sure Ervins wouldn't care as right now Ervin just isn't to well. He told Monroe the other day the medication isn't helping like it should and is also almost more than they can afford. It just hurts to see stress take over.

And don't ever get the feeling your sins are greater than can be forgivin. You know Jesus blood will wash the greatest sins clean. We had a great longing to come talk with you. But didn't know if you'd except us. But I finally told myself Ill write if you read it only by the grace of God it may help you. To God give the great honor I did not write to put you down and not to make you bitter. I guess only to try & do our part so maybe when judgement day comes we won't have to pay for this, by not trying to go to the second mile.

Yest. while in the garden my thots were like so much with Ruby. With tears I had to think yes I know how she <u>longs</u> to go back to her home & dig in her garden, check her flowers & have her dear husband back. Please just turn your pack to the world at the end of the road it as nothing to offer. My heart als breaks when I see the Schmucker cousins come together & you are not there. Ruby & Frieda have to go alone. And now with Elmer's baby I know that's what will happen again. Wouldn't you please wear your Amish clothes, just walk over to Elmers the eve. they go. <u>Everyone</u> would be so glad to see you!

I just will not give up on you. As long as theres life theres HOPE. Waiting for your return. The door is open 24 hrs a day.

Still praying for you & Ruby.

Monroe & Luella

The letter also contained the following note:

I keep clinging to a dream I had about you one night. I dreamed it was a cold rainy night you came into our house into the bedroom & just flopped on the bed & said I need help. Please Im sick and tired of this life. And you ask Monroe to help you on. Don't think we feel you just have to come to us for help help. As we by far don't have all the answers & do fail so much. But do bear in mind our hearts ache & would do anything to help you. Wear you Amish clothes. Walk over & help on Fermans house one day Mervin, Le Roy & Ferman are at it every day. I'd be glad to give you a *meal. Don't feel we'd turn our back on you. Remember there is a God who cares. And he does not turn anyone down who seeks for <u>true repentance</u>. I go to bed with you in my prayers & during the day I have you in my thots Please Please return.*

Ask yourself at the end of this life on judgement day. Which can you have to take with you. Your wife and child or your truck and electricity? Theres no way the truck & electricity can go with you. But your dear wife & child maybe able to if you just repent.

Not long after Ruby left me, her dad built a store for her. It's a white metal building set across the wide driveway from the house. Part of the building is used for inventory and storage. The other part is set up as a small grocery, with only about four short aisles, shopping carts, and a single cash register on a wide wooden counter. Beside the grocery items, there are also household and toiletry items, such as shampoos, razors, and baby supplies. Ruby's store specialized in damaged items, or seconds, and products that have been discontinued. All sold at reduced prices. The Bent and Dent. That's the name of Ruby's store. It's very popular with both Amish and English.

Word spread quickly about *poor Ruby* whose husband ran off with another woman...a loose Englishwoman. Amish usually keep their business to themselves, but this was different. This time someone from outside was involved.

When you live in a community where everyone, both Amish and English, know each other, there is a lot of gossip. It doesn't matter if the story is true. Some might claim they are only showing their neighborly concern, but too many people seem to enjoy spreading what they call news. The nastier, the better.

The Amish drivers, and the English who regularly deal with them, would have heard about my leaving. That news spread as quickly as darkness falls in December. For miles and miles around, everyone heard about Karrie shacking up with the Amish man who left his wife and baby girl.

No one seemed to care about the truth.

I hadn't left my faith. I was still a Christian. I just chose not to live as an Amish.

I hadn't left my wife and child. My wife broke her vows and left me. She wouldn't come back.

I hadn't left for Karrie. She was a co-worker and my friend. Without her help, I might not have made it in the outside world. We weren't having an affair. I had never had an affair with anyone.

I didn't want to leave my family and community, but when you leave the Amish, you don't have a choice. They leave you. They put you in the ban and excommunicate you.

I left the Amish.

I left because of all the stupid rules.

That was the truth.

Too bad no one cared about the truth.

Anyone who has met Karrie knows that she doesn't care what people think of her. Sometimes I think she gets a kick out of stirring things up and pushing people's buttons. But it's one thing to live your life as you please, not caring if people approve. It's another to have people making up vicious lies and spreading gossip.

It was a different for me. Karrie lived in the area nearly her whole life. I didn't know enough English people to care what they said about me. I knew the Amish would say anything. They would believe anything. It gave them an excuse. They would blame everything on Karrie. She was an easy target. The Amish could keep up the illusion of their quaint innocence with Ruby as the poor, suffering victim. I'm sure none of them minded the sympathy.

I'm sure it didn't hurt business at Ruby's store, either.

Twenty-two

My heart is in anguish within me;
the terrors of death assail me.
Fear and trembling have beset me;
horror has overwhelmed me.
Psalm 55: 4-5, *The Holy Bible*, NIV

Bill

Another letter from my mother arrived early in May:

5-6-03
Dear William,
Greetings of Love and in Jesus Name. This is Tue. toward eve. so I'll scratch a few lines while I rest a little. I was at Tobys today helping as they have church Sun. in 2 weeks and Millie plans to go with a load to Canistota S. Dakota next week for treatments again. Adlai's Both want to go also. I wonder if you would get good results there too if you could go. Last month when we were there one of the Ortman doctors had a speech one night and explained how our Bodies are made with all our joints, Bones, muscles & everything and how important it is to get treatments and good health care to just feel better and have a better outlook on life. People from all over go there for their kind of treatments and most everybody has an ailment of some kind and some very severe ones that they help. Then he Said even if a person thinks there is nothing wrong, he should still get treatments just to feel Better! Of course he was bragging on there own way of treating which is different and a good way lots of people think but we just to get away from the stress of our busy life a while and taking time to meditate and thing something else can do wonders. When he said that I had to so much think about you and your diving accident. I expect they could do a lot for you to get more strenghth Back in that hand!
Dad is working again today. Suppose Ruby prob. called & said that we got Lewis moved to Mo. and came home tired cause we traveled 2 nights in a row. So I hope they can make themselves at home And we wish them God's Blessings. We do miss them though but life is full of changes, as you well know!

This morning Jan Lant stopped in and said that Samuel Borntragers Chester Lee had a Bad accident yesterday. Something with a Big Hay Bale and is on life support machines in hospital Not expected to live. So around Noon William Bornt. then came & said he passed away. He was 10 ½ yrs old. and the 3ʳᵈ of their children. So I expect we want to go sometime. As I figure Chester & Amanda & fam. would be there as Chester is a Brother to Samuel Maryann. You prob. remember when they lived here, and Samuel prob. was your School teacher, Not so?? Lucky little lad that he can go be with Jesus and not have the further temptations of this sad world full of sin & Strife. The funeral is Friday forenoon.

Danny Joe accidently shot 2 pellets in his finger tip on Sat. fornoon with their air rifle. He had to go to Wild Rose Emergency & get it fixed. He thought it to be only 1 then when they xrayed they said 2 so the doctor dug them out and figured he had it all then yesterday he had to be Back for a check up & then x-rayed again & found that a little piece is still in, but the doctor says most times it will come out by it self so we hope so. But he has to be watched about infection very close. Tonight was the first time that he came back to Monroes to help chore.

Wonder where you are working now? And if there is anything you want to have done around there?? If so just let us know! We will gladly help wherever we can.

This is later now Wed. A.M and its raining again Which I was really surprised when we woke up this morn. to see it raining. I had wanted to plant garden today but it will wait until some other day. We don't have any seeds in the ground yet, which is a little unusual for me!

I guess Adlias & us & Tobys 2 Boys want to go to Evansville tonight for visitation at Samuels, so I want to clean up in the house today in case we get company. Thought maybe Chesters will come on up Sometime but don't know for Sure.

I'll send this little pamphlet along for you to read if you care too. I don't believe in all the tracts that people want to give and this I didn't order it just came for free. Some I look at & throw away cause they are misleading, but I thought if a person takes this one as intended it should be a help to us all so I'll share it with you.

My mind goes to a little verse:
Only one life, twill soon be past
Only whats done, for Christ will Last!

We really miss seeing you, so I guess if we can never find you at home you'll need to come visit us!

Psalms:145-17-18-19 17. Der Herr is gerecht in allen seinen Vegen, und hirlig in Alln seinen Verken. 18. Der Herr ist Nahe Allen near everyone, Die ihn anrufen, Allen, die ihn mit Ernst anrufen. 19. Er thut vas die

Gottesfürchten begehren, ist höret ihr schreien, und heißt ihnen. Several nice verses! Will close and we are still Praying for you as well as us all.
  Love,
  Dad-n-Mom

"I can't believe your mom says that about Chester Lee. A ten-year-old boy is lucky to have died? 'Lucky little lad' she says! Maybe a ten-year-old shouldn't be working on such dangerous equipment! Maybe then he wouldn't have an accident and have to be put on life support. I'm surprised they even allow him to be put on life support in the first place. What's the point? 'Lucky little lad' my ass! How can anyone say that? How can they consider a child dying as lucky? That's just totally screwed up."

It's funny how something can be right in front of you, but you don't see it. Like a rabbit perfectly camouflaged in a dense thicket. When I read that part of my mom's letter, I thought, "Poor Chester Lee, how sad for his family". That was the way I had always heard people talk. That's the way life is for Amish.

Karrie read the same passage and saw through the bullshit immediately. Her outburst changed everything for me. It was as if that rabbit in the thicket had twitched ever so slightly and in that instant, it had come completely into focus. I could see him as clearly as if he had just turned neon yellow.

The deceit.
The excuses.
The hypocrisy.

How had I missed it for so long? How could so many people continue to buy into such crap? Was their way of life so precious that they had to justify a terrible accident to a child as a good thing?

The Amish are masters of justification. It's their way of keeping everything under control. When I tried to find out if anyone knew anything about Karrie's attack, I asked several people. The most I could ever get out of anyone was that her ex-boyfriend was probably behind it.

"Bullshit!" was Karrie's reply when I told her the rumor about her former boyfriend. "He wouldn't do that. He was never violent. I know the girlfriend he was with before me and she agrees, he isn't like that. She certainly wasn't attacked when they broke up. He just goes on his way."

I didn't believe it either, but I wanted Karrie to know what the rumor was. After her boyfriend moved out, at the beginning of April, I knew it would only add fuel to the fire about the two of us.

"Did he leave because of me?" I asked her at the time.

"No, it's been coming for a while now. He didn't always like me helping you and David, but it was a lot more than the two of you."

It didn't make sense that her former boyfriend would attack her. Why would he? Why would he get some Amish guys to come do it? It didn't add up, especially since the purpose of the attack was so obviously intended to get me to return.

We might never know exactly who the guys and driver were, but we knew who was behind it.

There was no doubt in my mind about that.

But I doubted that he would ever admit it.

My father would never admit it.

Even if we could prove that he was behind it, he would only claim that he did it to save my soul.

That was all the justification he needed.

Twenty-three

You, therefore, have no excuse,
you who pass judgment on someone else,
for at whatever point you judge the other,
you are condemning yourself,
because you who pass judgment do the same things.
So when you, a mere man, pass judgment on them
and yet do the same things,
do you think you will escape God's judgment?
Romans 2: 1 & 3, *The Holy Bible*, NIV

Bill

In May I received a sympathy card. I had no idea why. No one died. But I guess they don't make cards with the proper message to send to a wayward Amish.

Printed on the front of the card was written, "With Deepest Sympathy" with a picture of a flower arrangement, two unlit candles, and an open Bible. Inside, the card read, "May you look to God above/And trust His love today.../In Him you'll find the peace of mind/The world can't take away."

A personal note was added, under the printed message:

William,
We feel so sorry for you that you, can't live with your Dear wife & children, we so often think of you, & pray for you. We aw have a son married to a English girl & it has broken our hearts so often. We feel so sorry for your dear Mom & Dad, but the most is your soul. Is there anything we could do for you?

On the left, inside the card, there was a printed verse: *"Our help is in the name of the Lord..." Psalm 124:8 KJV*

Above that, in the blank area, another personal message had been added:

Jesus will forgive all sins if we are truly Sorry & do Better
May you have a Blessed & happy Christmas.
Your Aunt
Alvin & Anna Miller

Why she was wishing me a Happy Christmas in May, I have no idea.

Another letter came from my mother a few weeks later. At the top she wrote the date, *5-23-03*, and also added *"Chester Alvin's Birth."* Chester Alvin is my nephew.

Dear William,

Greetings in Jesus Holy Name. This is another nice sunny morn. Hope this finds you well and on the go as leaves us. Dad went to work over at Harvey Gamolls tenant farm today. Don't Know what all he has to do but put in a new toilet stool & wreck an old garage. They moved another garage over last week out of Wautoma to replace this one.

He has been busy trying to get some of his job's completed that he had promised quite a while already.

I neglected from getting written to you the last 2 weeks as I thought I was busy last wk. doing Adlai's chores & had the Kids too while there were in S.D.

No lawn mowing & gardening is here so that keeps me a going plus I helped at Tobys several Past days this week getting ready for church.

Do I see you go past here the last several days or off & on for week now?? If so you could at least stop in some time & as much as say Hi to us! ☺

No, we haven't forgotten you, you are still in our prayers and constantly in our thoughts, plus wondering what have I done on my part to posess you to break our heats so bad? I am sorry for all the wrongs I have done to you and pray for forgiveness!

Today is Bake Sale Baking day for tomorrow so I Should get busy with that now too.

So take care and please write some time you surely can do that much for us.

Love Always,
Dads & Elvie
This is a prayer of Gods Love for us (by Phrofet Paul in the Bible)

Love is patient and Kind: "Love is not jealous or Boastful: it is not arrogant or rude. Love does not insist on its own way; it is not irritable or resentful; it does not rejoice at wrong, but rejoices in the Right.

Love bears all things, believes all things, hopes all things, endures All things. (1 Corinthians 12:4 –7)

And then another letter came, this one from my brother.

6-1-03

Dear William,

Greetings in Jesus name the one who accepts us as his children if we can with his help lead a life according to his word. Wonder how these lines find you in health & etc. We're all going with much to be thankful for, Esther has a sore spot in leg at present we are quite sure know it prob- is her vains a wk. ago we thought it possibly might be a blood clot. Today the 2 oldest boys & girls & me were over to Bloomfield for church was another interesting day. We've had quite a bit of rain since we're here so haven't been able to plow yet as we have some heavy bottom ground that lies along the river hasn't been worked for a year so it is packed pertty good and takes a while for it to dry out, hopefully we can start tommorow. We're trying to find a portable band saw I guess we'll go with a band saw instead of a circular for a few differnt reasons hopefully we can make things work out that way. Since we started looking for one we find that there are a lot of different makes & models right know we're checking for one from Canada called a cutting edge. It's kinda hard to decide whitch one we should get. With the information I get more people are leaning against bigger band wheels to extend band life. Sorry we didn't get to see you before we moved. Is quite a change in our life compared to what we had. Hopeing we can lead a life pleasing to God whitch is all that count's, only one life twill soon be past only what is done for Christ will last.

With Love & prayers, Lewis & all.

The Amish are never wasteful. Wastefulness is a sin. Lewis wrote that note to me on what was left of some paper from a letter that had been sent to him. The entire back page was blank, so he started with that and when he needed more room, he simply crossed out what Melvin had written on the front and finished. A big "X" marked through the original note from Melvin, but I could still read it.

126

Fri. morn.
Dear friends,
Greetings to you this nice spring morning.
Just a few quick lines in hope to beat the mailman yet.
If plans hold out we want to come to your place next Tues, the 27ᵗʰ early evening and we want to bring supper in for you. Thought if it didn't suit us to help when you moved maybe we can do this much.
Hope to see you soon!
Sincerely,
Melvin Schrock

In mid-June, a note came with two birds on the front that looked like robins. It was from my mother.

Fri. 6-13-03
Dearest William,
Greetings of Love and in Jesus Name. This is another warm day according to the thermometer. It says 79°, Partly cloudy so it prob. feels muggy outside. I should be out doors mowing lawn but grass is wet and I am doing inside cleaning getting ready for church. It will be here on June 22 Lord Willing. Last week Ruby & Frieda were here & helped me a day. Yesterday Millie & Rosanna helped. I feel I prob. can do the rest inside but then there is the yard to be cleaned up this time too so maybe Toby's kids can help a little with that next week again. The gardens are pretty welled cleaned for this week. Things really are doing good as of now. Plenty of yummy good radishes & lettuce to eat right now and I know you'd enjoy them too and I'd share with you if I could reach you. Dad happened to meet Jason W. the other day & he says your working down South so maybe you'll never get this note. Don't know if your coming home weekend or not, but will give this a chance for you to read. Hoping you'll receive it. I guess yesterday was little Frieda's 1ˢᵗ Birthday. You must of thought about it to and wished her a happy day. I suppose if she could write you a note – she would say, the best Birthday gift you can give me Daddy is come Back to us again and be my Daddy so we can all be happy together again! I know you are concerned about her and I hope you are feeling responsible for the one unborn too, and can come back & make things right with God & everyone. We would really like that. You Know God forgives us (all our sins if we confess). No one is perfect. I myself, have to battle constantly to try to do the best I know how. We can't understand everything but we are not either

supposed to be so smart that we can. Just try to live the way our parents, forefathers & everyone tryed to teach us, then still say – and pray we hope to have a home in Heaven some day, but only through the Grace of God for no one deserves it. Now I'm just talking about my own faults. So I need your prayers as well as you need mine.

I am also inviting you to come to church at our house on June 22. <u>Please</u>! Ruby says she wants to come too so we will see. I did not write this to upset you, Only out of concern, as a loving Mother's Responsibiys. We are still praying & have not forgotten you!

About a month later, a letter came from my father.

July 14 – 03
Dear Son,
Greetings of Love in Jesus Name wishing you the Grace of God to lead a Godly life to some day reap eternal happy heavly home.

We came here to the health mines at Basin, MT July 9 and plan to be home July 23 eve. Unless we get word of Lewis S. He is in very bad shape that as you probably know is Sister (Viola) husband although I called to the hospital Sat. and is a little better but am surprised if He will ever be well again, but again as we all know I or you can go in a twinkle of an eye.

Well time to go into the mine again the man wants us to sing some songs. Bro Levi then Mervin Ben Dienes, and Levi Otto of Ill are also here.

We sang quite a few songs this man cried so much the first song it touched Him so deep He had to leave. We feel a tough heart was touched the 1st song was If I could hear my mother pray again. Is an older man just wish He'd give His whole heart to God an sure He'd feel better is soft hearted yet swears and trys to talk tough yet also frienly als wonder how you are really feeling by now. Please don't deceive yourself.

Well believe Ben and I will go climb Mountain again this P.M. Had a beautiful climb the other day Friday I guess to much to write it all maybe can tell someday. Seems Levi is getting better can walk better but He is 73 so probaly won't get real good. Went by your place seen all the logs on east side. Did you cut up all the others already? Understood you sold the buggy horses was sorry to hear you actually sold Ruth and wonder what happened with the wedding present Dix.

You used to have the 3 – Rs Ruby – Ruth & Roxie. So sad. Als so wonder what the little one will be. Als spites me seems we don't see enough of Frieda that She can learn to except us yet but probaly will later. hope so.

But it's so nice to hold and play with them when they are small so they have a trust in gramps as they grow up.

Lewises Children als write wanting us to come visit so want to when Tobys move which is maybe the 1ˢᵗ week in Aug. They are down there now putting in the basement so they'll be gone soon too. Than only be Adlais & Monroes to visit and Council with.

Aus Liebe
Dad/Mom

My dad asking about what had become of my horses surprised me. There was a good chance that he heard I gave Dix and her foal to Karrie. If he knew, he would not have liked it. And he wouldn't have liked it if he knew that I had Karrie sell my buggy horses: Ruth, Randy, and Ricky. She sold them to another Amish who couldn't do business directly with me because I was in the ban.

My only other horse, Roxie, was the one Ruby took when she left me.

My dad didn't ask about Roxie.

He knew where Roxie was.

Another day, another letter. It had become a way of life for me and I grudgingly opened the latest.

Hello,

Bill __Please Please__ come back to your Sweet Wife and daughter oh Please. It's just not fair that they have to go through something like this – __All__ your friends would be so Happy if you'd only come back and be your happy self again – Hey we all make mistakes – what you done is done now, Please ask God for forgiveness and Please come back to Ruby! __Nobody__ would hold anything towards you, It's so hard for Ruby and you could make it __so__ easy. Please don't wait another day –

Tomorrow it might be too Late Your Sweet little Girly is going up __so fast__, she's just at the age where she's doing all the cute things – She say's __Dat__ __Dat__ Oh so sweet, Please Bill she needs you! Don't forget We're all human We All make mistakes! If we could cry Alittle harder, Get a little less sleep At night Would it change your mind?? If we'd have 2 dozen Roses – Would it change your mind????

Please Don't Wait another Day – Ruby needs you, Please put her out of her __Misery__!

From Friends that make mistakes too,
By God All Things are possible!
All your friends are wishing you Back!

Even though the letter wasn't signed, I had a good idea who sent it. Young Folks called me Bill. They also tended to know country songs. A lot of Young Folks had radios. As long as they weren't church members, the punishment wasn't as severe. Of course someone could hear English music while riding with a driver, so they might not be doing something against the *Ordnung*. Either way, my guess was the letter came from a Young Folk.

Next came another letter from my brother.

July 20, 2003
Dear William,
Greetings in our saviours name. The one who wants to live in our hearts if only we accept and let & him in. This is Sun. eve. after chores & supper we just had a day at home, a wk. ago we were to Bloomfield for church around 10 o clock word got to church that Melvin Schrocks house is on fire. so quite a few went to help with that the cause of it still not certain most of the upstairs had to be replaced. They were still able to save most of everything downstairs. By Friday afternoon the outside was pretty well finished. The past wk. was mostly spent on baleing wheat straw, including a baler break down of 2 ½ days. Wer'e still working on the shed for sawmill hopefully the mill will be here in a wk. or so. As of now we have a fair size order of custom sawing, we've done a couple of small orders so far, possibly another not sure yet. With love & prayers
Lewis & Family
Johannes 3:16

Also hat Gott die welt geliebet daß er seinen eingebornen Sohen gab, auf daß alle, die an ihn glauben, nicht verloren werden, sodern das ewige Leben haben.

John 3:16
For God so loved the world that he gave his only begotton Son, that whosoever believeth in him should not perish, but have everlasting life.

Soon after that one, another letter arrived. That wasn't a big surprise since a letter came practically every day. But this letter was different.

"There's a letter for you, Bill."

"So? What else is new?"

Karrie grinned and handed it to me, "The return address is 'Heaven'. Don't you think you'd better open it?"

I took it from her. It was just an ordinary white, business-sized envelope.

"Jeez, Bill, I didn't realize that God would take time out of His busy schedule to write to a wayward Amish. You think He's writing to tell you to go back?"

Rolling my eyes but cracking the slightest smile, I ripped open the envelope and took out the letter. It was written on wide ruled, three-hole punched notebook paper.

"Pretty plain stationery for the Supreme Being," Karrie continued with the sarcasm, "but I guess those stone tablets would have cost too much to mail."

My Precious Child,

I love you! I shed my own blood for you to make you clean. You are new, so believe it is true! You are lovely in My eyes, and I created you just as you are. Do not criticize yourself or get down for not being perfect in your own eyes. This leads only to frustration.

I want you to trust Me, one step, one day at a time. Dwell in My power and My love. And be free – be yourself! Don't allow other people to run you. I will guide you if you'll let me.

Be aware of My presence in everything. I give you patience, joy, peace. Look to Me for answers. I am your Shepherd, and I will lead you.

FOLLOW ME ONLY.

Do not ever forget this Listen and I will tell you My will. I Love You! I Love You! Let it flow from you – spill over to all you touch. Be not concerned with yourself – you are My responsibility. I will change you almost without your knowing it. You are to love yourself and love others simply because I love you.

Take your eyes off yourself! Look only at Me! I lead, I change, I make, but not when you are trying. I won't fight your efforts.

You are mine Let me have the job of making you like Christ. Let me love you! Let Me give you joy, peace, and kindness. No one else can! Don't you see?

You are not your own. You have been bought with blood, and now you belong to me. It is really none of your business how I deal with you. Your only command is to look to Me and Me only! Never to yourself and never to others.

I love you. Do not struggle, but relax in My love. I know what is best and will do it in you. How I want freedom to love you freely!

Stop trying to be, and let Me make you what I want. My will is perfect! My love is sufficient! I will supply all your needs! Look to Me!

I love you,
Your Heavenly Father

"The letter was postmarked in St. Louis," Karrie noted, "Maybe the Gateway Arch is really just a big mail slot coming down from Heaven above. They could change their advertising to "Gateway to Heaven"!"

Karrie had a lot of fun with that letter.

That letter pissed me off.

The harder they pushed, the more I dug in.

The longer I was out, the more obvious their bullshit became.

The hypocrites were now using God to try to get me back! They were pretending to speak for God. It was blasphemy! All this talk about "looking to Him." How did they know that I wasn't looking to God already? How did they know that God wasn't telling me to stay English!

When I was trying to figure out the right thing to do, I prayed to God for a sign. I believe God answered that prayer. I believe God gave me a sign. I even talked to my sister Rachel about what happened.

"Do you believe in signs?" I asked.

"I believe in signs. What was the chance of your pump going out right then? Why not believe it was God's work? There are other ways to serve God than to be Amish."

Having a sister on the outside made a big difference. I was lucky. I also had a brother on the outside, but no one knew where Lynn was. Karrie had been trying to track him down for me but wasn't having any luck.

I thought about Lynn a lot.

Where was he? How was he doing? Did he get letters after he left? Did God write to him?

Twenty-four

*Likewise, teach the older women
to be reverent in the way they live,
not to be slanderers or addicted to much wine,
but to teach what is good.
Then they can train the younger women
to love their husbands and children,
to be self-controlled and pure, to be busy at home,
to be kind, and to be subject to their husbands,
so that no one will malign the word of God.*
Titus 2: 3-5, *The Holy Bible*, NIV

Bill

A card came for my birthday. On the outside was printed:

Wishing you Birthday Blessings. The LORD will give grace and glory: no good thing will He withhold... Psalm 84:11

Inside was the printed message:

Because it's your birthday, these warm thoughts come you way as we rejoice with you on your special day. MAY GOD BLESS YOU AND GIVE YOU A HAPPY Birthday!

Above it, my mother had written, *"Dear William,"* She circled the inside message and drew a heart around *"May God Bless You..."* She also added *"And we wish you many more."* And also *"Love and Prayers"* Dad – N – Mom

On the other side of the card, she wrote:

"Hold Fast to God's hand and He Will lead you safely through all trails. Whenever you cannot stand. He will carry you lovingly in His arms." St. Frances de Soles"

Aug. 10, 2003
Oh my
Now your 25!

On the back of the card, she wrote out the entire popular passage:

"Foot Prints"
One night a man had a dream. He dreamed he was walking along the beach with the Lord. Across the sky flashed scenes from his life. For each scene, he noticed two sets of footprints in the sand; one before to him, and the other to the Lord.

When the last scene of his life flashed before him, he looked Back at the footprints in the sand. He noticed that many times along the path of his life there was only one set of footprints. He also noticed that it happened at the very lowest and saddest times in his life.

This really bothered him and he questioned the Lord about it. "Lord, you said that once I decided to follow you, you'd walk with me all the way. But I have noticed that during the most troublesome times in my life there is only one set of footprints. "I don't understand why when, I needed you most you would leave me."

The Lord replied, "My precious, precious child, I love you and I would never leave you. During your times of trial and suffering, when you see only on set of footprints, it was then that I carried you."

After all of that, inside was a letter.

Dear William,
First a greeting in Jesus Name. Its about 12 oclock & maybe I can jot a few lines before lunch as Dad isn't Back from Adlai's from helping unload 3 leads of oats to thresh. They did some Sat. & load 3 more loads & put in Sheds over Sun. Oats looks good this yr. Better then the corn & hay does.

Tomorrow (Tue.) Toby's plan to load truck & leave early Wed. morn for their new home in Mo. we will really miss them, but at least we can have hopes of seeing them now & then again even it its about 600 miles from here.

We plan to go along to help a day or so then back up to Arbela to Lewis s a few days, to see the new little one they were Blessed with on July 25 a boy named <u>Monroe</u> 7# 12 oz. 20 in. long. Now they have 5 girls & 4 Boys, just about same.

These 2 poems were in the Plain Interests paper & I thought how true they are and wanted to share them with you.

We had company for supper last nite from Kokomo, Indiana. Dads neice & family & one married dau., husband & 2 children, then our children, Ruby & Frieda, Levi Yoders & all their children living here, except David & Dena had gone to Clare, Mi. to visit Amosa over the weekend.

I washed this morn. but it's not drying fast as only once in a while the Sun peeps a little. Should go see if Millie still has something for me to do sometime this afternoon too.

Now why don't you take time and send us a few lines you Surely could do that much for us!

Well I must go, get other work done. This card will be early but I wanted to do it B-4 we leave & Knew tomorrow I won't have time. So take care and Remember we are still Praying for your <u>return</u>!

Lots of Love
Dad – N – Mom

My birthday.

It was hard to believe that summer would be ending in only a few more weeks. It was nice to get a card from my mother...even it was another attempt to get me back.

Nothing came from Ruby.

It wasn't surprising. The last time we spoke, back in early May, she told me, just before she hung up, that she would never call me again. That was a vow she seemed willing to honor.

I don't remember how the conversation began that day. Probably the way it usually did with Ruby asking if I was coming back. There had been so many times before that day when I pleaded with her to come back home or to move with me somewhere new. So many times when I felt down and lonely. If she had only given it the slightest consideration. If she had only said that she would meet me at our home, I probably would have gone back.

Back home.
Back to the Amish.

Instead, all she would ever say was, "I don't want to move. I don't want to leave my family."

Not only did she have her family, but she also had all of the community. Everyone was on her side. Everyone pitied her. She seemed to like it that way. She seemed intent on keeping it that way.

A few times she told me, "I'm afraid you'll kidnap me."

I never knew what to say to that. Did she really think I could do such a thing? Whether or not she believed it, whether it was just an excuse, it didn't matter. I didn't like it. I didn't like it one bit.

All I could do was to keep trying to make our life together work. She could be Amish while I lived English, or we move to a new community where I would be Amish again. I asked her so many times. I pleaded with her so many times. Why not try it?

Ruby always had the power to get me back, but everything had to be on her terms. She was never willing to compromise.

That day in May when we were talking on the phone, it all finally fell into place. I could see everything clearly, like the morning fog lifting with the rising of the sun.

Ruby was never coming back.

It hit me hard.
I realized something else.
She didn't want me to come back.

Ruby didn't want me back.

All of those times we talked on the phone, her voice was always so calm. It was always flat. Emotionless. Even when I was pleading with her to come home. It had never occurred to me before, but she was home. She was already home. Home with her parents. She obviously preferred that home to the one we had.

She didn't want to be a family if it included me.
She didn't want to be my wife.
She didn't love me anymore.

136

Maybe she never did.

"You aren't honoring your vows," I blurted out. I had never spoken so plainly and directly to her before.

"I don't know what you're talking about..."

"When we got married, you vowed to follow my leadership. You aren't. You aren't honoring those vows."

"I'm sure it doesn't mean leaving the Amish. I don't have to follow you if it means leaving our community and families," Ruby defended herself.

"No, that wasn't ever mentioned. You aren't honoring your vows. You're a hypocrite...just like all the Amish. You say one thing, like how you'll honor your marriage vows, but then you don't. You're a hypocrite!"

"Well, if that's how you feel, I guess we don't have anything more to talk about," Ruby challenged. In her voice I could also hear something else.

Relief.

"I guess we don't."

"If that's how you feel, I won't call you anymore."

"That's how I feel," I told her. I could be just as stubborn as she was.

The line went dead.

I knew at that moment that my marriage had died as well.

Twenty-five

Karrie

After I moved back into my childhood home, I was surprised to find so many Amish living around me. They intrigued me, just as they intrigued so many people, with their old-fashioned lifestyle and simple ways. I loved to watch the buggy parade on Sundays when church was held somewhere nearby. When we would hear the distinctive cadence of the buggy and the clip-clopping hooves coming down the road, my kids and I would rush to the front windows and watch as they went by. There always seemed to be something sacred in their procession.

At first we could only identify the buggies by the horses. We had no idea where the families had come from or where they were headed. After becoming friends with Amos and Verena and driving Lizzie Mae's kids, we were able to pick out those families. Over time, we recognized more and more of them, especially once I became more involved in the community.

After Bill first left, that same peaceful feeling would come over me when there was a church Sunday buggy parade. No one waved to me the way they had before, but the steady rocking rhythm of the buggy still soothed me.

But that changed once the Amish made it personal.

I wasn't surprised that they ostracized me for helping Bill. It wasn't unexpected that rumors and gossip would be spread about Bill and me. I didn't like it, but I could deal with that. But when the Amish came onto my property. When they beat me and threatened to rape me, that was when *everything* changed.

The sound of an Amish buggy no longer gave me a feeling of serenity and peace.

It made me angry.
It made me ear-smoking, fire-spitting furious.

I wanted justice for what had been done to me. I wanted those Amish men and their driver arrested and put in prison. I was beyond pissed at the person who had undoubtedly initiated the attack, and that also included the entire community for protecting the assailants and keeping it hush-hush.

I would never forget.
I would never forgive.

After the attack, the sheriff came out right away. He took my statement and had a detective stop by to dust for fingerprints on the skidder where the attacker may have touched something. I gave him a very detailed description of the men and their vehicle. Since the rear license plate had been removed, there was no telling where the vehicle had come from. It may have been from another state. The sheriff told me later that he questioned several of the Amish, including Bill's dad and brothers, but no one seemed to know anything about it.

No surprise there.

No one would ever admit to knowing anything whether or not they did. It was another case of convenient Amish amnesia.

"What a bunch of bullshit! Your dad knows damn well who they were. He's lying. He's lying to a sheriff! Doesn't he have to confess for that?"

"Probably not," Bill said in his typical low-key way.

"How the hell can he get away with it?"

"The Amish don't concern themselves with the English or the English law," Bill replied with a shrug.

"So that gives him the right to lie?"

"He wouldn't consider it lying."

Bill is still such a typical Amish sometimes. After spending some time with them, you become all too familiar with their ability to double-talk. They can weasel out of a direct question better than a seasoned politician.

I wanted to smack him.

"You're saying it's okay for him to lie to the police?" I said with great intent, never taking my eyes off his face, ready to explode.

"No, I'm not saying that," Bill sighed before he continued, "I'm trying to explain what *he* thinks, what they all think. When you're Amish, you're told not to trust the English. You're told that English are bad. The English are dishonest. Amish don't feel they have to tell the English anything. It's not about lying or not lying. They just don't believe they have to answer to outsiders. If the deacon or bishop asked my dad 'Did you have Karrie attacked', he would tell the truth. Of course, the worst he might get is two weeks in the ban, so why wouldn't he confess? Amish don't lie to other Amish."

"But they sure as hell will lie their asses off to the rest of us!"

My attack forever changed the way I saw the Amish. They had everyone fooled with their quaint way of living and their supposed higher moral standards. But they didn't fool me. Not any longer. I saw past the peaceful pastoral projection down to the rotten core. It was just the same as when I bored my chainsaw into a beautifully leafed out tree, appearing to be vibrantly alive, only to find that it was hollow inside from dry rot and decay.

When I learned that it wasn't required for them to be honest with anyone on the outside, it would alter the way I viewed all of my friendships with the Amish. Out of respect for my closest friends, especially Amos and Verena, I distanced myself from them after Bill left. I was an outcast from the community and didn't want to cause them any difficulties, even though my affection for Amos and Verena, David, and a handful of others, hadn't changed.

Now I was left wondering how close those friendships really were. To me, a friend is a friend regardless of religious beliefs, sexual orientation, skin color, or whatever other difference there might be. From what Bill explained, the Amish would always see me as English first. I would always be an outsider. And I wondered: if honesty with the English is optional, would any them tell me if they knew something about my attack? Would any of the Amish, even those I considered my friends, tell me? Where did their loyalties lie?

My loyalty would be to my friends, no matter what. Proof of that came only a few days, after David had gone back to the Amish, and I got a call from his mother.

"I heard David's thinking of leaving again. Please don't help him! Please don't take my boy away again!" His mother, Katie Ellen, sobbed into the phone.

Her call took me by surprise since I had no idea what she was talking about. If he was thinking of leaving again, David would have called. He would have called me. I was certain of that. He knew that I would help him anytime he needed it. This had to be gossip. Gossip, once again, intended to hurt me.

"Promise me that you won't help him, Karrie!" She pleaded, but it didn't touch me. Not from her.

"You've treated me like shit, Katie Ellen. I know you've said shit about me that wasn't true. If David wants to leave, you can damn well bet that I'll be there with bells on!" and I slammed down the phone.

David never called. Some time later, I heard that he had gotten married and ironically, it was to someone that I had suggested.

"There's no girls to date," he had complained one day, back before Bill left, when we were taking our usual break in the camper.

"Do you want to know who I think you should ask out?" I asked. I hate it when people try to tell me what to do, but David and I were friends, and if he wanted my advice, I would offer it.

"Yeah, sure. Who do you think I should date?"

"If I were you, I'd ask Marietta out." Marietta was the oldest of Lizzie Mae's kids, the one who did most of the talking that rainy day when their cart broke and I gave them a ride.

"Marietta? Why her?"

"Because she's a sweet girl. And she likes the outdoors, just like you do."

"Well, *if* I ever get married, she'll have to know how to make good bread."

"I'm sure Marietta knows how to do that. Her mom sure does."

David didn't say anything else then, but my suggestion obviously made an impression. When I heard that David and Marietta had gotten married, I was happy for them and will always wish them the very best. They should have a good life together.

While David never called me to come get him, there was someone else that summer who did.

"Karrie, I want to leave. Can you help me? Can you come get me?" A young Amish named Leroy pleaded, talking fast as if he was afraid someone was going to catch him.

Bill had given Leroy my number and told him that we would work something out. While I knew and had worked with Leroy's older brother Ferman for some time, I don't remember ever meeting Leroy. But it didn't matter. He needed help, and I would do whatever I could.

"You bet," I told him, "when do you want to leave?"

"Can you come tonight at ten?"

"I'll be there. I'll stop at the end of the driveway and you be ready, okay?"

"Okay, thanks," he sounded relieved and quickly hung up.

The late summer sun had finally gone down when I left to get Leroy. It felt as though I was setting off on a secret mission. Of course, it wasn't going to be a secret for very long. Someone would see me or they would recognize my car. Even if we got away undetected, suspicion would quickly fall on me anyway. The community would find a way to blame me whether or not I was the one helping. I was damned if I did, and damned if I didn't. So what the hell? I might as well!

As I got close to Leroy's house, I slowed down to nearly an idle. I wanted to be as quiet as possible and also needed to make sure that I didn't get there too early. The clock on the dashboard showed that it was nearly ten o'clock, so I continued to let the car creep slowly forward. At the end of the driveway, I stopped the car and in a flash, Leroy was out the front door, charging toward me with a duffel bag flung over his shoulder. He ran like a prisoner making a jailbreak. The front door had barely closed when it flew open again, and Ferman looked out.

"Hurry up!" I shouted out the passenger window.

Leroy threw himself into the car and before he could shut the door, I hit the gas, and we sped off. This was definitely a new style of Amish taxi service that I was providing these days.

Bill and I decided that it would be best to let Leroy stay at Bill's house. It was sitting empty and that way, if any of Leroy's family came looking for him, we could honestly say, "No, he's not here."

Leroy worked cutting saw logs for Bill. Twice he tried and failed on the written exam to get his learner's permit. About a month after he left, Leroy told us that he was going to Indiana to a much higher community. He was still a teenager and heard that they practiced *rumspringa*. That was the last we ever heard from him.

Finding out that the Amish feel no obligation to tell the truth to outsiders wasn't the only disturbing thing I would learn about them. Something else came up unexpectedly from the most trivial and unlikely of places: a televised beauty pageant.

"I can't believe she won," Bill grumped as he came out to join me on the back porch steps where I was sitting, enjoying the quiet of a summer evening.

"Who?"

"The black girl won. They're taking over the world."

"Well, more power to them!" I laughed thinking that he was kidding.

He wasn't.

"It's in the Bible. The blacks are meant to be slaves, they aren't supposed to be taking over everything."

"Who the hell told you that? That's not in the Bible!" It didn't seem possible that this was the same Bill who had been living under my roof for months now. Never, not once, in all that time had I ever heard him say anything discriminatory against any group of people.

"Yes it is. It's in Genesis. You know, where they found Noah naked, and Ham went to get his brother. It says that they and all their descendants were damned for all eternity. Blacks are to be the servants of all servants."

"That's bullshit."

He looked at me with that 'you poor English don't know the Bible' look. That was all the challenge I needed. I hopped up and went into the house for both of my Bibles, the King James and the New International versions.

"Here, smart-ass, show me where it says that," I said as I dumped both books in his lap. "You show me where it says that God turned them black!"

"If you don't believe that God can do that, then you aren't a believer."

"I'm not saying I don't believe God can do that, but I also know that He *didn't* do it!" I yelled at him and stomped back into the house.

I was pissed. Not at Bill as much as all of the Amish. What kind of religion teaches crap like that? Why preach that one race of people should be slaves to another? Why preach that God ordered it!

Looking out the window, I could see Bill walking out toward the barn with both Bibles under his arm. I went to the phone and called his sister Rachel.

"Do you know what your brother just said?" I asked before launching into what just happened.

"I don't believe that," Rachel said after I finished, "We weren't taught that!"

"Well, your brother sure as hell says differently!"

"Let me call Amanda. I'll call you right back."

Their sister Amanda is still Old Order Amish but in a higher community that permits telephones. Only a few minutes passed before the phone rang.

"Amanda says that we *were* taught that...just like Bill says. I can't believe it. I sure don't remember it that way."

"Here comes your brother back from the barn, I better talk to you later."

From the way he came walking toward the house, I could tell that Bill hadn't found what he was looking for. He came into the kitchen and took a seat at the table.

"It's not in there," he said, setting the Bibles on the table. Disappointment and confusion were clearly written on his face. "I found the passage that they always referred to, but it's not like what they said. It's not at all like what we were taught. They changed it."

Right in front of me, I watched as someone's entire world turned upside-down. Bill had gotten used to their illogic and hypocrisy, but this went deeper. This went to the very foundation of the Amish faith. They had altered and distorted the Bible.

"You get used to hearing stuff that you don't understand," Bill explained.

Church services are spoken in what they call "high" German, what would be considered proper or formal German, so most of it goes over the kids' heads. Before they start school, Amish children learn to speak their dialect, Germish, as I call it. Germish is most commonly spoken in the home and while it comes from German, there are unique Amish words and pronunciations. When the kids start school...Amish school...at six, they learn to speak English and on Fridays, and only on Fridays, they have German lessons. For the most part, Amish are fluent in speaking both English and Germish. They can read and write English, but most Amish can't write in high German and while they may be able to read it, most of them don't truly comprehend it.

Bibles used by the Amish are printed in English or German. Most Amish don't have a German dictionary to go with their German Bible. Having the church services in high German means that very few in the congregation fully understand what is being read. But it's certainly a good trick to have up your sleeve. It's not too hard to twist things, or give them a different slant, or even to lie. How hard can it be when no one understands the real meaning of the language? Who knows how many generations have been deceived?

I became aware of this lack of education when I wanted to make the signs for my car, the ones telling the Amish to speak English. That was all I needed my sign to say. Just two words. Speak English. It seemed like such a simple thing, but it wasn't. I couldn't believe how many of them I had to ask before someone was finally able to tell me how to write those two words so the Amish would understand it!

It isn't surprising that the Amish don't educate their kids past eighth grade. The less you educate children, the harder it is for them to know when they are being deceived. Just when the kids are moving into their rebellious teen years, they are taken out of school, and away from their peers. Girls are sent home to help their mothers with the housework and care for their siblings. Boys go off to work, apprentice style, usually with their fathers or older brothers. They get paid, but typically the child will hand over his pay to his parents, with the boy only keeping some, if any. Child labor laws don't seem to apply to the Amish.

Something else came up that summer that had to do with Amish and money.

One day Rachel called, "You aren't going to believe this one, Karrie!"

"Now what?"

"They're sending out a chain letter asking for money for Ruby!"

"What the hell? You're kidding!"

"No, can you believe it? Amanda got one in the mail today. She was so mad that she called me. She's sending me a copy and when I get it, I'll type it up and email it to you."

A few days later I got the promised email from Rachel:

Lets have a cheer up $5.00 shower for Ruby Hersberger, Her husband left her! And shes alone to support her little girl. She has no income except for some quilting. So lets send her a few lines of cheer along w/$5.00.
Send a copy to 6 of your friends
Keep goin' till Aug. 2003

Unbelievable!

The Amish started a chain letter campaign for poor Ruby. She probably netted several thousand dollars, all unreported and tax-free. The letter claimed that Ruby had no income except for some quilting. There was no mention that she was living with her parents. There was no mention that Bill had repeatedly told her to use whatever she needed from their account. There was no mention of the Bent and Dent store where everyone in the area was already encouraged to shop to support poor Ruby.

Poor Ruby indeed!

Someone was certainly taking full advantage of Bill's leaving. Poor Ruby wasn't just getting her bread buttered on both sides of the slice, but all four edges as well!

Twenty-six

Bill

Fri. 8-29-03
Dear William,
Greetings on this nice & cooler day. Thought that we were gonna get a good rain last night but just sprinkled a little so its still dry. Grass is Brown so it doesn't need mowing every week.

Today I'm Baking Rolls, pies & Bread & in the morn. Want to put some donut dough together to Send to Monroe Schmuckers to the Bake Sale.

Its so quiet around here as Monroes and Adlais all went down to visit Lewis's on the weekend, Dad at work & of course Elvie at W.I. so at recess I hear the school kids play. School started here on Tues. Seems like only yesterday the last day was this spring. My My where has the time gone!

Its been some time already now since I wrote last but that wasn't because we forgot you, we well never do that as long as life and memory last. We still love and miss you so much! Why don't you come over for supper Sunday nite the 31ˢᵗ? Please! We would be glad to have you here for a nice visit. Monroes & Adlais Both gone is So lonely around here so you could come Brighten our day.

Maybe you would even like to come help us do Monroes Chores, you'd be more then welcome too. We have some Yummy fresh garden tomatoes to

*eat so just come! And we will fix something. You don't work on Sunday so
you really don't have a reason to not come Do you? ☺ So just do!*
Its nearly mail time So I'll close and hope to see you Sunday nite.
Love and Prayers
Dad – N – Mom

By September, there didn't seem to be any point in keeping my house
standing vacant. I would have gladly sold the house and moved to another
community. Move somewhere where we could start fresh. But my wife and
daughter weren't ever coming home.

I still wanted them back more than anything. But it wasn't going to
happen. I knew it.

If only she would honor the vows she took when she married me. She
should have honored those vows and come home. She should have moved
with me. She should have done whatever she could to bring our family
back together.

After I left, I hoped that she wanted our family to be together. I hoped
that she loved me. But the summer simmered on with no word from her. It
was hard to keep hoping.

Since I was staying at Karrie's full-time, I offered to rent my house to a
friend when he told me that he was looking for a place. Karrie helped me
type up a letter to my parents asking them to tell Ruby to move her things
out.

Part of me thought...part of me hoped...that it might finally convince my
wife to come home.

It didn't.

I never heard a word from her, but my mother had something to say
about it.

Sept. 13 – 03
Our Dear William:
*We just got back a while ago from taking Rubys things out of your house.
A very <u>heart Breaking job</u>! But so it is! Still hoping you will wake up to the
fact what you are doing. This is no laughing matter.*
*We left around half of the canned goods in the Basement out of Love for
you to use for <u>yourself</u>. But if for some reason you do not want it. Let us
Know so we can go get them as it Should be used. Better yet just do a very
simple thing and come back home to where you belong so Both of you can
use it.*

I also left some cups in the cuboard I Knew were yours the clocks I knew were yours we left and the flashlite, elec. Coffee perk., & soap under the Kitchen sinks, plus your things in the office room & on that desk I figured you to get that. The one closet & Bedroom still has a few items for you too & the couch & table & some chairs, in the basement & L. Room we left & also some of your items in (Sorry we didn't have time to clean up the mess Better but had to leave.) Bathroom mirror & etc. Its for you to go get & use. Also we left the curtains on the windows & if the guy moving in doesn't want those, please have them taken off and either store them in a safe place or Bring them here or to Ervins as those are near new curtains. By the way who is the guy moving in if we may Know??

You did a very good job of typing the letter if that was you Wm. So you can now write us more letters if you think we are not fit to speak to in person. We still love you, and want to be your friend if you can except us as your Parents Altho we must of made lots & lots of mistakes in trying to raise our family for the ones that just simply left us do not know what they are doing and probably can't realize how heart Breaking it is to their parents. Out of love that I wrote this I do not want to make you feel bad, just wish that some day we can be back together as a family on the side of eternity! So I guess you all would better be happy now for after this life you will not be if you don't make a change for the Better.

I must get Busy – we still love you – from Dad – N – Mom

Rachel called on September 21st, to tell me the news. Ruby had given birth the day before to our second child. A boy. She named him Paul. Everything had gone well. Ruby and Paul were both doing fine. I was happy but heartbroken. I was excited by the birth of my son, but it ripped me apart.

Why hadn't anyone let me know?
Why wasn't I told sooner?
But I knew why.
I wasn't welcome.
I was being punished.

Maybe their plan was that by treating me this way, they could get me back. I would finally see the error of my ways.

It didn't make sense. They should have let me know. They should have told me when Ruby was in labor so I could rush to her side. Or tell me after his birth to get me to come see him. To have me come bond with him. They had another lure to dangle in front of me. To use as bait to lead me back. But they didn't even tell me about him.

Instead they punished me by remaining silent.

They just kept on cracking that whip, trying to force me to submit.

About September 23rd, my son's baby announcement arrived at Karrie's with only simple request:

"Please give to William Herschberger. Thank You."

A Precious Baby Boy
Name: Paul
Arrived: Saturday, Sept. 20, 2003, 12:58 p.m.
Weight: 7 lb. 6 oz. Length: 21 inches
Parents: William & Ruby
Sister: Frieda

On the front and back were my son's footprints. Also on the back, someone had added his hand prints and another short note:

"Hi Daddy- From: Your son Paul"

Another letter arrived about September 25.

Dear Son
Greetings of Love in Jesus Holy Name. Wonder als each day how it finds you. We're just home tonight. Had been to middle Church then went over to see your little Son. A very adorable baby has features that look like some more of our Grandchildren A heavely gift for someone to take care of and try to lead Him where He can someday live in heavenly Bliss.

So hopefully We can all do that but I on my side have to als vidder kemph against Satan. But enough of this as you don't want to be reminded of these things. Aber Gott laszt sich night spotten.

We've been filling silo the past 2 weeks. Hope to finish here at Adlai's by Tues. Hope so as will need to help Ruby more yet. Oh yes that plow als thought I'd get a chance to go pull it home had pulled it out there with intentions to hook behind the furniture wagon but didn't work out. Well I have to get to bed soon as want to go bender corn for Adlai early tomorrmorn if possible maybe it will rain could use more. Now wasn't this a dry summer just hope the Boys can make it thru the winter as have to buy hay and corn both but guess that it will all make it. Anyhow whatever happened with Dix & Colt. Will close wishing you the enlightment of Gods gifts Jesus Christ that He gave to redeem us poor sinners.

Aus lieb

Dad & Mom

P.S. Tues. morn. Just thought of what you said about Rachel maybe you know something we don't She didn't write us about that would be a help to Her and us. But even than we still have to give account of what we are now doing regardless of what others have done. But it helps a lot if the wrongs are made right with a heartfelt words of really being sorry. Well so it is. So I say sorry. Mom doesn't.

Ruby and the children are here a few days so mom can help take care of Her as Ervins are getting ready for Church Sun.

Another letter followed that one.

Oct. 10 – 03

Dear Son

Greeting of Love in Jesus Name. Looks like another nice day. But hope the bugs stay hid it makes a person think of the Plague God sent over Eygept in Isrial time.

Was so glad you got to talk with the Boys Yest. And hope We can all come to an understanding and be together again somehow. We can see Satan is trying so hard to make misunderstandings.

Hope you can get some good from this book as you can see it was written long ago and still stands for what a true Christian should be. I've personally know people who left the church and at the time of death regretting, screaming and crying to no avail. But I've never heard say of anyone that remained steadfast that regretted it at death door and I realize this culture or way of life has stood well over 400 years. Must go to work wishing you the Blessing of God so yearn to see you again and have a peaceful talk. Oh yes I believe you told Adlai all sins can be forgiven. Yes if we repent from it and quit doing it otherwise it comes under what we read the unpardable Sin. So let us all be careful we don't do that.

Aus Groza Lieb
Dad & Mom
P.S. This Book is for you to keep and do please read it as it quite plainly
answers lots of questions.

The book was a small, red hardcover book titled *1001 Questions and Answers on Christian Life*. Mom added an additional postscript.

P.S. Will scribble a few lines. Adlai did call Ruby last nite. She is at David & Ednas for the weekend as its Ervins Council Church & the Baby would be 3 wks old but I guess she didn't care to go sit in ch. all day the 1ˢᵗ time. He told her to call you and incourage you to come to Davids so hopefully she can get the call through he told her to keep trying as at times the connections are poor. Hoping you will go see them sometime. Think she'd go back to Ervins Mon. or maybe even Sun. nite (no not sure). The baby is such a sweet, cute, little one and really grows or I think so. Als were there again on Tues. Dad did some work for her & I sewed carpet rags, yes, we all want to help you the guidance of Gods power & hand in these trying times. Sorry we didn't Call you when Paul was Born but at the time we thought you just wouldn't answer but found out different! Come see us sometime. We still love you!

It was wearing me down.
Not seeing Ruby.
Not seeing Frieda.
Not seeing my newborn son, Paul.

Part of me wanted to go back. There was so much I missed. So many things I would continue to miss. My son would soon be a month old. I still hadn't seen him.

There are men who don't get to see their children right away. Men serving in the military. That is unfortunate but understandable when someone is far away.

But I wasn't.

My son was only a few miles away. Only a few miles!

As long as I wasn't Amish, I wasn't welcome. I might as well have been on the other side of the planet.

I couldn't stand it any longer.
There was one option.
On October 7th, I met with an attorney.

After Paul was born, I knew I had to see my kids. I hadn't seen Frieda since February. I didn't want to think about how much I had already missed of watching her grow. I couldn't stand not being a part of her life. And now I had another child. The attorney told me that the only way I could get legal visitation rights was to file for divorce.

Divorce.
The word rolled out of her mouth so easily.
It sounded so simple.
File for divorce and see your kids.

My body went numb. It went against everything that I had ever been taught. It was something I could never do as an Amish. Could I do it as an ex-Amish?
It wasn't that I was against divorce.
Divorce made sense when two people don't get along. Divorce was a good thing when someone is abusive or unfaithful. Divorce makes sense if two people don't love each other anymore.
None of that applied to Ruby and me.

I loved Ruby.
I thought she loved me.
I hoped she loved me.

Our marriage had been good, at least it had seemed that way. We got along and were loyal to each other. Why should I divorce her? I didn't want to divorce her. I wanted her back. I wanted her and our children to come home.

It would be much simpler for me to return to the Amish.
If I went back, she would have to come home.
To me.
It would be so easy to go back.

Get out my old clothes. Quit trimming my beard and shave my mustache. Give Karrie my truck just as I joked after I bought it. All my family and friends would be so happy. They would all welcome me back. Sure, I would have to go into the ban for a few weeks. I had been put in the ban before. It hadn't bothered me then. Wasn't it worth it to see my wife and children? Visit with my nieces and nephews and my brothers and sisters? My best friend, David, and I could work together again.

I thought about all of it.
It would be easy.
It would be so easy.
All I had to do was to take up the reins and return to my old life.
My Amish life.

The problem was that nothing would have changed.
Nothing.
All the things that had caused me to leave were still there.
Waiting and watching for me, like a wolf in the cover of the woods.

But maybe having some time away had helped.
Maybe I only needed a break.
Maybe it was time to go back.
Back to the Amish.

Twenty-seven

Karrie

"Karrie, I'm going back."

It was coming. I kept waiting for it.

Every time the phone rang, I knew it would be Bill calling to tell me that he was going back to the Amish. It was only a matter of time.

For weeks, the battle raged inside of him. Not knowing how to help, I watched and waited. It was even worse after his son was born. It was so hard to see him looking so torn and confused, like a man caught in a cross-fire.

He's going back, I was sure of it. I kept waiting. Expecting the call from him. Telling me that he was going to be Amish again.

If Ruby had contacted Bill when their son was born, it might have tipped the scale. But she didn't. No one did. Not Ruby, not his in-laws, not even Bill's parents or his other brothers or sisters in the area. No one in the entire Wautoma Community had called to let him know the special news. Instead, it had been his sister Rachel, who wasn't Amish, who called from Missouri. It didn't seem right, and Bill was furious.

"I don't get it. You'd think that they would want you to know," I said to Bill one evening after supper. "Someone could have called when she went into labor. You had a right to know. What better reason did they have to get you to come over?"

Bill nodded his head and dragged deeply on the cigarette he held to his lips. His quiet nature was usual and familiar, but this was different. I could see it on his face and in the droop of his shoulders. He looked weary and defeated.

"Why don't you go over and see the baby?" I suggested. "They'd have to let you in, wouldn't they?"

He didn't say anything right away, he just stared at the table for several minutes. Then finally, he stubbed the end of the cigarette in the ashtray and asked, "Would they? Would they let me in? I don't know." He looked at me, his dark eyes anguished, "Ruby's told me over and over how she thinks that I'm going to kidnap her. You think she'll let me hold my son? I don't know. Maybe. But it would be in a room filled with all her family. Them all watching me...and praying the whole time. That's not the way I want to see my son."

We sat there at the kitchen table for several minutes, neither of us saying anything. It wasn't an uncomfortable silence, only a lull, and I tried to process what Bill had just said.

Then the haunting jangle of an Amish buggy coming down the road creeped into the room, disturbing our peace.

"Speak of the devil," I couldn't resist saying, with added emphasis on that last word: devil.

There was no escape from them, not even inside my own home. Their calls and letters came regularly for Bill. Two Amish men had come onto my land and attacked me. Even the sound of them traveling past by home disrupted our thoughts and disturbed our peace. They were a constant presence in our lives, one way or another.

"Did I ever tell you about what happened with my niece?" Bill asked while lighting another cigarette.

I shook my head, "No."

There was a long pause before he continued, "I always had a lot of fun playing with my nieces and nephews. One day...when I was probably about fourteen...my father came up to me. He said he heard that I touched my niece...you know...in a bad way."

"What the hell?!"

"It didn't make sense. I mean I hadn't, there's no way. It made me sick just thinking about it. I remember standing there, staring at my father. Trying to figure out why he would say such a thing to me.

"He just glared back at me...like he totally believed it...like I could do such a thing. He told me that I needed to confess. I told him I didn't do anything, that it wasn't true. But he didn't believe me. Then he said, 'I can tell when you're lying because you blink a lot.' But I just kept staring at him, and finally, he walked away.

"It ruined me. Even though it wasn't true, and no one ever said anything more about it, I always felt Dad watching me, his eyes boring into me. After that, I wasn't ever comfortable being with the kids, not my nieces and nephews, not even Frieda."

"Jeez, Bill, that was a shitty thing for him to do. It's not right. Your dad is such an asshole."

"Yeah, he can be," he nodded, "And now I can't see my son without feeling like I'll be in a room filled with my father's eyes watching me the whole time. I can't do it."

"Why don't you talk to an attorney?" I asked. "You could go talk to Bev Fleishman, she was my divorce lawyer. She could tell you what your parental rights are. You're the father. You should be able to see your kids when you want, without any supervision."

Bill didn't say anything. We both looked out the kitchen windows and watched a flock of geese fly low over the field and then disappear into the trees surrounding the Mecan. The migration south had begun. Fall had arrived.

"Okay," he said at last. "Can you get me an appointment as soon as possible?"

"You bet," I answered, already out of my chair and on my way to get the phone number.

After meeting with Bev, I could tell that Bill felt better. He knew there was a way for him to be able to see his children on his terms. But along with the relief, I also sensed his continuing turmoil. Bill is very accepting and open-minded for someone who was raised in such a restrictive environment. Granted, there was the incident with the African-American beauty queen, but even that hadn't really been because of his personal beliefs. Those were lies that had been drilled into him over the years by others. Lies presented to him as the word of God.

Even before he left the Amish, I never felt that Bill judged me because of my divorce. There were plenty of others in the Amish community who did. Hell, there are still English people who look down on divorce, or at least my divorce, but then some people are too eager to find something... anything...they can, just to put you down.

As Bill and I got to be friends, especially after he left, I told him about my marriage and divorce. Divorce is never easy, not even when it's necessary. No matter how badly you want the divorce, it is still a failure and loss. The realization that a dream has died.

Bill always seemed to accept my divorce as something that I did for good reasons, but I'm sure that he never thought of it as something he could consider for himself. While he was Amish, it wasn't an option. It was also pretty obvious that he didn't want a divorce. Until he met with the attorney to find out about getting visitation with his kids, I don't think it ever entered his mind that it might be something he would *have* to do.

It was very clear to me how much Bill still cared for Ruby. It seemed as if he had been waiting for her to show him that she wanted him back. Sure, she might have asked if he was coming home every time they talked but from what he told me, there had never been anything in her voice that told him that she wanted him back. Never any sign that it mattered to her. That she missed him. That she loved him.

When Paul was born and Ruby didn't even call, it seemed as if Bill finally realized where he stood. He had another decision to make: go back or get divorced.

According to Amish rules, Ruby would have to go home to Bill if he returned. But would he return? Could he return? If he didn't and if he wanted to see his kids, he had to file for divorce. Was that what he wanted?

Day after day, I could see him struggling with the burden he carried. It was hard watching him suffer. Not being able to help. Not knowing why it had to be like this.

How could they treat him this way? How could they keep his children from him, dangling them like a carrot from the end of a stick? No one seemed to care if Bill saw Frieda and Paul. They just kept the kids hooked like a fat worm, waiting for him to nibble so they could set the hook and reel him back in.

Back to the Amish.

Twenty-eight

Enjoy life with your wife, whom you love,
all the days of this meaningless life that God has given you
under the sun—all your meaningless days.
For this is your lot in life and in your toilsome labor under the sun. Whatever your
hand finds to do, do it with all your might,
for in the realm of the dead, where you are going,
there is neither working nor planning nor knowledge nor wisdom.
Ecclesiastes 9:9-10, *The Holy Bible*, NIV

Bill

It was one of the longest weeks of my life. My brain buzzed constantly, trying to figure out what I should do. Should I go back?

Should I file for divorce?

What was the right thing to do?

I was at a crossroads. Again.

Only this time, it felt much more permanent.

It had taken many years for me to decide to leave. Years of telling myself that someday I would be out. All those years. Waiting for the day when I could finally leave. Waiting until I could be free. Waiting for the day when I could live a life that felt right. Live without being forced to conform to the *Ordnung*. Live without feeling like a hypocrite. Live a life that was honest. Live a life that I could choose for myself.

The first time I thought about leaving was when I was about eleven. I would think about it over the years, whenever I was unhappy or in trouble for doing something that was considered wrong. I would tell myself that as soon as I was able, I would leave.

Thinking about leaving was my relief valve. Letting off steam. Venting my frustration with a life that I had no control over.

Finally one day, I was old enough to leave. My "someday" had arrived, But could I do it? Could I leave? What would I do without my family and community? Could I make it on my own? Could I trust anyone to help me?

I was old enough to leave at last, but I was also old enough to know that having a dream is one thing. The desire was still just as strong, but it was different once I knew that I *could* leave. The reality of leaving was overwhelming.

Sometimes there is comfort in a cage.

You know where the boundaries are.

You know what to expect.

Instead of doing what I had promised myself that I would do as soon as I was able, I did nothing. Nothing except continue to plan and plot. And continuing dreaming of being out. I would tell myself that it was something that I would do "soon" or "the next time I got really mad." I kept postponing it for one reason or another. Maybe I was waiting for a sign. I don't know.

After Ruby and I got married, I set aside my thoughts of leaving.

Ruby was the first girl I dated.

She was my first love.

I was surprised when she agreed to take me on and become my wife. We were happy together. Maybe I didn't need to leave, I thought at the time. Maybe I could be happy with an Amish life. I had Ruby. Then we had Frieda. It was a little sooner than we had expected to become parents, but Frieda's arrival made our family complete.

It was much harder to allow myself to think of leaving after I had a family of my own. How could I? I had a wife and child.

When those thoughts came up, I quickly pushed them aside.

I did my best to be a good Amish and live a simple life.

I really tried.

But it all changed that night in the fuel shed. That night, from out of nowhere, it all crashed like the foundation of a poorly stacked logging pile giving away. I knew that I had to make up my mind once and for all.

Would I continue to live a life that I was born into but never believed in? How long could I go on, feeling that I wasn't really living? How long could I keep on just going through the motions? How long could I continue to live a life that had always felt wrong to me? How long could I pretend to be someone that I wasn't?

After wanting to leave for so long, especially after I got married and became a father, it didn't seem possible that it could ever really happen. I thought the fire of my life-long dream had been snuffed out. But then an ember, still smoldering under the ash, had sputtered and began to burn anew. Just like those birthday candles that keep relighting after you blow them out. A flame had flickered back to life and quickly grew stronger....stronger than ever.

On that bitter cold night back in January, I decided to do what I had always planned to do. To do what I had always wanted to do. I chose to follow a different path. I made my decision that night, knowing that I could not face another fifty, sixty, seventy more years of feeling the way I did.

In the end, there was only one thing that had ever stopped me from leaving.

Me.

I knew it was the right decision. And it was surprisingly simple. All I had to do was to say, "I'm not Amish". That was all.

I was out.

The relief I felt after finally making my decision, proved that it was the right one. Of course, telling my wife, and David, and later dealing with my family, and the rest of the community, wasn't so easy. It definitely wasn't fun.

My only regret is that I didn't do it sooner. I never should have become a church member. I never should have married. The guilt ate at me like termites in a pile of seasoned lumber.

It was hard enough leaving the Amish. I hated letting down my family and friends. Worst of all, I hated hurting Ruby. I hated losing my wife and child. My children. But I did not leave them. Ruby left me. That was hard to bear. But if Ruby had given me the slightest encouragement, I probably would have gone back. Even a hint that she missed me and wanted to be with me however she could. But she didn't. And that left me with only one other option.

Divorce.

Divorce was very different from leaving.

Leaving didn't have to be a permanent thing. A lot of Amish leave and return.

Divorce was forbidden.

Divorce made everything seem very final and concrete.
I left the Amish, but did I want to divorce my wife?
Did I have a choice?

Ruby left me. Refused to ever be alone with me. Admitted that she expected me to kidnap her. Broke off all contact with me months ago. But even with all of that, I didn't want to lose Ruby.

I wanted her back. I wanted her and our children back together. I wanted us to be a family again. Probably not in this same community, but somewhere. Somewhere where we could make it work.

Ruby was the one to draw the line. Either I was Amish, in the Wautoma Community with her, or she wanted nothing to do with me. She wouldn't let me see our children. She felt no need to let me be a father to Frieda and Paul. She didn't care about the vows she had sworn. She obviously had no desire to be with me.

The attorney explained that under Wisconsin law, in order for me to have any visitation rights with my children, I had to file for divorce.

In order to see my children, I had to file.

I had to see my children.

I had no other choice. I told myself that filing was only a first step. Maybe filing would make her see that she couldn't have it all her way. Ruby had taken vows. If she expected me to return, then she should at least uphold those vows. If she didn't, I could hope that her father, or the bishop, or others in the community would make her. Someone would tell her that it was her duty to come back to me.

Maybe filing divorce papers would get my wife and children back.

In the end there was really nothing else I could do.

I had no other choice.

On October 13, 2003, I filed for divorce.

Twenty-nine

Karrie

"I'm going to file for divorce," Bill said nearly a week after we met with the attorney, Bev Fleishman, "I don't have a choice, not if I want to see my kids."

We went in the next day, and he signed all the documents.

"The papers will have to be served on Ruby," Bev told him. "That could take a few days, but after that, it shouldn't be much longer before you can see your kids."

"How long?" Bill asked in a tone that made it clear that he felt he had waited long enough already.

"Why don't I serve the papers?" I offered, "That way it'll be done right away, and Bill won't have to pay the extra fee."

"Sure, I don't see why not. We have to send them over to the courthouse for recording first, and that can take a few days. It shouldn't be more than a week before they'll call and have you pick them up to serve Ruby."

On October 21st, I drove over to Ruby's parent's farm with the divorce papers lying on the seat next to me. It was a perfect fall day, the whole world was painted in various shades of orange. I appreciate all the seasons, but spring and fall are my favorites.

In the spring, I can't wait to see all the flowers and trees come back to life, as if Mother Nature is putting on a fresh new, brightly-colored dress. Down at the Mecan, the animals begin to pair up and make nests. They seem to celebrate the return of the sun and the warmth. Spring thrives at the Mecan.

Fall also brings a renewed friskiness in the animals after the summer heat finally breaks. The robins and hummingbirds quietly disappear, unlike the geese that loudly announce their winter departure. Instead of new life and bright colors, fall brings its own somber beauty with the changing leaves. Mother Nature has traded in her now-faded spring dress for a comfortable old sweater, wrapping it tightly around her, trying to hold off the chill for just a little longer.

Fall is focused on the woods for me. Once deer hunting season begins, I have a reason to sit in the woods. It is all the excuse I need to bundle up and sit in my stand for hours, listening to the stillness of my woods, watching the squirrels leap through the snow and fallen leaves, and waiting for a buck with a big rack to appear.

With a smile still on my face thinking about that big buck, I parked my car and walked to the door of the main house. Glancing over toward Ruby's store, I noticed several cars and a buggy parked outside. Business was booming.

Ruby's father, Ervin, opened the door before I was even close enough to knock.

"Can I help you?" he asked, his tone harsh and demanding, leaving no doubt that he was not at all pleased to see me.

"I need to give this to Ruby."

"Give it to me," he stuck his hand out, looking like I was about to hand him something disgusting.

"I have to give it to Ruby. It's the law." I knew they didn't care much about our laws but as Americans, they should honor them.

"You can either give it to me, or not at all."

"I can't give it to you. I have to hand it to her. No one else. If you don't let me give it to her, then the Sheriff will have to come out and have to do exactly what I'm trying to do right now."

"Fine, then let the Sheriff come out," he said as he stepped back and shut the door with a decided thud.

It had been worth a shot. It would have saved Bill some time, and after what they had done to me, I didn't mind poking back at them.

As I pulled out of the driveway, I dug out my cell phone and called Bill.

"Ruby's dad wouldn't let me give her the papers, so I'm heading to Wautoma. I'll take them straight to the sheriff's office, and then they can come out and serve her."

"What did he say?"

"Not much. He wouldn't let me see Ruby. He said that I had to give the papers to him, even after I said it was the law and that if he didn't let me do it the Sheriff would come out. So now the Sheriff can do it."

"I guess I'm not surprised that he didn't let you see her."

"But why the hell not? I haven't done anything to Ruby!"

"You've helped me...and you know they think we're fooling around."

"To hell with what they think. I'm not going to stay away from doing what I had a legal right to do just because a bunch of assholes make up lies about me."

"When do you think the Sheriff will get out there?"

"Probably later today, maybe tomorrow. I'll find out and let you know."

Bill didn't understand why I had been willing, even glad, for a chance to serve the divorce papers. Part of it was for him, to get the ball rolling so he could see Frieda and Paul sooner. Part of it was that it was easier. There was no reason why I shouldn't serve the papers and save the Sheriff a trip. And part of it was because I've never been someone to back down from confrontation.

Maybe Ruby and her family weren't directly involved with my attack, but there was a good chance they knew something about it. They had all done their part in casting me in a negative light by spreading lies and rumors about Bill and me. They had all done whatever they could to make Ruby the victim. "Poor Ruby" meant more "cheer up" cash donations. It meant more customers to show their support by shopping at her Bent and Dent store.

Poor Ruby, my ass.

If serving divorce papers to Ruby was the only bit of retribution I could get, then so be it. Considering all they had done to me, at least it was something I had every legal right to do. I wasn't spreading rumors and lies about her. I didn't hire some goons to beat her up and try to rape her. I hadn't done anything but help a friend...my friend...the one she vowed to love and honor and obey.

As Bill's friend, I was furious with her for what she was putting him through. Bill was a good person. He deserved to be treated better. And she left him! She walked out first thing the next morning. She refused to go home. Not when she had permission to live with him if she was Amish and he was English, not when she realized she was pregnant, not after Bill asked her to consider moving to another community, not for any reason.

From everything I saw, Ruby appeared to be glad that Bill had left. Well, maybe glad is an exaggeration, but she definitely seemed...relieved. She was content to live in her little house that was attached to her mommy and daddy's. She had the store and several thousand dollars that had undoubtedly come in from the "Cheer up Ruby Shower."

Ruby definitely seemed to be cheered up.

She obviously didn't care about Bill's happiness. If she did, she wouldn't have been so quick to run home to daddy. She would have gone back to Bill when she had permission to live with him even if he remained English. She should have considered moving to a different community, if that's what it took to get him to be Amish again. If she loved him, she should have wanted to be with him. She should have done whatever she had to do to be with him.

And yet, all everyone ever heard was how her husband had left her because of me. Others might be saying "poor Ruby," but I knew it was total bullshit. I knew the truth. I also had a pretty good idea about Ruby, and the only thing that made sense was that Ruby didn't want to go back to Bill. She didn't want to go back to being his wife. She didn't want him to return to the Amish. She didn't care about him or his soul.

It all seemed to fit, but there was no way I could say any of this to Bill. He had been hurt enough already.

She didn't deserve him.

As Bill's friend, I saw the hurt and pain she inflicted on him. Sure, he hurt her when he decided that he didn't want to be Amish, but it had been all too easy for her to run home to her parents. It was almost as if she was glad to have a reason to go back home. She would never admit it, but it didn't seem that she was doing everything that she could to get Bill to come back. She hadn't even contacted him to let him know that his son was born! If that isn't a good example of someone writing you off, I don't know what is.

I knew Bill still cared for her. He probably always would, especially since she was the mother of his children, and I guess that's why they never made Ruby go back home. The bishop and others must have figured that she was good bait. They probably figured that eventually Bill would bite. He had certainly nibbled when the bishop gave his permission to Bill to live as an English with Ruby. When it was suggested for them to move to another community. There were other times when he probably would have returned if she had agreed to meet with him or if she had simply moved back into their home. Wasn't that the nibble they were waiting for? Didn't they know that when you get a nibble, you give the line a tug to set the hook?

After we met with the attorney, I could only wait and watch as Bill decided what to do. I wanted him to do whatever was best for him, whether it was filing for divorce or returning to the Amish. I would support whichever path he chose, even though I knew our friendship would be over if he went back. There was no way he would be allowed to have contact or work with me again. Ever. It didn't matter that we weren't involved romantically. We had already been judged and damned by both Amish and English.

A week or so after the papers were served on Ruby, I stopped at her dad's house again. It was meant as a neighborly gesture.

"Here's some of Ruby's mail that was delivered to Bill by mistake," I said to Ruby's mom when she answered the door.

"You've got some nerve coming here," she said, her eyes glaring at me and her thin lips pinched tight, as she snatched the mail from my hand. "William would come back to the Amish if you let him, but you've got your hooks in him..."

"You think I've got my hooks in him?" I asked, stunned. My pissed off scale going from zero to ninety in a heartbeat, "If I had my hooks in him, you'd know it! For one thing, he'd have those kids!"

She snatched the mail from my hand and disappeared into the house, not quite slamming the door in my face, but almost.

Storming back to my car, I fumed all the way home. So I had my hooks in Bill? What a bunch of crap. Anyone who knows me realizes that I'm much too strong and too independent to ever need a man so much that I would force him to give up his wife and children. It was entirely up to Bill to make up his own mind.

If he stayed English, I would continue to help him in any way he needed. I had already been beaten and nearly raped by the Amish, but I wasn't afraid of any of them. It wouldn't stop me from continuing to help him. But if Bill decided to go back, I would help him and give him a ride home. It was always entirely his decision.

The accusation that I had my hooks in Bill is just a classic example of the pot calling the kettle black. Instead of looking at themselves and how *they* drove him away, they projected all their guilt on me. I was an easy target. Blaming me was so convenient....oh so much more convenient.

If only I had a mirror with me when Ruby's mom said that to me.

"You want to see who's got the hooks in him?" I would have asked, "Take a good look. It's you. It's all of you. It's ALL the Amish. Who the hell is it who keeps telling him that his soul is in danger if he doesn't return? Which of us is offering him everything they own just to get him back? Bribing him? Who keeps him from seeing his wife and children? Which of us got attacked for helping him? Tell me again who it is that has the hooks in him?"

I would have loved to ask her, or any of the Amish, all of those questions as well as a couple more.

Who is it that has had their hooks in Bill since the day he was born?

Who is it that keeps on ripping at his flesh?

Thirty

To the married I give this command (not I, but the Lord):
A wife must not separate from her husband.
But if she does, she must remain unmarried
or else be reconciled to her husband.
And a husband must not divorce his wife.
And if a woman has a husband who is not a believer
and he is willing to live with her, she must not divorce him.
But if the unbeliever leaves, let him do so.
A believing man or woman is not bound in such circumstances;
God has called us to live in peace.
How do you know, wife, whether you will save your husband?
Or, how do you know, husband, whether you will save your wife?
1 Corinthians 7: 10-11, 13, 15-16, *The Holy Bible*, NIV

Bill

When Karrie wasn't allowed to serve the divorce papers to Ruby, the Sheriff went out the next day to do it.

I'm not sure what I expected.

Maybe a call. Maybe Ruby agreeing to move to a new community. Maybe my wife crying and pleading with me to come home. Telling me that she didn't want to lose me. That we could be a family again.

That she loved me.

I still had hope.

A letter came only a few days later. I held the envelope in my hand for a few moments, studying her neat handwriting. Except for Paul's birth announcement, I hadn't heard from her for nearly half a year.

Did she realize now that I was serious?

Was she finally ready to be my wife again?

I ripped open the letter and found a brief note inside, dated the same day that she had been served.

October 22, 2003
Hello William,

I got a letter from your mom, and Adlai had also called me, saying you wanted to talk to me. So the question is if you would maybe still consider coming back to an Amish life? So write and let me know when to call you as according to what your mom and Adlai say its hard to get hold of you.
Ruby

Ruby.
Just Ruby.

Not "Love, Ruby."
Not "I miss you."
Not "Let's not get divorced."
Not "We should be a family again."

She wrote because my mother had written to her and my brother had called her. She felt obligated to do something. She wrote as little as possible, but enough so that she could say, "Yes, I wrote to him." She hadn't written much, but she said plenty.

She didn't want me back.

It hurt.
It hurt more than I realized it could hurt anymore.
Our marriage meant nothing to her.
I meant nothing to her.
Why did she marry me?

I remembered a time, not long after we married, when a nerve must have gotten pinched in my spine. The pain was so sudden and severe that I fell to my knees and rolled onto my back, lying as still as possible on the floor, afraid to move. I didn't know what to do. It hurt to breathe. I was scared. But Ruby was right there, kneeling beside me, her brow creased with worry.
"What can I do? Should I get someone?"
"I don't know, give me a minute..."
The pain in my back only last a few minutes. Then it vanished. I continued to lie flat. Hesitating. Still afraid to move.
"It's okay, I'm okay," I muttered to Ruby.
"Oh William! Are you sure? I don't know what I'd do without you!"

I don't know what I'd do without you.

Never before had I felt so cherished or loved. What a lucky man I was to have such a wife.

I don't know what I'd do without you.

Ruby said it, but remembering it now, the words sounded hollow. They mocked me. It hurt as much, maybe more, than that pinched nerve in my back that had knocked me to the floor.

If she meant what she said then, how could she not feel that same way now?

If she didn't mean it then, why did she say it?

Why did she marry me? Did she ever love me?

Was she only doing what she felt she should? Was she only doing what was expected of her as an Amish? Did Ruby marry me because she knew she was supposed to get married and make Amish babies? Did she marry me because she knew that she eventually had to marry someone?

Re-reading Ruby's letter, one thing was clear. Ruby had figured out exactly what she would do without me.

Thirty-one

Bill

Soon after Ruby's letter, I got one from my mother with sad news.

10-29-03 Tomorrow is your Bro Adlai's B.D.
Dear William,
First a greeting of Love and in Jesus Name. This is Wed P.M. at 4 oclock and it's beginning to be kinda dark in here, but I'll try to jot a few lines your way <u>finally</u>. Its been quite some time since I wrote, was going to last week, then about this time last Wed. we found out about the sudden death of Eddie & Amanda's dear little Baby – 13 mo. old. So we made arrangement to go to her funeral the next day. Adlai called you Wed. nite & left a message on you're A.M. so we hoped you found out about it.
Eddie Amanda was at her Moms house that day and when she went home she also made a stop at the salvage store and Bike shop so at 6 oclock that nite when she got home (she had a driver with a van) as it was quite far to her folks house. She set off the groceries & a new bike for them and the older children were all excited about their bicycle & run in the house to tell Eddie as he was at home from work & had supper ready by that time, anyway little Jeremy just older then Leanna Kay was asleep so she set Leanna off & reached in to get Jeremy and closed the van door and started for the house & the driver started to go & she had not given a thought that the other kids didn't take her in until she heard a crunch &

knew right away what it was & screamed so loud the driver stopped & Ed came out as he Knew right away what that scream meant so she laid Between the 2 sides of the van wheels w/ a wheel hitting her head & she must of got killed instantly as when they picked her up no life was there anymore. My what a shock that would have been. But this happened for us all to from time to time to realize that our time on earth is but a twinkling of the eye away from death and eternity so the Good Lord looked down and picked a sweet little rose Bud out of our midst. She looked so sweet and pure and no scars of this life in her heart! She actually reminded us of little Frieda if you looked at her from the Side and across the eyes. So it gives us all reason to try and live a life pleasing to God so we can, only by the grace *of God inherit a home in heaven some day where we all want to be, but I on my part am such a failing human and need constant prayers for us all. I didn't know what I was going to write but just thought I'd let you know, then am also gonna send a card that has a nice poem on about a Baby's message.*

Do wonder how you are? We are on the go but yesterday at Joe L.B's frolic Dad accidently hit his next to the little finger on his L. hand with the hammer & he said was a hard Blow and crushed the tip of the finger so it bled & this morn. was still Bleeding some, but went on to work with Rick & Linda's, old barn putting in some new sills I think it was. As for myself I'm hobbling around with a Bad Knee, so don't know for sure what all it is. If it's Bone on Bone or arthiratis or a combination of Both so my going outside isn't the best. I went out to the garden & got a hd. of cabbage & some Chinese cabbage in, a while ago. Its still very good & there is plenty here so stop in sometime soon *& I'd be glad to Share some with you.*

Last nite on the way home from Joes, Dad stopped at Ervin M's & got a few items at there Bent & Dent then went in to see Baby Paul again and also the other. My that little one really grows, he said it weighed 11# already. If he keeps that up B-4 we realize it he will be caught up with Frieda. He is such a sweet, sweet *little one I just hope you've been there to see it already and have a nice talk with Ruby. If you haven't been,* just go *you'll be glad that you did & I guess if you don't find her at home you can Keep going Back until you do. I sewed a little shirt for Paul which he doesn't need now but time has a way of going on that before we know it he will be old enuf if the Lord see's fit to let him live that long. Yesterday, Rosanna & I helped Lydia Ann butcher their 20 old hens to can for Broth, now tomorrow we'd like to do Adlai's too, Lord willing. Then its time to get yards cleaned as church is coming around soon too.*

Sounds like Monroe Millers fam. is planning to move over to Elkhart Lake, W. on next Tues. so once they've gone, none of Eli Yoders children would be left in Wautoma. So that brings a change also as Eli's plan to go to, too where some of the Children live, but not sure where too yet to our knowledge.

When Dad came home tonight her finger was in a mess & still draining Blood so there must be a lot of pressure in it. Hope we can get it healed soon.

Oh yes, from what we gather that you told Adlai on the phone several weeks ago – that you really do want Ruby back, then you don't want to file for divorce as that is not the Christian way to get her Back and if you truly do want her, you would be glad to come Back to where you left off on that fate ful day in Jan. of 2003. Nothing could keep you from it if your heart really & truly wants this. Of course we know that there is always 2 sides to a story so each would need to compromise and seek the Lords will in everything and you Know as well as we do that you were Born into the Amish Heritage and that is where you belong. Not that, that name will get you to heaven but that is where you grew up in & is the way that is the right way for you. No I'm not judging you and didn't mean to preach at you, just out of love & concern from you still crying mother almost daily for my little Baby which has grown into a man.

So please do _stop_ that divorce deal as if you go on with that and should marry someone else that is so _final_! So please take heed of all the warnings, as you know how Lynn started out and now he is in a terrible, terrible situation and his family is not even allowed to Know where he is at.

So stop and think _deeply_, it's for your own good that I am writing this, and it was out of my own mind I just wrote what the Good Lord gave me to think and write. And again I'm so sorry for all the wrong things that I did in my life that misled you! Hope to be forgiven by our heavenly Father as well as all others concerned.

Well you are probably tired of reading my scribbles so I should quit. But now its your turn to answer & better yet _do_ _stop_ _in_ sometime we are anxious to talk to you again. Do you Know what I did Sat. nite after I left the message on your answering machine? Came home & cryed, cryed, cause I once again heard your voice if we are not allowed to see you! Must quit & this is written Love for you as we still Love you.

Dad & Mom

P.S. You might think that if you served papers to Ruby already & have a date set for the hearing that it can't be stopped, but it _certainly_ _can_! Up to the day and remember please go see your cute little Boy.

172

Around November 3rd, 2003, a letter from my sister Millie arrived. Millie is my oldest sister, the third child after my brothers Elvie and Lynn. Millie is married to Toby, and they have five children.

Sun. eve.
Dearest Brother,
First a friendly greeting from us all here in MO! Wonder what this will find you doing? We were just at home today for the 1rst time since we are in our own house. Wm Lambrights 2 boys came over a while this afternoon then Perrys & Amoses brought supper over so we ate around 5:30. Is now 7:30 & all have gone home dishes done boys playing checkers & girls Life. Oops! Sounds as thought Elvie got beat in the checker game & thinks it's not fair that Danny Joe always won so far tonight. Is tearful to him, a problem he still has & hope he can get over that someday. D.J. told him he often got beat by you & Monroe or Toby, that he'll learn but so goes, guess he's got to learn to give in at times too, but so how our lives go to at times, seems so unfair yet a lot or most of it is our own fault if we only admit it, not? Better communication would be a lot.

What are you working at this time? Still in the woods I assume. I've tried to call & have a chat with you but seems I never get to you, don't I have the right number or what? Would you rather I'd just not even try? If you don't mind send me your number & we'll talk sometime. In the next 3 wks. our phone should get hooked up but don't have it as of yet, so always go to one of the others if we need to call.

We all have our own phones in an outside shack. Wonder have you seen your 'sweet little ones' lately? Would like to see them myself but don't know when. Toby maybe going up taking care of our property matters sometime next week, doubt I'll go along.

Wm. I don't think I need to & I don't have that ability too either to tell you how much we all are praying for you & hope you will someday take us, Ruby & your children all back as 'Family'. So please Pray & give yourself a fair chance to see whats happening to your life. I feel I have myself to better & can't feel right correcting anyone else but if I'd do as I like to I'd just bring you down here & try to help you find a different home & area, with different attitudes we're all sinful humans but need other to help us through our struggles. I hope I have not written too much, but felt responsible to let you know we CARE about YOU, too. Remember Wm. You need not live in the area you do now & it's really something how different areas have different feelings for a troubled or sin weary person, I know, I've been there in different ways than you ever knew. We've had our *struggles & only God knows but he also helped us when we listened to him & gave in from both sides. I think you 2 want the same so <u>please</u> pray B-4 you can't turn back. I've even had mental problems thru it all as you probably knew. Talking would go better so I'd better stop B-4 I confuse you more or make you upset about me. There are only 2 sides to this life the dark & bright. So we make it for ourselves.*

Pray for us too, Want to do the same in our weakness,
Lovingly, A Sister,
Millie & family

Millie's letter was upsetting, especially reading about what she calls her mental problems. I couldn't help but wonder if her problems came from living a life that she felt trapped in. Had my sister also considered leaving? Has she wished for a different life? How many others were there? How many others were living a life that made them miserable?

I could only hope that she was happier in the Missouri community.

Millie wrote to get me to come back. Her plan back-fired. Her letter proved that my leaving was the right thing.

Within only a few more days, another letter from my mother arrived.

11-10-03
Dear William,
Greetings in Jesus Name. Hope these lines will find you in Good health. We are as older people get with ups & down, some days the pains are better than others. Guess my knee legs are giving me fits now for the last several months. Hopefully Someday it will be better.

This is with great concern for you and Ruby that I am writing this, seems I just can't get it off of my chest that you are actually planning on filing for divorce. You know that, that is <u>NOT</u> nesacary and pray that you can dismiss that all from your mind. As you need to give her another fair chance.

Sure you can say your not gonna be Amish anymore but – God can change that for you if you are willing to accept it.

I don't know if you found out how it went with one of your first cousins or not? But will try to explain it a little on who was told to us. It's been a number of years ago already am not sure but more than then 10 (nearer 15) I'd say.

It failed on Both his & also his wifes side but he left her & the family (had quite a few already & went out into the world & thought he was gonna do what he wanted, and lived away from the family for a number of months (at least 5) maybe more. But praise the Lord he saw his mistake and came back and Both had to make things right with God & the church. Today he is a devoted husband and Daddy again and they have several married children and some grands too. So I'm sure if you could talk to him he would give you some good advice. This was Levi Herschbergers son Raymond, the live in the Arthur, Il. area.

So please, I plead again as any mother would to her wayward child, Consider coming back & both make things right with each other if there were things and start a new life in Christ. Now Jake & Rosanna are living over there on his place. It would be so nice if you and Ruby could be there again on your place like you were a year ago, we'd only be to glad to help in anyway to make so you could have a job at home & if you don't want to live here w/ the Amish there are lots of other places to live where there are good Christian people to associate with (I mean Amish).

Monroe Millers moved over to Elkhart Lake area last week and now Eli Yoders plan to leave to move to Crab Orchard, Ky. To Bruces & Amos's by today in 2 weeks so the Eli Yoder fam. will all be moved out again which makes it so sad on our part as we were or still are close to Eli's, but we can not Blame them for going if all of there children went so they can be with some of them again. We will greatly miss them.

We would probable do the same thing, and it sounds if we might have to as Monroes here are interested in going else where & if they go it prob. Won't be long before Adlai's go to. But we don't want to move its just according to what the others do. And maybe the Good Lord will make the end come for us all before they ever get that done. We never Know! Now, please don't get upset that I wrote this as it's just out of Love and Concern and I pray for forgiveness if I offended you in any way. Keep looking up and on the Positive side of Life instead of the negative. We still Love and Care about you. Let's Pray for each other.

From Your Mom

Soon after that, about November 13rd, 2003, a short note came from my father.

Dear Son,

Greetings to you in Jesus Name. I'll get to the point right away. Our mind is much with you. We understood there is to be a hearing next Friday.

Just one last time please reconsider. You surely realize where this will put you before the Almighty God. He tells us plainly in the scriptures. Read Matt. 13. What and how can we except if we neglect so great a salvation. This will be a case of a people judge but someday we will <u>all</u> stand before an almighty judge and it will be in all eternity either a beautiful bliss of Heaven or an everlasting torment of fire in Hell. We will never be able to say we weren't warned which will make it yet worse. I know you said you don't want to be preached at but consider I do want to be a loving father that still cares for you or I most certainly wouldn't be writing this. Please think and think and think then come let us try to reason with each other and the script if you can find anything there that justifies these things please tell and show us where.

Aus groza liebe.

Dad

Herr Gott durchich deine liebe fur mich der recht weg. Also read Mathew 15:4

Filing for divorce got them all stirred up, like angry hornets when their nest has been disturbed.

My brother Lewis also wrote, concerned for me and shared something surprising.

11-18-03

Dear William,

Greetings in our savours name. Wonder how these lines find you? We're all going with much to be thankful for. Today is a rather rainy day we're having little showers since yesterday afternoon. Deer season is open here since last Sat. so that's what we've been doing part of the time, still haven't filled any tags. Larry missed one other than that we've never had a chance to shoot.

Hello this is Thur. A.M. around 9:30 want to try and get this in mail today. Larry is plowing the rest are cutting up the last of the deer that Larry got Tuesday afternoon a fair sized 6 point.

I want to take plowing on so Larry can go see if he can get another deer. We've been sawing some off & on hopefully we can finish a job tommorrow & move mill home and start sawing at home there are at least four different people that want our lumber so we have to decide what will fit on sceulde

best. We've heard that you are thinking of getting a divorce. I hope you can see differnt before you make the final descion I don't believe that is acually going to bring you true happiness. We think & pray for you it still causes nights of wondering what did I do wrong. The other night I dreamed that I wanted to make a move similiar to what you did & I did, but it made me awful miserable, and was very glad to wake up to find it a dream. So I kinda know how you might feel, and there is no need of it if you are willing to do your share I'am confident the other people will too.
With Love & prayers,
Lewis & all

My attorney contacted me about that time.

"Hi, Bill, it's Bev. I just wanted to let you know that I've spoken with Ruby's attorney. We're trying to get a conference set up to get your visitation started."

"Ruby has an attorney?"

"Yes, as soon as we get something arranged, I'll let you know."

Ruby has an attorney.
This was unexpected.
It went against everything the Amish stand for.

As an Amish, Ruby should not have gotten involved with the English legal system. Going to court is considered to be judgment by man. The Amish believe that God is the *only* judge.

She could have done a non-contested divorce.
She *should* have done a non-contested divorce.

That would have been the proper Amish thing to do.
Instead, she hired an attorney.
It was just more Amish hypocrisy.

They make all these rules. They create an entire *Ordnung* for the community. Rules they are supposed to obey. Rules they are supposed to live by. But when the rules don't suit them, they don't have any problem breaking them.

Our lawyers scheduled a teleconference for Friday, November 21st, to work out my visitation. Teleconferencing made a lot of sense, since my lawyer was in La Crosse, a town about a hundred miles away.

"After you get your visitation arranged, the lawyers will start ironing out the other settlement details of the divorce," Karrie explained to me, "Who gets what, who pays what, all that. As soon as the two of you and your lawyers have things worked out, they'll ask for a trial date. Everything is worked out before the trial, so the trial is just the two of you and your lawyers telling the judge the final details. The judge signs off, and then it's official."

I had taken the first step toward divorce.

In six months, it would be over.
Ruby would no longer be my wife.
Not according to English law.

Ruby would always be my wife according to the Amish.
The Amish might not recognize divorce, but they would have to abide by the judge's ruling giving me visitation with my children.

I was going to see my children, at last.

Thirty-two

Train a child in the way he should go,
and when he is old he will not turn from it.
Proverbs 22: 6, *The Holy Bible*, NIV

Bill

Almost ten months.

The last time I saw my daughter was on February 10th. Nearly ten months ago. How did so much time pass?

The morning after I left the Amish, the morning that Ruby left me, I had kissed Frieda good-bye. I could still see the way her face had scrunched up when my whiskers tickled her. I didn't know then that it would be two weeks before I would see her again, when Ruby stopped by the house with Frieda when I was changing to go bowling with Karrie and David. At that time, I could see changes in my daughter. Changes that I missed.

And now ten months had passed. What had I missed? I didn't like thinking about it.

It wasn't that I hadn't tried. There had been so many times I wanted to see Frieda, and later to see Paul, but Ruby always found a way to put me off.

"You can come over," she had said, "but I want my dad here."

"I'm not coming to see your dad, I want to see you and Frieda."

"I don't want to see you without my dad here," she responded, her tone making it clear that there would be no compromise.

Luckily, the state of Wisconsin didn't have to compromise. After I filed for divorce, I was granted mandatory visitation. I would finally see my children. Ruby couldn't stop me.

Then the day that I had been waiting for arrived.

Sitting in front of me on a small stool was a little girl. She looked at me with such big brown eyes, like a young fawn, curious but wary. My heart ached, both with the happiness of finally seeing her and for all that had been missed.

Nearby was a crib. I walked over to it and looked down. At long last. My son.

Two months since he came into the world.

Two months that I missed.

He looked so peaceful as he slept. I gently dressed him as best I could, trying not to wake him. When Paul was ready, I turned back to Frieda.

"Hi, Frieda. You get to come for a little visit with me." I said to her in our Amish dialect.

It was awkward. I had been gone nearly half of her life. She probably didn't remember me at all. Would she come with me or would she run away? My heart pounded in my chest while her wide eyes studied me.

This first visitation took place at Ruby's parents' house in a room filled with her family and other Amish. I don't know how many there were, I wasn't going to look around long enough to count, but it was a lot. They all sat quietly. Praying. Any space not filled physically with their bodies, they saturated with their silent presence.

I was unwelcome.
I was unwanted.
I was trespassing.
I was no longer one of them.

I did my best to pretend they weren't there. I tried to ignore their disapproving eyes while I got my kids dressed and ready to go. I resented having to do all of this in front of an audience.

I was thankful that my voice sounded strong and steady when I asked Frieda, "Would you like to take a ride with Daddy?"

I held out my hand to her.
Waiting.
Afraid to breathe.
Hoping.

Then her face lit up with a big smile. Frieda reached out her small hand to take mine.

"I'll have them back in a few hours," I said at the doorway, without looking at Ruby, or anyone in particular.

It was Tuesday, November 25th. I was finally getting to spend a couple hours with my children. I would have them again on Thursday, which happened to be Thanksgiving. My visitation was arranged so that I would get Frieda and Paul on alternating weekends. Paul wouldn't be able to spend the night while Ruby nursed him.

Walking out to my truck, I carried my son and daughter. I liked the feel of them in my arms. It was reassuring. They were real.

One of the rules of my visitation was that I had to pick up the kids by myself.

Alone.

This rule was obviously directed at Karrie. I didn't like it, but I agreed to it. I didn't have a choice.

"I can still ride along with you, if you want me to...just in case. You'll just have to leave me out on the road," Karrie offered.

"I doubt there'll be trouble, but it would probably be good if you came along," I agreed.

Karrie had been standing out on the road in the dark and cold while I got my kids. As soon as I stopped at the end of the driveway, she hopped in.

"It seemed like you were gone forever. Did everything go okay?" Karrie asked.

"Yeah," I replied. I would fill her in on the details later, but not now.

No one spoke the rest of the way to Karrie's. Paul continued to doze while Frieda sat quietly but taking in everything. Her reaction had worried me the most. Would she fuss and cry? Would she refuse to go with me? All sorts of scenarios had run through my mind since my visitation was arranged.

But it went fine. They were both sitting in my truck with me. They were mine. For the next three hours, they were both mine.

Before I got them the next time, I was going have my attorney contact Ruby's. There was no way I was going to repeat this scene every time. There was no reason I should have to go into a roomful of mournful Amish and have them watch while I get the kids ready. Next time, Ruby could have Frieda and Paul ready and waiting for me by the door. They were pushing me too far. It was time to push back.

The headlights sliced a wedge in the darkness outside. Inside the truck, by the faint glow from the dashboard, I glanced over at Frieda. She looked at me and smiled, her face lighting up, and my anger vanished. It was worth it. It had been worth all of it to finally see her and Paul.

Thirty-three

Karrie

It was nearly Thanksgiving. That meant the start of hunting season. Bill took a few days off so we could be out in the woods. We hadn't seen anything that morning and would have stayed out longer, but a cold front came through, dropping the temperature nearly thirty degrees. The sudden cold meant more layers of clothing would be necessary when we went back out later. It also meant there was a chance that there could be snow. Hunters always welcome snow to help with tracking.

While we took a break in the house, Bill watched some television and I decided to clear off some of the clutter on my desk. The letters, from both of Bill's parents and his brother Lewis, lay on the top of one pile. I opened the desk drawer and pulled out the designated manila folder.

So many letters came for Bill after he left, but he never seemed to care what happened to them after he read them. He just tossed them aside. Sometimes I wondered if he even read them.

"It's the same old thing," he would say as he handed them to me. "Do what you want with it."

After the initial flood of letters, it gradually tapered off with only his mother being the consistent writer. Now that Bill filed for divorce, the letters rushed in again.

As I opened the folder, the lone letter from Ruby caught my eye. That one more than any other had surprised me. It was amazing that she finally wrote, but shocking in her cold and indifferent tone. She made it clear how little she cared. So little effort went into the note that it hardly seemed as if it had been worth the bother.

Ruby had been obligated to write. If it hadn't been for Bill's mother and brother putting pressure on her, it was obvious that Ruby wouldn't have written at all.

Usually, I don't save letters. I might keep a special mother's day or birthday card from my kids, but pretty much everything else gets tossed. But not this time. Something told me to hold on to the letters from the Amish. Maybe Bill would need them some day. The latest letters got tucked in behind the rest, all in chronological order...just in case.

In a separate folder were two letters that hadn't been sent to Bill. They came from the Amish for me. Both had arrived back in the spring, between the time when David had gone back and before those two Amish guys attacked me.

The first letter was from Aaron Beechy. He wrote in response to a note I sent after talking to my chiropractor friend, who also treated him, and who told me that Aaron was spreading rumors about me. My note demanded that he knock it off. I told him that I would sue his ass for libel and slander if he kept it up.

3 – 27 – 03

Hello Karrie

This sure was a cool damp day. But am ready for this spring weather.

Recieved your letter today and yes I was shocked. As Becky sure did a good job of turning things around.

I had (or we) had our mind made up not to say anything. But then She opend it up. I did NOT. I'll try and put in words as near as I can remember the way it was.

She said what is Wm doing. Then I said Still living over here as far as I know. Now I don't remember really what was said next their But I know I then said, There are some that think if it wasn't for a Devors Lady in the neighbor it mite not have happened. And right away she said thats Karrie. And what I had said about you drinking yes I know you don't or didn't think So as I was told already. But I said a (man (English) told me with her drinking problem Wm could loss his farm yet, If he got in a accident driving & drinking with her. I know I should have told him. then I don't think she drinks.

And then she also said Karrie does not drink. And about your children All I said was I have wondered if you leave them alone?? And if you do I think it should be reported to the authorities. Now why did I say that, because I think you have 2 nice children there. And I'd hate to see someone walk in and get a hold of them. But what really got to me is that Becky would turn around and twist things all around then say them to you. And most of All NOT say what All She said about you??!! And I have NO Idea what you are talking about spreading lies in letters and have hear (very very little) of any one talking about you.

So am wondering if you are maybe imaging some of it???

But want to for give Becky for this as its no way of getting done with this if we just keeping digging and digging. Want to forgive and for get. But don't think she has to give me any more treatments.

And this is not the first time I have been blamed for things I didn't say. But try to always think. They hurt them more then me and God knows and takes care of this. But now if you really think this letter is being past around. You'd Better just guess again.

Not even our Dau. will read it That would just be a way of getting roomers started and people going

Want to try harder to stick with what we had planed on, to not say anything to any Body

O yes I know I had also said to Becky I feel sorry for Ruby as young as she is yet.

Again I'm sorry for all the things said and hope you can forgive me and <u>WANT TO DO</u> <u>BetteR</u>

Aaron

When Becky came we were just ready to have a sandwich of fresh meat so I gave her mine to eat and made me another one. She liked it so well we then gave her some yet to <u>take home. Now what a reward</u>!?

Fri 28th ready to put this in mail. And Now just found out That <u>you</u> went and told around what Becky had said about me!!?? So you are doing the SAME think that you So put down all of us. Now whos _____??

The other letter was very strange. It was a brief note from Monroe Schmucker, Ruby's uncle and a bishop, and written on an invoice slip.

Monroe Schmucker

4 – 7 - 03

Mrs. Karrie Stevens

Good Morning a very snogy Morn.

I want to apologize for anything that I said about you or Bill that is not true I am Sorry

I have been telling people to quit talking about it and as far as I know we have

I or my family have not talked to any body at Evansville about this as people are saying we did. If you still have something against Willard I think you should be man enough to go tell him about it

Monroe

'I should be man enough.' That line always made me smile. I should be man enough to go talk to the man who spread the lies that I was the one who ran over the Amish kid's volleyball. As far as I was concerned, I already said everything I needed to say to Willard that morning when I cussed him out.

The papers on my desk were sorted into neat stacks. I was about to tackle the bills next when I heard the crunch of car tires on my gravel driveway. Moving into the kitchen, I watched through the window of the door as a strange car came to a stop. It was a surprise to see Bill's dad and brother Monroe get out and come up onto the porch.

"Monroe wants to talk to William...and I thought that I'd come along," Chris said to me, without any other greeting, when I opened the outer door to them.

"Let me see if Bill wants to talk to you," I answered coolly and closed the door, leaving them standing outside.

"Hey, Bill. Your dad and Monroe are here to see you. Do you want me to let them in?"

"I guess so," he uttered, getting up off the couch where he had been napping. He switched off the television and went to let them in.

"Monroe wanted to see you, so I came along for the ride," Bill's dad repeated as he entered my kitchen.

What a crock of shit, I thought as I went back into the office and sat down at the desk. I wanted to give them some privacy, but not too much. A badger doesn't invite a fox into its hole.

At first, I didn't pay much attention to what was being said, especially since Chris and Monroe spoke in Germish. Bill would always answer them in English, so I had a general idea of what was going on. Chris had been so quick to announce...twice...at their arrival that it had been Monroe who wanted to come visit, but it was Chris who did all the talking. Not that I was surprised.

From the bits of conversation I picked up, the visit seemed to begin with the typical chit-chat and catching up on various family members. Bill asked how Ruby was and then told his dad and brother about work and how hunting was going.

But then it changed.

Chris asked some things in Germish and when Bill answered, his tone sounded testy with a very short and curt "I don't think so" or "I don't know."

Chris said something in Germish and again Bill answered in the negative, "No, that's not possible."

From the way he spoke, I could tell Bill was irritated, but he sounded as if he was handling it. I continued checking my email.

Again Chris spoke and this time Bill answered, "There's no way her boyfriend would have done something like that. The guys who attacked her were Amish."

Now they had my attention!

Chris probably wasn't happy that Bill had clued me in on what they were talking about and he mumbled something else in Germish.

Whatever it was, it was too much for Bill, "Jeez, Dad, she knew they were Amish. She could smell them!"

"Good one, Bill!" I wanted to shout, but managed to control myself. He's doing great, I thought, let him deal with it.

Once more Chris mumbled in Germish and this time, Bill replied, "Well, why don't you ask her?"

That was obviously my cue. There was no need to call me twice.

"Ask me what?" I asked, out of my chair in an instant and joining them in my kitchen.

"I'm wondering about this attack you claim was done by Amish," Chris said very seriously, as if it was a great mystery for us to consider.

"What do you want to know about it?"

"Why would you suspect they were Amish?"

"There is no doubt in my mind, no doubt at all, that they were Amish. They had a hired driver with them and like Bill said, I could smell them," Chris only rolled his eyes, so I turned the tables on him, "Besides, who else would do something like that?"

Chris didn't answer, but would only look at me with an expression that I was either lying or delusional. His holier-than-thou attitude really pissed me off. As if the Amish were too good to stoop to doing something violent or criminal. I had enough of his bullshit.

"Well...we'll know who it was since the sheriff had the skidder dusted for fingerprints. If the guys have committed any other crimes, they'll be in the system." I paused, but when no one said anything, I continued, "What? You don't think they can figure out who did it by the fingerprints?"

Again no response.

An idea came to me. I set out the bait as I continued, making my tone very casual, "But of course! I don't suppose too many Amish have been fingerprinted."

While I left that dangling, I glanced over at Bill. There was the faintest hint of a smirk on his lips. He knew where I was going.

Still no nibbles, but I had my prey in my sights. I looked Chris straight in the eyes and asked, "Have you ever been fingerprinted?"

"I...ah...I don't recall," he stammered.

BAM! I had him!

"Bullshit! You can't tell me that you don't remember whether or not you've been fingerprinted! You don't forget shit like that! You'd remember all the details...them taking each one of your fingers," and I went for high drama here, demonstrating with my own hand, "Them putting your finger in the ink and rolling it across the paper. No way in hell someone would ever forget that happening to them! You would not forget getting fingerprinted in a police station!"

I was on a rant. How dare they! How dare they come in my house and treat me like a liar! How dare they sit there so innocently, when the only thing that made sense was that Chris had orchestrated my attack, just as he had when Rachel left.

"If anyone around here did know anything about my attack, would they tell the authorities?" I asked.

"I don't know what you mean," Chris replied. Evasion was always the most common Amish answer.

"What would you do if you knew anything about those guys coming onto my land and attacking and threatening to rape me if I didn't make your son go back to the Amish? Would you report it to the authorities?"

"I haven't heard of anything..."

"If you did! Have you heard anyone confess to my attack? Have you ever heard anyone confess to anything illegal? Ever? You know you're supposed to report it, don't you? Otherwise you're just as guilty as they are under the law. Do you know that?"

My questions must have made him uncomfortable since he motioned to Monroe and they got up to leave.

But I wasn't through with them.

"Tell me, Chris, how come I'm not welcome in your home while you are welcome here anytime?"

There was a pause, a moment of anticipation, of wondering what Chris might say. I expected some more of his typical grumbled muttering, but instead, his reply was surprisingly direct and honest, "Well, I wouldn't be welcome if I was doing damage to your children."

"DAD!" Bill reprimanded, disbelief and embarrassment clearly written on his face.

Chris mumbled something in Germish and left with Monroe following like a well-trained dog.

Thirty-four

Even in laughter the heart may ache, and joy may end in grief.
The faithless will be fully repaid for their ways,
and the good man rewarded for his.
A simple man believes anything,
but a prudent man gives thought to his steps.
A wise man fears the LORD and shuns evil,
but a fool is hotheaded and reckless.
A quick-tempered man does foolish things, and a crafty man is hated.
The simple inherit folly, but the prudent are crowned with knowledge.
Proverb 14: 13 – 18, *The Holy Bible*, NIV

Bill

Only a few days after he and Monroe stopped by, a letter arrived from my dad. It would not be like him to let someone else have the final word. Karrie put him on the spot about the fingerprinting. He could never let someone get the better of him. He couldn't stand for that.

Nov. 27 – 03
Dear Son,
Greetings to you aus leibe in Jesus Name. Looks like we will have a cloudy Thanksgiving day. We're just at home. The Lambrights are gathering at Adlais also Roman Schrock and several of their Children. Eli Yoders loaded out Monday and left for Crab Orchard Kentucky to Bruces. My thoughts have often gone to the other eve. When we were there am sure yours did too. You said something that I wondered about later. You asked if we thought Ruby was OK, I got to wondering later So I'm asking now, is there something that She does or did that isn't right?? Except of course the small mistakes we make in every day living and need to get on our knees and ask God for forgiveness every day.

The questions Kerry put to us that I didn't know how to answer cause I wasn't sure, so I asked Mom and She wasn't either but we think pretty sure we were figer printed either about Rachels deal or when we had a hearing to make us guardians of Elvie. The other ? if we ever were where someone made confession of sinning that also violated the law I didn't dare say cause 40 years is a long time to remember plus I want to forgive and forget as that is what God does if we admit sin and turn around and do repent. Anyhow To my thinking and knowledge No I never was in such a situation that we know of even if someone calls me a liar that will have to be rechoned with them not me. Another thing that was said, that Jesus condoned or o'ked divorce, no never!, no where, much more He points out the outcome of such. Again am sorry that didn't get the right Christian teaching into your mind. But am sure that you've learned enough that living to satisfy our flesh isn't the way to heaven. Please feel free to write or better yet come talk about you problem than maybe we can better understand why things are as is.

Aus Groza liebe.

Dad & Mom

Read Mark 10 – Matt 5 Ephsins Chapter 5 – 3 -5 Exodus in eight 2 books Mose 20 – 14 Leviticus eight 3 book Mose 3 – 9-10

My mom added another bible verse to the letter:

Read Sirach Chapter 23

"Rachel's deal. That's what he calls the kidnapping of your sister and the attack on the man who is now her husband. Rachel's deal. He got arrested and put on probation!" Karrie said with disgust as she tossed the letter on the table.

"He justifies it," I agreed, "It was okay because he was getting Rachel back to the Amish and saving her soul. To him, that was more important than any English law."

"He sure weaseled out of the bit about whether he'd heard any confessions of anything illegal. 'Forty years is a long time to remember...' What a cop-out!"

"Forgive and forget. That's the Amish way," I added. How many times had I been told that?

He twisted a question Karrie had asked him, about Jesus forgiving sins, to once again hammer home his point that divorce is forbidden.

"What's up with that bit about Ruby?" Karrie asked.

"What do you mean?"

"He asks if there's anything that she does that isn't right? Is he looking for some dirt on her?"

"Probably. He and Ruby's dad never got along very well. I always figured he would have been happier if I'd married someone else, anyone besides Ervin's daughter. It was also hard on him when my brother Lynn left. The bishop there gave him a lot of grief, put him down for allowing his son to leave. I'm sure that's a big part of why we left Iowa. Dad got fed up with being bitched at. Lynn's leaving was hard on my dad since it was the first. Rachel's leaving was also bad, but mine is probably the worst."

"Yours? Why?"

"I'm the only one who left him with in-laws."

Karrie nodded, "I'm sure that kills your dad having to constantly deal with Ervin."

"There seemed to be friction between the two of them right from the beginning, pretty much as soon as Ruby's family moved into the community. Now, thanks to me, Ervin has something to hold over my dad. I'm sure that pisses him off."

"Yeah, well, Ruby isn't innocent in all of this," Karrie reminded me. "She had permission to live with you, and you offered to move somewhere new."

"I don't feel bad about my dad getting shit from Ruby's. It serves him right. If he hadn't always been pushing me, always keeping the reins so tightly pulled...maybe I could've stayed Amish."

The phone rang and Karrie left the table to answer it. I lit another cigarette, my eyes wandered over to my dad's letter lying in the middle of the table. It was as if a bit of him was here in the room with me. Stern and disapproving.

Grabbing my jacket off the back of the chair, I felt in the pockets for my keys. I needed to get out. Might as well run in to Coloma for some cigarettes. Outside, the wind was crisp and cold. It would be nice to get some snow for hunting. It certainly felt as though snow was coming.

As I drove, my mind went back to my dad's letter and his visit a few days earlier. I knew as soon as they showed up that day that my dad had some sort of agenda. He could say that it had been Monroe's idea to come over, but it's always my dad behind everything. He's the one always pulling the strings.

What I told Karrie was the truth. I didn't feel bad for my dad, having to deal with Ruby's dad, or anyone, because of me. He brought it all on himself. Three of his nine children left. One third. And several others have probably seriously considered it.

My friend David had left, but only for a short time because in the end, his family was too important to him.

I missed my mother and my siblings. I missed my nieces and nephews and other family members.

But not enough.
Not enough to go back to being miserable.

I lost my wife.
Ruby didn't love me enough to want to stay with me.
She didn't want to find a way to make it work.
She didn't love me.
Not enough.

But thanks to the state of Wisconsin, I didn't have to lose my children.
I wouldn't have to miss Frieda and Paul. I could see them grow.
The situation wasn't perfect.
I would have rather been a family, but Ruby had drawn the line.

I was getting over missing her.
The hurt was easing.
My heart was healing.

Thirty-five

Then you will understand what is right
and just and fair—every good path.
For wisdom will enter your heart,
and knowledge will be pleasant to your soul.
Discretion will protect you, and understanding will guard you.
Wisdom will save you from the ways of wicked men,
from men whose words are perverse,
who leave the straight paths to walk in dark ways,
who delight in doing wrong and rejoice in the perverseness of evil,
whose paths are crooked and who are devious in their ways.
Proverbs 2: 9 – 15, *The Holy Bible*, NIV

Bill

A new year had come. At last. The longest year of my life was officially behind me, but some things hadn't changed. Another letter from my mother arrived, the first of the year, but written at the end of the previous year.

Dec. 30 - 03
Dear William,
Greetings in Jesus Name. Want to forward this envelope that came one of the days we were gone to Il. The Herschbergers Christmas get-tog at Bro. Eli's. Bro Levi is poor from a heart condition and Ervin has Both Knees fixed a week Before & Ervin Ester was also sick so they and Levi's couldn't be there at anytime. Monroe Mary was to sick w/ flu to be there for dinner but felt good enuf to be their for Supper. Andy Schrock were also there from Blm F. IA. & Andy Yoders recently moved to Ava, Ill but were also Back & Levi Y went with us, We also took Elvie along. He did fine but was a very tired Boy by the time we got Back as he never slept on the way to & fro. Traveled early morn. & late night. Want to invite you to come to our house on Sun. Jan. 4 for the noon meal as that is when the others are coming for our Christmas dinner so please come. Its been so long since I saw you last. We will do Best we can about the eating part so its not embarrassing to you. Want to have a turkey meal at noon. Our church is on Old Christmas the 6th then so we will try Sunday. Of course you know your

*welcome to come to <u>church</u> <u>anytime</u> <u>also</u>! Well I'd best get this in the Box
and hope to See you on Sunday. Take care.*

   Lots of Love, Mom

   P.S. I hope this audit letter will not be to complicated for you!

My mother wrote the letter on the front, the back, and along the sides of
the paper. It was a bit of a mess, but I managed to read it.

It wasn't long before another letter arrived. This time it was from
someone new.

Jan 15 - 04

Dear William,

*How are you? Have not seen you for a long time We miss you & would
welcome you back if you change your mind completely.*

   *I'm writing in regards to your Social Security exemption I'm quite sure
you are aware that you are not eligible to be exempt anymore since you do
not belong to the Amish Church. But I do not know if you are aware that
you could get in deep trouble if you do not report it. (See inclosed form that
you probly signed) If you have not and do not report it I as the Bishop of
the church feel I should report it out of respect for our Government. If you
have reported it please accept my apology.*

   Sincerely

   Eli Byler

When I left the Amish, I did everything that I needed to do to be English.
To be proper English. I changed my Social Security status without having
to be told. It was the right thing to do. The Bishop had nothing on me, but it
still irritated me, especially the part about how he would report me.

After I read it, I handed the letter to Karrie.

"What the hell?" She always had a way of saying exactly what I was
thinking. "He's going to report you if you aren't paying Social Security?
'Out of respect for our government' what a bunch of bullshit! They'll report
you because they want to stick it to you anyway they can!"

"Pretty much."

"He's acting like he's so concerned about English laws! The Amish only
follow the laws they have to and try to get out of as many as they can!"

Everything Karrie said was true. Amish lived by their own rules as much as possible and believed they had every right to do so. It was another item in the long list of examples of what hypocrites they are.

Several more letters arrived over the next few months.

2-11-04
Dear William
Greetings in Jesus name. Hope these lines find you well & going, here we're all in good health, did have a round of flu earlier. Here we have approx 6 – 8" of snow with weather temp. high twentys to a little below zero. We are busy with sawing most of the time we are just about out of logs approx ½ day of sawing, hopefully more coming today. We are in the process of getting a resaw whitch will be used to cut small ½" boards out of the cants. So far we've pretty well cut a semi load a wk. of long cants since mid Dec.
Dad & Mom were here for a wk. 2 wks ago they had Elvie along too. I'am not much of writer as you can see. I'am sorry for not being a better example for my brothers & sisters. Hopeing with Gods help we can lead a life according to his word. Lets live everyday as if Christ died yesterday, arose today, and is coming back tomorrow. Hopeing & praying that things will change.
A brother & family
Lewis

Sat 2-28-04
Dear Son,
Greetings of Love and in Jesus Name. This looks to be another fairly nice winter day. The daylight is getting longer so B-4 we Know spring will be here and with it the outside work which I always enjoy doing especially the gardening (that is if I'm able). Don't know yet how my Knee will let me work this summer as its Bone on Bone. I can still go fairly good but need lots of rest and during the night it's very painful to the point where sleep isn't always very good, But still I don't have reasons to complain so I'd best grin & bear it.
Dad has been laid up a few days with an infection on his foot (just started by itself) but is going again but on infection pills for 2 weeks. Today he was hoping to finish his job at David L. Yoders he was doing on a heifer

194

Barn. He also went to Coloma this morn. first. Is using a Tennasee Walking horse of Adlai's that he is Breaking for an English man. He has all Kinds of gaits including galloping!! But Dad said last nite he is inproving. Well I should soon go over to help Lydia Ann again as I'm supposed to be there maid since they are at home from the hospital with the little Baby. Ruby surely told you that Monroes have a new little miss – named Millie. But she has problems which is called a cloaka for an infant – a big person it would be a colostomy – which is a side opening for the Bowels and has a sac – where her wastes go. The doctors say it can be fixed to normal again but will need to do 2 more surgerys B-4 it is. And no more surgery before – after she is 2 months old. Don't Know what takes so long but I guess the doctors do, so the tiny one needs special care but so far she has been fairly Brauf – She still weighs under 7# & is only 18 ½" long so is tiny to hold. Probably about the size Frieda was when she was a Baby is she weighed 6# 12 oz?

You should just come and see her! Would be nice if you would for the sake of Monroe as you Know how close you 2 were before you married.

Now, get back home – fixed a lunch for Elvie & me and cooked some custard so Monroe can freeze some ice cream – (B-4 the snow all melts) its 50° at Noon so if it Keeps this up – well I guess theres still plenty of snow for more ice cream later.

I expect you probably figure we forgot about you? But no we certainly didn't – each day I think about you and <u>wonder</u> what you are doing.

It would be so nice if you could just come for a friendly chat once. Its been soo – long since I saw you I don't think I can remember how you looked!

As you prob. Know in Jan. we were in MO. with Tobys – 10 days & a little over a week at Lewis's so we were gone a day close to 3 weeks.

Tobys had plenty of work for Dad – Hang sheet Rock in Basement, as that's where they live until they have money to fix the main story of their new house. He also taped & doped it, plus hung the soffit on the outside. At Lewis's he helped saw at the sawmill, so that will now last for a while.

Then when we got home Monroes & Adlais Both had a cow to Butcher & Monroes also a hog so we just barely had that done until the baby came along so we are kept busy. Monroes and baby were in hos. 8 days.

Hoping we can go visit Ruby & the children soon, Saw Frieda on the 12th but Paul was not since I think it was the 5th of Jan so I expect he is getting bigger too.

I found this letter to you, at the time you had your diving accident the other day as we were clearing out the desk so I thought maybe you'd want to read it again. It would do you good.

Also these tracts I'll just send along. Now don't think that I ordered these, I didn't we just get some every so often – free so I thought they have good reading for any body and especially so for myself. I find I am such a poor sinner I just pray for faith and that God may forgive me a poor sinner only by his grace. So please don't forget your parents and other family members at the hour of prayer!

Please come over for a visit or then send us a letter in the mail so we know what you are doing & thinking. God Loves You and We do Too!

Out of Love,
Dad & Mom

Sat 4-10-04
Dearest William,

Greetings of Love and in Jesus Name. Do hope this find you in good health and "a going".

We are on the go. Dad went over to where Eli Detweilers used to live to help take down the red pole type Barn. Its a school project. I need to make 5 doz. Donuts for Phil Golke who has been getting donuts here for quite some time already for their Churches Easter Sun. services. Also want to make some xtra for Monroes & us. Little Baby Millie now weighs 7# 3oz. At 8 weeks old so has gained back to her birth weight. Well I must get to what I'm after as not much spare time for me Today. We got a letter yesterday saying that your Uncle Monroe's and Jonas Schrocks of Ill want be here by the night of the 15ᵗʰ so please come on over as they surely want to see you too. They are invited to a wedding at Hillsboro Wi. so thought as long as they are that close they'd come on over for a little. It won't be long she said as they'd go home again either Fri. P.M. or Sat. morn so come on over for supper then! Must go & hope to see you then. Take care

Lots of Love,
Dads & Elvie
P.S. Also Ola's Steven has Cancer! don't sound to good.

4-22-04
Dearest Son, William,

Greetings of Love and in Jesus Name. The Lord is my light and my salvation; whom shall I fear? The Lord is the strength of my life; of whom shall I be afraid? Psalms 27 -1

A nice verse if I could just life up to it better, maybe things would be better also. I will start a letter for you, probably won't get it done today, or if I ever will, I'll give it a try.

Its been on my mind so much that I'll just write a little to you, (while I sit and rest a spell) and realize you probably won't enjoy it. But out of concern for your soul and I guess mine too, I feel I should as its out of Motherly love and my responsibility. If you can't see it now, maybe if the Lord lets you get old and grey and have no one to go to for help you can know what I mean!

First, you Know you are living in the Sin of adultry plus not honoring your Father and Mother. And don't for one minute, no not one second think that you and Ruby were not meant for each other, as you well Know the Bible says "What therefore God hath joined together , Let not man put asunder." And this was done before God and many witness's on your wedding day. So please, I plead <u>with</u> <u>you</u> <u>to</u> <u>give</u> <u>Ruby</u> <u>another</u> <u>chance</u>. Try coming back and make things right with God and the church and everyone would be so happy! <u>We</u> <u>all</u> <u>need</u> <u>you</u>!

This afternoon I want to take some eats down to Adlai's for church on Sun. the 25 as we will take communion there this round and it just hurts my heart so to know you'd also belong there and <u>ar'nt</u> so please don't think we forgot you, as often Sun. Mom's we think of you as well as the other wayward ones, and wonder do you ever think where you should be?? Do hope you do! No life is'nt easy but we need to strive to do what we were taught and daily ask for guidance and also for forgiveness as we all fall short of being perfect, and I for myself <u>fail</u> <u>often</u>!

I was reading in Matthew 24 – where the words are spoken by Jesus himself – verse 11-12-13 and many false prophets shall rise, and deceive many. And because iniquity shall abound, the love of many shall wax cold. But he that shall endure unto the end, the same shall be saved. So beware there are many false prophets in this day and age trying to mislead whoever they can! So please think some sense, think for yourself, you know you were not taught to live the way you are living.

This is now Monday April 26 – 04

Why don't you visit with Ruby some more on the nights you go to get the children? You should, so as to get relaton ship started, or I'd think so.

Last week on Mon. nite Toby, Millie, Moses, Anna Mary (Tobys folks) came here at midnite & was a bed then Tues morning they went on over to Wilton, area to the funeral of a young mother that died at Child Birth of her 13th child. Her husband is 1st cousin to Toby & she is near Millie's age so they came with Moses. They then said their David (Mose) is thinking about coming Back to the Amish, really do hope he will, that would be Such a joy for there fam. Mose Said that at the same place where David stays in MO.

Where Ex amish Boys live one of them got killed just several weeks ago – when he was on his way home from a party <u>sad</u> <u>sad</u>! Funeral was at Windsor by his parents. It was Earl T. Millie's Boy from Windsor, MO – but they had just moved down there from Kalona, IA less then a year ago. So this got David to do some serious thinking & he went home to visit & also his Brothers Called him. Mose & Anna Mary were going to sell there home there in Verona & move over to one of the other of there Children as they both are not healthy anymore & they should live with 1 of the children, so he David wants them to wait a month or so to sell as he is interested in coming home to be with them then. Oh what joy that would be for us all and remember each of us can die in the blink of an eye, so be a man & do some serious thinking about yourself. No, no one is perfect that we do know but we all must live with the talent that the good Lord sends us. So please <u>reconsider</u>. You do Not want a divorsce! You Know you don't, you just <u>think</u> thats the way to do, but it isn't, cause you married Ruby and she is your wife and no one else can be your wife rightfully until she dies and you Know that much too.

Be not deceived what so ever a man soweth so he shall reap, is a biblical proverb. I really do wish you could take the time to come over for a visit. I especially invited you several times and you didn't come so just come anytime. Your always <u>Welcome</u>!

Its now a year I saw you last so its about time you come! I saw Roxy & your buggy yesterday & it made the tears come to think who should have been at church also. I will close now and please don't blame your heart Broken Mother to much for writing this as I felt it to be my responsibility to admonish again. Will close with a prayer in my heart for you.

Love you,
Dad - & Mom

My divorce from Ruby would be final in less than a month. The hearing was set for the morning of May 21.

The pressure from my family was increasing. They were trying their best to stop me before it was too late. I was the water leaking from a crack in their carefully constructed dam. They were scrambling around. Doing everything they could. Trying to patch the break. They had to stop it. My leaving threatened them. They had to stop me. They were trying their best, but they didn't seem to understand that the dam was already damaged beyond repair.

That dam had been constructed hundreds of years ago, when the Amish began separating themselves from the rest of the world. What they tried to create was like quiet lake, where we Amish could live simple. But it was all so misleading. Underneath that placid and still surface were layers upon layers of muck and filth. Anything trying to grow in that foulness became stunted and withered, until the toxins finally choked the life out of everything. One way or another.

Only a few of us were able to escape.

My brother Lynn had gotten out, but those early years had already ruined him. He moved from one poisonous lake to another. One of drug abuse and bad choices. I didn't even know where he was.

My sister Rachel and I had gotten out. It was a struggle, but we were both doing our best to overcome and adapt.

Someone else had gotten out.

She was from a community that was in a different part of Wisconsin, but very similar to my community.

She had been dragged down into the deepest, dankest depths of the lake's foulness.

Her escape was a miracle.

Thirty-six

Karrie

Spring was coming. It was finally coming! A late snowstorm had made me doubt that winter would ever end. I enjoy winter, but I was ready for a change, ready for warmer weather and longer days. Spring was coming. That's what I kept telling myself. I was ready for it.

One sunny but still chilly day, I made my annual pilgrimage down to the Mecan. The trees were still bare, keeping their buds safely hidden from the icy winds. Snow lingered in the shady slopes, and fragile sheets of ice covered the tiny streams.

No matter how many birthdays I have, and this was the year I would turn the big "four-o", I will always enjoy playing in the river, just like I did when I could count my age on only two hands. It is my playground and my kingdom. Down there at the river, everything was perfect. It is nature; both simple and complex.

If a place can be your soul mate, the head of the Mecan is mine. Hours slipped by before my growling stomach finally forced me to return to the other world. A world that was also beautiful, but cruel.

In a very short time, I would be reminded just how terribly cruel it could be.

Not long after Bill left the Amish, I began searching the Internet for information about the Amish and ex-Amish. At first it was to try to locate his sister Rachel and brother Lynn but soon enough, I became interested in contacting others who left and finding out more about their experiences.

The best website I found was created by a man, David Yoder, who left the Schwartzentruber Amish, one of the strictest sects. David updates his website with recent news involving the Amish, especially cases involving abuse.

About the time that I made my Mecan mecca, David Yoder posted a story that immediately caught my attention. A young Amish woman living near La Crosse had gone to the police to report terrible abuse. She was only about a hundred miles away! I quickly did some other online searching and turned up another article with more information.

This young woman, barely out of her teens, had gone outside of the Amish for help, something that is strictly forbidden. It was unheard of for someone, especially a woman, barely even a woman, to get the English involved. Keeping separate is the core Amish belief. Not many can appreciate the amount of courage this takes, the amazing bravery it took for this young woman to go against everything she'd ever been taught.

While reading the article about the young woman, it struck me that there would be very few English who would realize the challenges she was facing or fully understand the world she was coming from. Not many people know the Amish as I do, both the good and the terrible.

I wanted to help her.

The young woman's name was not being released, which is the law in sexual abuse cases, but that didn't slow me down. From the article, I knew the location of the case, so I found the listing and called the Vernon County District Attorney's office and asked to speak to whoever was in charge of the case.

They put me through to the Sheriff.

"I'm familiar with the Amish," I explained, after introducing myself. "I've lived around them for years and used to be a driver, but that changed when I helped someone from the community who wanted to leave. Please tell this woman that she can call me if there's anything I can do to help her...if she needs a place to stay, or wants to talk to someone, or anything."

After I gave my name and phone number, the Sheriff said, "Thank you, I'll see that she gets this information."

I didn't have a clue if anything would come of my phone call. The sheriff might not pass along the information, or the woman might not want to talk with a stranger, but I knew that I had to try.

A few hours later the phone rang.

"Hi, this is Mary Byler, you left a message for me with the sheriff." It was the young Amish woman. Mary is very social and talkative so we chatted for a long time. I was surprised at how open she was.

The article only stated that her three brothers were arrested for sexual assault. That was bad enough, but hearing the details directly from her was heartbreaking. She endured vile acts of abuse, beginning when she was about three or four. Her first abuser was her father. He was killed when his buggy was hit by a car. Mary's mother remarried, and the family moved from Pennsylvania to Wisconsin. But the abuse continued. Mary was first raped when she was about six or seven and then was repeatedly raped, and gang raped, by her brothers and cousins.

Mary asked for help, something a lot of victims are unable to do. She told her mother what was happening.

"You aren't fighting hard enough," Mary's mother, Sally Kempf, told her. "You need to pray harder."

Fight harder.

Pray harder.

That was the help Mary was given by someone who should have protected her.

When Mary reported the abuse and assaults to the bishop and other leaders of her community, her brothers were punished severely according to the Amish standards. They each had to confess and were given the maximum: six weeks in the ban. Six weeks. Six weeks for years of rape and abuse and torment. All that pain inflicted and they were punished with only six weeks.

For six weeks they were not allowed to interact with others outside their immediate family. They had to be served their food first and their plate and utensils washed last. They had to miss any weddings or social events. Six weeks of some relatively minor inconveniencing and just like that, they were absolved of all the years of abuse and depravity they inflicted on Mary.

Mary was expected to forgive them.

Mary was expected to forget.

Mary was expected to never speak of it again.

Only she didn't forgive.

She didn't forget.

And she spoke of it.

First, Mary spoke out in a support group for women of domestic violence. With the encouragement of friends in the group, she went to the Vernon County police.

An English friend Mary met in the group helped her leave and gave her a place to stay. That woman became a better mother to Mary than her biological mother had ever been. Mary was used to hard work and quickly found a job and began studying for her driver's license.

We talked a long time. I promised to go visit her soon and offered to bring her back home with me, if she wanted to get away for a little bit.

"It's disgusting," I said to Bill later that evening. "Mary had to sleep with the windows closed all summer or else her brothers would crawl in and rape her. She'd lock her bedroom door, but they'd take the hinges off to get at her! She finally gets the courage to tell her mother, as if that woman shouldn't have done something when Mary's door was being taken off the hinges, and you know what the woman says? Fight harder. Pray harder."

Bill just nodded his head. What could he say? What words are there for a mother who doesn't protect her daughter from her own brothers? How could such a woman look herself in the mirror? It was despicable.

"It's bad what happened to Mary. The worst part is that it's not uncommon."

"What do you know about it?" I asked.

"It's just that there's a lot of bad stuff like that."

"Like what?"

Bill looked out the window. He had already told me so much about the Amish, but this was new. This was different. He looked uncertain and uncomfortable, as if he was about to speak the unspeakable...and I realized that he was. He was about to tell me the darkest secrets of the community.

"One time, I got caught smoking...actually, I got caught smoking again. It was my third offense, so I had to confess at church on my knees. It was the most severe punishment that I ever got. I wasn't looking forward to it. But at that same church, the deacon's son and son-in-law had to confess, one of them for smoking and masturbating, and both of them for drinking and having sex with animals."

My face contorted as if a foul odor had suddenly come into the room. "They have sex with their own animals?"

"Yeah. We used to joke about how those guys were real farmers, that they even fertilized their animals."

"That's disgusting."

"I know...and there were more of them doing crap like that. I guess with the wives pregnant all the time, they decide a farm animal is an okay substitute."

"That's really sick," I repeated. "And they freely confess for doing it?"

"They might. They might be feeling like they've got to be a good Amish and confess their sins, but I always figured that it was more likely that someone saw them."

"What happens when they confess? How do people react?" I couldn't imagine it. At least if you're Catholic, only the priest would know, and you had a screen between the two of you so you wouldn't have to see the expression on his face.

"I don't know...no one says anything, they just sit there...all frozen...like zombies. I didn't hear about stuff like that until I became a member, and then I'd tell my buddies what happened, and we'd laugh about it."

Bill was quiet for a few minutes before he continued, "But there's other stuff, too."

"Like what?"

"You hear stuff."

"What kind of stuff?"

"Like fathers who mess with their daughters."

"You've heard stuff like that?"

"I never heard anyone confess for anything like that, no, but I've heard rumors...and, well...there was one time...when my dad said something to me...he told me that I might hear that he raped my sister."

A cold chill rolled over my body, settling in the area of my stomach that suddenly felt clenched and tight. It took a few moments until I was finally able to ask, "What happened?"

"You remember me telling you about the time Dad accused me of molesting my niece?"

I nodded.

"Just before he got into that, he said, 'You may hear some things, you may hear that I raped your sister, but it's not true.' He said it just like that...out of the blue...and before I could say anything or ask anything, he switched topics and started accusing me of messing with my niece."

"Do you think he raped his own daughter?"

"I don't think so...I know that I didn't believe it could be true when he told me, but then he distracted me pretty quick about my niece, didn't he?" Bill took a long drink of the beer sitting on the table in front of him, before he continued, "You don't want to believe that your dad is capable of anything like that, and I never did hear any rumors or anything.

"But I remember one evening, I was lying on the trampoline...my brother and I were goofing off after we'd finished chores...and Dad came out yelling for her. I remember thinking at the time, 'Why does he want her?' He never kept track of any of us kids. He found her across the road, in the woods. Later, I asked her why she was in the woods, and all she said was that she didn't want to talk about it."

Again there was a long pause, and then Bill sighed, "I've been thinking about it a lot these last few days...and I don't want to believe it. It may have all been nothing, but...I don't know. I just don't know what to think anymore."

Over the next few months, Mary and I talked a lot. I kept my promise and went to visit her, and she came back to stay with me for a little while. Her story got picked up in the media, and she agreed to be interviewed for ABC's *20/20* news program. They filmed Mary's interview in my kitchen with my old wood stove making the perfect, quaint, old-world backdrop.

The media was also there for the trial. I sat next to Mary and held her hand when she needed comforting. It was the least I could do to give her the support she certainly wasn't getting from her family. Her family, and over a hundred other Amish, packed the courtroom. They sat there, an undeniable force and presence. Even though no one could speak, their presence filled the room as if they were shouting, but the only sound was that of the women sobbing for the "poor boys" who were being mistreated by the English and our strange laws.

Why aren't any of you crying for Mary? That's what I wanted to ask. That's what I wanted to scream. Who's the one who put up with abuse for her entire childhood? Who's the victim here?

I wanted to punch every single one of them for what they'd done to Mary and for what they continued to do to her.

One of Mary's brothers, Eli, was charged with five counts of second-degree sexual assault, a lesser charge than sexual abuse. He received eight years in prison with four years of supervision.

David, the youngest brother, was charged with both first and second-degree sexual assault of a child. The second-degree charge was dismissed, and he was sentenced to four years in prison, with four years of supervision.

Two other people were charged in the case as well. Mary's stepfather, William Kempf, received one-year probation for battery, and Mary's mother, Sally, received two years probation for failure to protect a child. Mary's stepfather was later quoted as saying that if it went on that long, it wasn't rape. He said that Mary was probably asking for it. Since taking him out for a long, slow beating isn't an option, I can only hope that he gets what he deserves someday.

Mary's brother Johnny had been her most frequent attacker, admitting to raping her about a hundred times. He was charged with five counts of sexual abuse of a child. A huge crowd of Amish turned out for his sentencing, but because Johnny was married with a child, they pleaded that it would be a hardship for him to be locked up.

The judge should have made certain that justice, above all else, prevailed. The judge should have known better. The Amish always take care of their own. There was no way...no way in hell...that Johnny's family would have starved. Family and other Amish in the community would have provided for them. Hundreds, if not thousands, of "We're having a cheer up shower" notes were undoubtedly sent out to all the Amish communities across America for them. Just as it had for Ruby.

Of course, the Amish believed that Johnny had already been sufficiently punished after being placed in the ban for six weeks. The other brothers had also been severely punished, by Amish standards. Eli confessed his sin and was put in the ban. Since David was too young to be a church member, he only had to stay at home until he showed signs of character improvement.

Johnny's sentencing was for one year in the county jail with *Huber*, or work release privileges. What that means is that he was let out each morning so he could go home to work on his farm but had to return to the jail at night. Basically, he served his sentence by sleeping at the jail each night for a year. He would also serve ten years probation. Three of the charges were dismissed.

We were shocked when the judge gave Johnny only a year with work release. Rape your sister for years, but if you're Amish with a family, you only have to go sleep in jail. You can go home each morning and carry on as if everything is normal.

Talk about injustice. Talk about justice being blinded by some misled nostalgic compassion. Fill a room with weeping and wailing Amish and the judge completely forgets that he is supposed to be fair and give equal treatment under the law. What English person would get off so easy?

Furious with his decision, I vented my anger in a letter to the judge. It was a disgrace and a miscarriage of justice! Mary's brother had *admitted* to raping her. How could the judge not treat him like any other U.S. citizen? That judge was just another buying into the "but they're poor Amish" way of thinking. Put them on a pedestal. Aren't they quaint? Aren't they so virtuous and morally superior to us?

Bullshit!

Sure, I believed the Amish fairy tale at first. It seemed so long ago when I was helping Amos and Verena with the haying and those early mornings of driving the kids to school and playing volleyball or round-town with them. That was back when I felt connected to them, even though I could never be one of them.

But then the mirage of their perfect world and harmonious existence had been shattered after Bill left. A line was drawn. For the sake of one friend, I became as much of an outcast as he was. I would never understand how those I considered to be my friends could so easily cut me from their lives. How could they blindly follow what the community demanded? How can you shun family and friends just because they disagree? How could they so easily cut people out of their lives?

That wasn't the worst.

The worst was finding out about Mary and too many others. All the abuse that is allowed to go on. Fathers raping daughters. Brothers raping sisters. Victims ignored. Victims told they didn't fight hard enough or pray enough. There were so many rumors, too many to be ignored or discounted.

The Amish are no better or worse than the rest of us. There are good and honorable Amish, just as there are good and honorable English. The problem with the Amish is that the victims have nowhere to go for help. Everyone they typically encounter is Amish. Their teachers are young adult

Amish with only the same eighth grade education and who answer to the community. No Amish teacher is required by law to report suspected abuse. Amish children, from their earliest years, have it drilled into them that the English are not to be trusted. They have nowhere to go and no one to ask for help.

And we allow it. We allow the Amish to remain separate. We permit the Amish to only educate their children to the eighth grade. We patronize their businesses and treat them as an acceptable family tourist attraction. We don't hold them to the same standards under the law because we're too busy putting them on a pedestal and buying their quilts.

There are other things besides sexual assault and abuse going on, although that alone is bad enough. There are many things that none of us, the English, would get away with. The Amish can bury their dead in simple pine boxes in their own cemeteries. When the English have a burial, the casket has to be placed into a concrete vault to prevent groundwater contamination. Amish can send their children out to work full days after eighth grade without a work permit and the child's earnings going to the family. Tell me any English person who could get away with what is essentially child slavery?

The weekends that Bill has the kids, the first thing I do is to get them cleaned up. I can wash their clothes several times, hang them outside to dry, and still not get the stink from them. Even worse than that is the condition of the children themselves with gunk coming from their ears, cavities in their teeth that need fillings long before a child should have to, and just being dirty.

At least now Bill's kids have options. They have someone outside the community they could go to.

That's more than most of the rest of them have.

It's more than Mary had.

Thirty-seven

Blessed is the man who finds wisdom,
the man who gains understanding,
for she is more profitable than silver
and yields better returns than gold.
She is more precious than rubies;
nothing you desire can compare with her.
Proverbs 3: 13 – 15, *The Holy Bible*, NIV

Bill

The day arrived.
Finally.
I was due in court.

Today was the day that I would appear before the judge and tell him that I wanted to divorce my wife.

The early morning sunshine disappeared behind dark storm clouds as we drove to Wautoma. I didn't mind. The weather matched my mood. I didn't want to be doing this. Why couldn't Ruby have just agreed to an uncontested divorce? According to the Amish rules that we had always been taught, she should not want any part of English world. She should not want to appear in an English court. But she hired an attorney and insisted on having a hearing.

I dreaded it.

Karrie told me about the trial of Mary Byler's brothers. She told me about the packed courtroom and the weeping women. I knew the Amish would come out in force for my trial as well. They would do their best, one last time, to try to convince me that I was being misled. They had to stop me before it was too late.

The temperature dropped about twenty degrees in the time that we drove from Karrie's to the courthouse. We hurried across the street into the courthouse to escape the frigid wind.

"We're supposed to meet Bev in the conference room before we go into the courtroom," Karrie reminded me.

I nodded. It was all that I could do to keep my teeth from chattering from the chill that had seeped into my bones.

I wanted to have it over with. Why couldn't time suddenly leap forward several hours? Why couldn't we be walking out of the courthouse? Why couldn't it all be done and over with?

Very faintly, I heard the clip-clop of hooves and the clatter of a buggy. They were coming.

It was about to begin.

Thirty-eight

Karrie

"What are you going to wear today?"

"I don't know. Am I supposed to dress up?"

"I think neat and clean is fine. Maybe a button-down shirt and your new jeans," I suggested. We would be leaving for his divorce hearing right after breakfast. Bill is always quiet in the morning, but I could tell that this morning was different. To lighten the mood, I asked, "Are you going to wear your black shoes?"

Bill looked at me, clearly puzzled, but then the slightest smile came to his lips, "I just might."

For his sixteenth birthday, Bill had asked his mom to buy him a pair of shoes that he wanted.

"They were plain," he told me several months earlier, "All the stitching was black...and there weren't any decorations, or logos, or anything on them. I showed them to Mom. She said if that was what I wanted, she could get them. She said they looked okay to her. Dad said they were okay with him.

"I don't think I had them a week, but not more than two, when it was time for church. I remember kneeling down to pray and having this feeling that someone was staring at me. I glanced over my shoulder. It was the deacon right behind me. I thought I saw him looking at my shoes.

"The deacon stopped by our house later. I was gone somewhere, I don't remember where. He asked to see the shoes I wore to church, so my mom got them. On the backs, there was some padding that came up a bit over the back of the heel...there were two bumps that made sort of an "M" shape...like two camel humps. The deacon looked at the shoes and told my mom that she had to cut those humps off so it was straight and then she had to sew it closed."

"What was the reason?" I asked, not seeing how two bumps on the backs of a shoe could cause such concern.

"Same as always. It was too fancy. Those two little humps were black just like the rest of the shoes. Two little bumps. But they were too fancy."

Bill shook his head before continuing, "When those shoes finally wore out, I got another pair. I was about nineteen then, and a church member. One morning, I went to get ready for church and my shoes were gone. I couldn't find them anywhere, so I asked my mom if she knew where they were.

"'Lewis came and got them. Get your old ones.' That's what my mom told me."

"They took your shoes away?"

"Yup. I had to wear these old, hard leather ones. The new ones were nothing fancy either. They looked nice and plain and were comfortable. But it was just like always. They can't let you get too close to the line. They've got to keep you tightly reined in.

"I didn't have anyone to support me. I couldn't fight it. Later, some of the other young folks bought the same shoes. Once there were a few of them, and they stuck together, they had to let it go through. It was so ridiculous."

"If I didn't know you," I said to Bill, shaking my head, "I would swear that you make this shit up. Just like what happened with your hunting stuff."

"That was another thing that really pissed me off," Bill said, suddenly sitting up in his chair. It was strange to see him this worked up about something. "Why did I have to go out hunting with a cold neck? Rip up a perfectly good jacket just so it was *plain*."

Back before Bill left the Amish, he called me one day when I was out shopping and asked if I would get him an orange hunting coat. "Something cheap," was the only instruction he gave me.

I found something and also happened to find a nice orange, flannel shirt. When he showed up to go hunting a few days later, the collar on the coat was missing.

"What the hell...?" I asked, pointing to his coat.

"Collars aren't allowed," Bill said and rolled his eyes. "We're only supposed to wear the orange vest. I could get in trouble if someone catches me, since I didn't rip the arms off."

"You have to rip the collar and the arms off a perfectly good coat? How are you supposed to keep warm?"

"If you'd got me a hooded coat, I would have had to rip the hood off. It's little things like this that piss me off. It seems stupid to destroy a perfectly good coat."

Amish were allowed to wear camouflage until word got around that some, like Bill, were buying $400 Scent-Lok camouflage clothing. Not long after that, the rules changed. No more camouflage.

"Can you believe it? I'm not supposed to wear camo when I hunt anymore!" Bill had been really pissed. Bow hunting is Bill's favorite and it's pretty hard to have anything to shoot at if you aren't camouflaged.

"What are you going to do?" I had asked.

"I'm not giving up my camo. I guess if I get caught I'll have to confess and take my punishment."

"What do you say when you confess? 'Dear Lord, I'm sorry for hiding from the food that I was trying to provide for my family. I guess we'll go hungry. I won't do it again.'"

"Yeah, something like that," Bill answered with a smile.

The next hunting season, after Bill left the Amish, he joked about getting to wear a collar at last, "I finally get to have a warm neck this year."

"You're just living it up now that you're English, aren't you, Bill? A coat with a collar and sleeves!"

"Don't forget the zipper," he added.

As we walked out to the car, I noticed that Bill was not wearing the black shoes. He let me drive while he sat looking out the side window most of the way to Wautoma. I knew Bill was nervous and dreading the court appearance. There was nothing I could say to distract him or take his mind off it, so I let the radio fill the silence.

Several days earlier, I told Bev that it would be best if Bill didn't have to stand around in the hallway for a long time. Mary's trial had opened my eyes to some of the tactics of the Amish, and I wanted to protect Bill from any of that.

"We'll have a conference room assigned to us, so we can wait in there," Bev had reassured me.

When we got to the courthouse, I was relieved that there was no sign of any of the Amish yet, but by the time we reached the courthouse steps, we could hear buggies approaching.

"It'll be okay, Bill. Just ignore them and keep walking."

"I know."

We waited in the hall until Bev got there a few minutes later and led us to a conference room. It was still too soon to go into the courtroom, so I went out to use the ladies' room. That was when I saw it.

Filing single file into the courtroom, their heads bowed, and their hands clasped in prayer, came the Amish procession. They looked as if they were going to a funeral. No one raised their eyes to look at me. I didn't count them, but there had to be seventy or eighty of them.

When I went back to the conference room, I didn't say anything to Bill. What would be the point? He knew they would be in there.

And then finally, it was time.

"It'll be best if you wait here," Bev said to me as she stood up from the table.

Staring at her, I felt completely torn. I wanted to be there for Bill, to sit next to him and give him support. That's what I had done for Mary and no one had given my being there a second thought.

But it would be very different in this courtroom. I couldn't deny that my presence could be distracting and possibly even be used against Bill somehow.

Bev was right, so I nodded and to Bill, I said, "I'll see you in a bit. It'll be over in no time."

He didn't respond, he just looked very lost and alone as he left the room.

Pacing like a caged animal, I waited and waited. Time can play tricks on you. A minute can seem like an hour, but something was wrong. This was taking too long. My divorce had taken about five minutes, and checking the time on my cell phone, Bill and Bev had already been gone half an hour. What could be taking so long?

Finally, after nearly an hour, the door opened and Bev walked in. My eyes remained focused on the door, waiting for Bill to come through.

No Bill.

A couple more seconds passed.

Still, no Bill.

"Where's Bill?" I said, my heartbeat increasing.

"He was right behind me..."

"We can't leave him alone out there!" I said, my voice rising with alarm, "We've got to get him!"

Thirty-nine

*"Again, you have heard that it was said to the people long ago,
'Do not break your oath, but keep the oaths you have made to the Lord.'
But I tell you, Do not swear at all:
either by heaven, for it is God's throne;
or by the earth, for it is his footstool;
or by Jerusalem, for it is the city of the Great King.
And do not swear by your head,
for you cannot make even one hair white or black.
Simply let your 'Yes' be 'Yes,' and your 'No,' 'No';
anything beyond this comes from the evil one."*
Matthew 5: 33 – 37, *The Holy Bible*, NIV

Bill

It seemed to go on forever.
Karrie told me that her divorce hearing took five minutes.
I looked over at the clock again. Twenty minutes.
How much longer could it take?

The Amish had come out in force. So many familiar faces. Ruby's family. My family. The community. They all came to support Ruby. The room was full of them. There weren't enough seats. Some stood along the back, leaning against the walls.

They looked as if they were at a funeral. They looked as if they would have preferred to be at a funeral. At my funeral. They would have preferred that I was dead. My death would have been better than my divorcing Ruby.

How warped is that?
How twisted is it to think like that?
That it would be better for someone to be dead than not Amish.

Everything seemed to be dragging on. The judge asked Ruby so many questions. He asked if she was aware that she may be entitled to more property.

All of this had been worked out by our attorneys months ago.
Back and forth.
Back and forth.
It had gone back and forth for months.

There had been so many details of the marital settlement agreement to work out. One day, I would feel as if things were moving along. That things were going well. Believing that it would all soon be over. Then something new would come up. Ruby even asked for my sawmill! That request took me completely by surprise. The sawmill was mine before we got married. She knew that. She had no claim to it. But I knew what was going on. Her dad or her brothers told her to try to get it for them.

After my attorney said no, Ruby's attorney came back with a request for the sawmill or $10,000. Greedy Amish bastards. Ruby and her family were determined to put a knife in me and keep twisting it round and round.

My attorney again denied the request.

Nearly everything was mine before I married her. The house. The sawmill. The horses and the buggy.

I found out after the trial, too late, that I probably could have filed for a "short-term marriage" divorce. If I had done that, Ruby would have only gotten what she brought with her. Her clothes. Some dishes. A few pieces of furniture, including the curio cabinet that she hadn't been able to move that day she ripped up the carpet in the living room.

Ruby ended up getting the horses and buggy even though they were mine. I guess the judge figured that I wouldn't need a buggy anymore if I wasn't Amish. I would have sold them, but I was okay with letting her have them. Maybe it would ease some of the guilt I still felt. The guilt that I would probably always feel.

I will always be sorry for hurting Ruby. But over the past year, I knew that she wasn't a complete victim. She made her choice. She chose to not honor her vows. She chose to live without a husband. She didn't want to find a way to work things out with me so we could be together.

What was Ruby thinking now? How did she feel about being here in the courtroom with the judge? Did it seem real to her? Did she feel like a failure? Did she have any regrets? Did she wish she would have tried to get me to come back? Did she have the urge to stand up and say, "Stop! I've changed my mind!"?

Did her heart ache as much as mine?

Glancing over at the table where she sat with her attorney, I expected her to have her head bowed like all the other Amish in the courtroom. I expected her to look sad. Or lost. Or confused. Or blank, as if she had tuned everything out.

I didn't expect her to be smiling.

I didn't expect to see her giggling.

But she was.

Her attorney had just said something to her, and Ruby was giggling about it. The judge noticed at the same time I did, and she quickly covered her mouth with her hand.

The judge went over how much money was owed and how much various things would be worth if they were sold. All of this had already been covered in a teleconference.

He asked if she was okay with the profit, *my* profit. She said she was.

I didn't get that. He seemed to be intentionally giving her an opening to ask for something. To ask for more.

But she passed.

I noticed that there was never any mention of *her* house or *her* store. Those things had been kept out of her name just so I wouldn't be able to make any sort of claim on them.

She didn't give a second thought to trying to get my sawmill.

Finally, the judge ruled.

It was the longest forty-five minutes of my life.

Then it was over.
It was over, at last.
Ruby and I were divorced.

"William! William!"

As soon as I stepped out of the courtroom, my dad called to me. He grabbed my arm and roughly pulled me over to him. He shoved a piece of paper into my hand.

"You read this. Karrie is a liar. I can prove it."

What was he thinking? Seconds before I was in court, in front of a judge, getting divorced. Did he give any thought to what I just went through? Couldn't he give me a moment? Couldn't he give me a moment of peace? Did he really think that I even gave a damn?

All my dad cared about was trying to prove something. Make me think that Karrie was a liar. I already knew who was the liar and deceiver.

"You're reading that wrong," I said, pushing back at the letter he held up in my face as I glanced around for Bev. She had already disappeared.

The letter that got my dad so stirred up was one that Karrie wrote him. I knew what had probably set him off, but it was nothing. Nothing except my father trying to find something. Something to put Karrie down. Something to make my father right.

I tried to step away. Tried to get to the conference room. But my father's grip reined me back.

"No! You read it! You'll see that she's a liar. You shouldn't trust her, William!"

Then on my other arm, there was a tug. And a voice that I was relieved to hear.

"Come on, Bill, we're going," Karrie said.

We went back to the conference room and talked with Bev. We took our time. We waited for the others to clear out.

"Let's just go," Karrie said after what seemed to be long enough.

The halls were empty of the mourning Amish masses. I felt myself starting to relax as we reached the front doors. Just a few more yards, and it would all be behind me.

A shocking cold blast of wind pulled the courthouse door out of my hand. Rain lashed in, and my shirt was instantly and completely soaked. It was nearly the end of May, but it felt more like a November storm. The kind of storm you expect to turn to snow.

Shivering uncontrollably, I would have given anything for a coat.

"William! You've turned into a wuss!" a voice called across the courthouse steps. I recognized it immediately as my brother Adlai.

"Don't listen to them, Bill," Karrie said, picking up her already quick pace.

"William! William! Do you know where you are going? You are going to straight to HELL!" A cruel voice that sounded familiar yelled at me. There was too much rain. I was shaking too hard. I didn't bother to look around to see who it was.

It seemed to take forever before we finally made it to the car. Karrie cranked up the heat, but it took ages before any warmth penetrated my frozen body.

"I'm sorry about all that, Bill. At least it's over now."

"Yeah. It's over."

On the way back to Karrie's, I told her more of the details of the hearing that she hadn't heard while we waited in the conference room.

"Ruby swore an oath?" Karrie asked, surprised, "I thought that was against some Amish belief."

"It is," I said, "She should have done uncontested. That's what she should have done according to the rules. She would have got exactly the same as what she got by going to trial."

"She didn't sign the papers, did she?"

"No, her attorney did that. For that, she followed the rules, although she shouldn't have had an attorney in the first place. They're such hypocrites! They pick and choose the rules they want to follow. They get out of stuff by hiding behind their rules and then break the rules when it doesn't suit them."

It was the same thing. Always the same thing.

Three days later, my mother called.

"I want to apologize to you, William. I'm the one that yelled to you the other day. I said that you're going to hell. I don't want to go to hell for saying it, so I had to tell you. I need to free my soul."

I didn't know what to say.

What could I say? What could I say to my mother? What could I say to a mother who could yell such things to her child? What could I say that she only called to apologize in order to free her own soul.

It wasn't much of an apology.

I don't remember what I said to her. I probably just mumbled something like, "Okay."

It was over.

I was out.

I was English. I had a driver's license. I paid Social Security. I trimmed my beard and grew a mustache. I wore hunting coats with collars. I wore jeans with zippers. I was still Christian and still believed that Jesus Christ was the Son of God.

I was no longer Amish. I didn't have to follow the *Ordnung* or any of their strict rules in order to get into heaven someday. I didn't believe that I would go to hell just because I wasn't Amish. I didn't have to feel like a hypocrite. I didn't have to live a lie.

I believe that it is more important to live a good life.

To do my best. To be a good man. To be a good father.

My life as an Amish was over.

No more living by someone else's rules.

No more following the road that had been paved by someone else.

No more traveling in my *Ordnung*-approved black buggy with the battery power light and "slow moving vehicle" sign on the back.

I was free.
I was finally free.

Free to find my own destiny.
Free to go wherever the road took me.

I was letting go.
Letting go of the reins.

Forty

Wisdom has built her house;
she has hewn out its seven pillars.
She has prepared her meat and mixed her wine;
she has also set her table.
She has sent out her maids,
and she calls from the highest point of the city.
"Let all who are simple come in here!"
she says to those who lack judgment.
"Come, eat my food and drink the wine I have mixed.
Leave your simple ways and you will live;
walk in the way of understanding.
Proverbs 9: 1-6, *The Holy Bible,* NIV

Bill

Over the next nine months there were a few more letters that came. Most of them were from my mother.

5-26-04
Dear William
Greetings of Love and in Jesus Name. Hope this finds you feeling well and on the go. We are Busy. Dad went to work again this P.M. In A.M. he was fixing Balers, elevators & harrow for the Boys as they started mowing hay Today. Seems theres always something to keep him Busy. Yesterday I finished the garden & mowed the grass with the help of Adlais Boys in the P.M. Adlai got hurt by a yearling colt outside (as it had stomach ache) and all of a Sudden she or a he am not sure which jumped up & knocked Adlai face down & stomped of his upper Back to where he has a very stiff neck & is quite sore. He Said he heard his neck pop when it happened so I hope he can heal soon. It was Bad enough but it could of also killed him if it would of Broke his neck. But his time wasn't here to go yet.
Here is the scrap Book sheet – now you can fix it yourself as am sure you prob. have seen some already. A few get well wishes, nice pictures, card, and also some Bible verses are what is usually put on Sheets. So show us that you care.

I guess you don't have any idea where Lynn is do you?? There is also a sheet here for him but I don't Know where to send it too so sad! If you Know, let us Know so I can send it to him. Well good luck and hope you can get it done before you forget. Its up to you where you want to send it but Ola's address is on the paper. Thanks very much.

Love you,
Mom

6 – 16 – 04
Greetings of Love – In Jesus Name. Hope you are well as leaves us. Just a friendly reminder about the scrap Book sheet I sent for you to fix for Steven.

May be you've got it done and good if you do But I guess next week is the time to have them sent Back! Hope you understand.

Love and Best Wishes
Mom

P.S. Its up to you, if you want me to send it to Ola's that's fine. Just get it here so I can!

A birthday card arrived in August. The outside was printed:

Happy Birthday
May thy life happy be
Is my dear wish for thee

Inside was the printed message with "*Dear William,*" added above it:

May your birthday be as special as you are!

My mother added inside:

Live For Jesus, Serve Him Daily
As The Path on Earth you Trod,
For Lifes Greatest Plan and Purpose
Is, "Prepare To Meet They God!"

Draw Nigh To God and He will draw nigh To You
James 4:8
A few of the sayings and verse that were on my Birthday Quilt from the
neices and daughters on my 60th.

On your 26th Birthday!
"Aug 10, 2004"
"Love and God Bless You"
Dad – N – Mom
and Elvie
"We Still Miss You"

October 15, 2004
Dear William,
Greetings of Love and in Jesus Name. Hope these few lines will found
you in good health and on the go, as leaves us. Except yesterday it seemed
like I had the 24 hour flu or something. Achy Bones & just not feeling up to
Par so I really didn't get very much done except rest. Little Millie had
another few days at the Madison hospital again from Mon. nite to Wed.
P.M. She was having a temp. so they had to check her out & she had
urinary tract infection & I kidney puffed up so they had to release that &
put her on medication again. Poor little miss has to suffer so. Wish I could
do it for her.
You probably figure we forgot you? No we didn't & never will as long as
life and memory last. Sorry for not writing sooner. Sun. Monroes had
Communion & now on the 24 Oct. we are to have church at our house, so
you are more then welcome to come for that as well as any other time you
care too. The Boys are done w/ silo filling and Adlai did make some fire
wood. He made a nice little pile for our Wood Shed. We were out and Dad
helped silo filling for 3 weeks so I guess thats his pay which is plenty good
enough. Dad went to the funeral in Bonduel Tue. of Wm. Yoder, he was an
uncle to Rubys Mom so lots of others went to. Was a very large funeral like
1200 people. Dad and Wm. had lots of heart to heart talks when they
happened to meet each other the last several years, so this was also very
hard on Dad. But at least we can have good hopes for him as he tried to
lead a God fearing Life. He left a big family behind and also a very
bereaved wife. So I hope God will See her through her lonely days. Now
your turn for a letter to let us Know how you are.
Take care – Lots of Love & we are still praying for you and your family.

On floral notepaper with "Love Never Fails" 1st Corinthians 13:8 printed at bottom was another letter.

12 – 20 – 04
Dear William,
Greetings. Got some winter now, Eh? At least Today is milder then it was yesterday. We had -7° the coldest that we saw in our Thermometer yesterday, so I guess we thought it was COLD!
Just a line to invite you over to our house for Brunch of Breakfast haystacks on Sat. Christmas Day. Do hope you can come as its nearly 2 years that you were here and that is way to long! So please come and be with us & the family for a few hours.
Sorry for not letting you know sooner but we didn't decide it until last week, we first usually need to see if the other side of the families have there day planned so we can go accordingly. Would of course have the candy, snacks & games in the P.M. I'll set a plate for you so please come! See you then.
Lovingly,
Mom

A month or so after my divorce was final, Karrie and I became more than friends. No one will believe that it didn't happen sooner. Everyone had us sleeping together before I left. But that was just vicious gossip and outright lies. I was faithful to my wife until after our divorce was final.

That's the truth.

There was always a connection between the two of us. I have always been able to talk to her. We both loved to hunt and fish. We never got tired of talking about it. But I was able to talk to her about other things. She always listened. She got it. We had a solid friendship before we became lovers.

"I had a bit of a crush on you," I admitted to her one day, "Before you started driving for me."

"It was probably those halter tops I wore," Karrie said with her typical sassy attitude.

"Maybe," I agreed, smiling at the memory.

"Yeah, I remember seeing you in a buggy once. I noticed those sexy brown eyes and wondered who you were," Karrie said. "I asked several people who it was in that buggy, but no one would tell me."

My sister Rachel and her kids came up for a visit that summer for our mom's birthday. It was great seeing her again and meeting her family at last. They came only a few weeks after Karrie and I became a couple. Everything was still very new between us, so we kept our relationship a secret.

"Rachel called," Karrie said, "They got back home okay."

"That's good."

"I told her that we're a couple."

"What did she say?"

"She was surprised. She said, 'You're kidding, really? I would have never guessed.'"

Besides Rachel, who was back in Missouri, we didn't go out of our way to tell anyone else. But by winter, everyone seemed to know. Of course, most of them already thought they knew long before it happened.

That Christmas, Karrie sent my parents a card from all of us. As a family. We were both surprised when it came back. The card had been opened and put into a different envelope. There was no note included. No explanation.

A letter from my dad arrived about December 22nd.

Dear William

Aus Groza Liebe in Gottes Namen dich der sege gewüncht.

A beautiful scene this morn with the snow. Don't know if I'll work much this A.M. as my body just can't take a full day to much pain yet so will maybe try to save it for P.M. as Monroe & Adlai want to go finish loading Gary Bladers semi with tin and lumber. Took down the Poy Sippi elvator lots & lots of material it is going down. Already one load went last week to Bloomfield Iowa for Lewis & Monroes to put up buildings as they're both buying land without much on it. So hope it can be a silo in it for them.

About the greeting that was sent we didn't send it back about from who it came but it came as a Family package and you know in your own mind or at least used to, that it can never ever be right before the eyes of the Almighty God, who will be the judge we will all face on that great judgment day in spite of how we let our mind be led. Yes Jesus Loves Us all, including the very worst criminals in the world. But He also says Who lives in Sin will die in Sin, and we also all know will arise on that day in Sin. I have Sinned as well as All other persons on this earth But what Jesus says

224

repent meaning quit doing sin and ask forgiveness and try to not sin again.
Yet if we fall again, rise again, & cry for forgiveness. Put away world.
Jesus said He who loves the world, in Him is not, the Love of God. I just
felt with a heavy heart to remind you we feel you did at least know better at
one time. And I'm not asking and don't want an answer from Kerry on this.
This will probably be the last plea to you from me directly, want to plea on
your behalf to Jesus.

   Aus Liebe
   Dad – Mom
   P.S. Just a poem that was read off at Wilbur Dayes services – a good one
for us all to read and study.

Followed by a note from my mother soon after.

12 – 28 – 04
Dear William
   Greetings of Love & in Jesus Name. Hope you are well and on the go.
Once again we need to Change our Christmas gathering as Amos & Rose
of Lamar Mo. came as a surprise to everyone on Sun. the 26 so the
Lambrights plan to gather at David Yoders the 29 (tomorrow) as they'd
leave again on Thurs. so we didn't want Monroes & Adlais to take off 2
work days in one week so now we plan for Old Christmas Jan 6 in the P.M.
and you shall also please come! We went to have finger foods & Candys &
play games or whatever for a few hours so I thought I'd best let you know
right away.
   So will we see you then? Hope so! Must hurry on. Dad & the other Boys
went to Poy sippi to work on that elevator again today Am glad when they
are finished with it, which shouldn't take to many more days.
   Take Care – God Bless You.
   Love you,
   Dad & Mom

Another note from Mom arrived with Valentine stickers "A Valentine for
you" and "You are so Special"

Jan. 29 – 05
Dear William,

Greetings of Love and in Jesus Name. Hope this will find you in good health and on the go. As leaves us much to be thankful for. Seems like Dad just can't get his strenghth Bach like he wants it Since he got Kicked in Nov. Now he also has an awful cold. But still Keeps a going. He thought the orange juice & oranges were gonna Keep him healthy all winter then Bam suddenly he started w/ a cold the 1ˢᵗ of this week.

If he goes to church tomorrow his singing will prob. be sorta squeaky.

He is quite Busy rebuilding hay loaders, which is a good demand for them in some areas close by. He has 4 done & is working on 2 more. So far since his Accident he hasn't been back to his carpenter work so its good he has this to Keep him occupied.

Wanted to let you Know that we got the shocking news on Wednesday that Ervin Jess has Cancer on his liver & pancreas. So that doesn't sound good at all. Doctors say just Keep him comfortable at home with pain medication as they can't do anything for him. So we never Know who will be next with that dreaded disease.

If he should Happen to pass away would you probly want us to let you know?? And if you'd want to go to the funeral which would be nice if you would. You'd be welcome to go with the others of here if you don't want to go alone.

Oh yes, don't Know if you've found out yet or not that Monroes are buying a place in Bloomfield, IA. Same area Lewis a are?? Want to be, moving by last of April or 1ˢᵗ of May is what there plans are as of now. Allen Yoders are buying this place. So I guess we will also need to move out of this house (which spites me) but so it is mol. Guess Allens parents of Jamesport, Mo. would want to live in here part time. Prob. in the summertime. So we haven't decided yet where we will go as don't want to move out of this area as long as Adlais & Yours are here.

So time will tell – But decisions need to be made B-4 Long. Monroes want an auction sometime in April to sell excess items & some horses & Adlai also has horses to put on the sale. We pray for the Lords will in this all. I guess we lived here for over 21 years now and it just seemed more like home but so be it.

Well it's Sat. & need to do cleaning & Bake Bread & put all the stitches in the quilt I can plus get drawers & thinks cleaned out with junk & etc.

Had meat to put up this week. If you'd stop in I'd give you some. Is Beef, made chili, & Bolona also. Very good. Little Baby Millie is still waiting on her last surgery. Weighs 15# & the 12ᵗʰ Feb. will be a year old. Is a cutie.

Take care – Love you!
Love & Prayers
Dads & Elvie

My family was gradually moving away from the Wautoma Community. Now Lewis. Later Monroe. Soon my parents would be gone as well.

I remember my grandfather saying, "You can't run from your problems." My dad didn't seem to believe that.

They were moving again.

Just like when Lynn left.

And they were still trying to get me back. It had been nearly two years since I left, but they kept on trying.

They never seemed to get it through their thick skulls that the harder they pulled at me, the harder they pulled the reins, the harder I fought.

It never made sense to me. All that time, they had a carrot. Something to offer me while I bucked. Something that could have settled me down. Something to lure me back.

Ruby.

So many times, if Ruby had given me even the slightest encouragement, I probably would have gone back.

She always had that power.

She was the only one.

But she never tried.

Never.

One other letter arrived. It was dated the exact two-year anniversary of when I decided to leave the Amish. The letter was from my Uncle Andy, the husband of my father's sister. I missed Uncle Andy and was glad to hear from him. Even if he was only trying once again to get me back.

Jan. 30, 2005

Dear William,

Greetings to you from Bloomfield, Ia in the name of the Dear Lord & Savior Jesus Christ. This is Sunday forenoon and Irma & I are at home today. Something that very seldom happens. Usually we are either in church or Sunday School. We here in our community have Sunday school from spring until Thanksgiving in the fall but not during the winter months. So during the summer we have church one Sunday and Sunday School the next Sunday. Since we now have 7 church districts here we have the priviledge of going to church every Sunday even in the winter when we don't have Sunday School. So now today we chose to just be at home for once and it doesn't quite seem right. Do want to use it in a way that can be pleasing to the Lord. Such as reading upbuilding material, writing letters and spreading good cheer to others.

Today is just an ordinary winter day. Is over cast and about 30° with a light blanket of snow on the ground. We have had a fairly nice winter so far. Did have several cold snaps but didn't last long. Our coldest I believe was 8 below one morning. We've had several weeks of ice which was a little hard to get around but it is lots better now again.

I suppose you know that your Brother Lewis & family live here in our area now. Felt sorrow for them that no one else moved in over at Arbela, Mo. where they were and had hoped to start a settlement. Well any way they now live here in our area but still haven't got a home of their own. Just rent where they now live with hopes of being able to find a farm some time in the near future. Lewis likes Dairying and I'd be glad for them if they could find something suitable to buy and get back to milking again. I believe it would be good for the family. The farm seems to be as good a place to raise a family as can be found but ofcourse not everybody has that opportunity and also other occupations can support Christian principles.

I've been helping son Kenneth here at the feed mill now for close to 10 years and find that this also gives a person the chance to meet up with all kinds of people and challenges, to live a life so that others can see the goodness of Christ in my life. Not as a show off but as Jesus said in Matthew 5 – 16th verse "Let you light so shine before men that they may see your good works, and glorify your Father which is in Heaven" Ofcourse we should be more concerned to live a righteous life for Christs sake than just so people can see our goodness but the two go together in a Christians live. It is sad to think how Satan lures people away from God with all his enticing ways and after he leads people astray he offers no way of repentance but often leaves them in a miserable and discouraged state even after offering a person all the liberties the world has to offer. In Galatians 5 v19 we read of the works of the flesh. (The things that Satan lures people into) then as we read on we come to the fruit of the Spirit v 22 (The things that God wants us to do) Quite a contrast. So the Bible tells us we are servants. Either servants of God or the Devil depending on our works.

I wonder what you are working now? Are you still sawing pulp wood? It would seem that with so many logs being cut all the tine the world would run out of wood but that is another wonder of creation that trees are growing all the time and replacing those that are harvested. We have a number of saw mills here in our area but are having some trouble getting enough logs at present. We have 2 mills sawing furniture grade lumber but the others saw mostly custom or pallet & crating lumber.

228

I mentioned that I help Kenneth here at the feed mill. It is about all that 3 of us can keep up with. Kenneth & their oldest son Ervin (16) & I. We do grinding, mixing, & delivery of bulk feeds and have a line of bag feed that can be picked up here and we also deliver some. There are various other businesses in our area. A shop just west of us that manufactures truss rafters, several furniture shops, bulk food grocery stores, salvage store & welding shops to name some.

There is a Goat cheese plant in Wisconsin that has been buying goat milk from some of the Amish in Kalona Iowa area which is about 100 mi north of us now they wanted more milk to fill their demand so they had a meeting in our area to see if enough interest here to justify hauling milk to Wis. So now there are 10 families that have committed to start milking goats by this spring some time, an average of 100 each so that will be a new source of income for here.

Also have 4 layer houses going up to furnish organic eggs for some group in Kalona area. Seems like there is something for every one to do here and is enjoyable to see that the community is surviving.

From what we hear your Bro. Monroes are also expecting to move here to our community by spring. Is nice to see more of the freundschaft among us. Maybe then we might get to see you too sometimes.

Will close in Wishing you God's Grace
Andy & Irma Schrock

Folded separately was another letter.

Want to share with you a little of our concerns we have for you. Hopefully I won't write anything to make matters worse for that is not my intention. Often do think of you and Ruby. Of how it is that youns are not to-gether and how we all so wish something better for both of you. Marriage is so "precious. Something that God so ordained and is so sad when Satan interferes and breaks marriages up. I know very little about your life at home and also your marriage but when we were als at your folks when you were still at home I always thought you were so reserved & quiet and felt that surely you would some day be rewarded for your attitude in not being loud & boisterous. So now I also think what were you thinking what happened in your life that lead you to do what you are now doing. Was it partly my fault? Did I act in a way that was a stumbling block to you. I ask your forgiveness if I did. I do think of several things that took place in your community as you grew up as told by your Dad that could perhaps have given you a bad taste of the Amish Church which is sad. A young person growing up in such an environment could surely get a feeling of wanting to get away from it all but like the Prodigal Son that we read about in Luke 15 there is really nothing out in the world that is going to treat us good either. Usually we just sink deeper and deeper into sin. Satan helps us in but never helps us out. Only God can do that. Reminds me of the Devotional Booklet we read this morning Philippians 4 – 13 "I can do all things through Christ which strengtheneth me"

    Feel so sorry for You & Ruby to think how nice it could be for both of you if youns were together again and in good standing with God and the Church and in contrast how sad it is this way. God gives a choice. We can choose to live for him but we don't have too. We do have to suffer the consequences though if we don't live for him. I think some times we in our Amish circles don't teach enough on why we believe as we do and maybe too much on our sichtbare ordnung. I think we need a guide line to help us stay out of Satan's luring territory but also we need to grasp the importance of having a clear conscience and proper respect for God our Creator. We were all condemd to eternal punishment because of human sinfulness but then God saw it fit to redeem us human beings by sending his son Jesus to die on the cross to free us from …hell if we repent and live a righteous God fearing life and we all know that this can not be done if we live like the "works of the flesh". As we read in Galations 5. So the way I understand it is if we willfully live in sin and don't repent and lead a better life we are helping to crucify Jesus again and there is no heavenly hope after death. How sad. Something that I have learned over the years is that the 'Grade Gottes' "God's Grace" as a gift to us humans so it can't be earned, it is free 2 any one doing the will of God. Now we can't be good enough even with our best intentions to really earn our way to Heaven but God is good enough to grant us heaven after death if we live a life pleasing to him like "The fruit of the spirit" in Galations 5. I don't know how much you read in the Bible and I'll admit there is much there that I don't fully understand but wish I could get you to read the 4th 5th & 6th Chapters in Romans and study them some what. It tells a lot of how a person can come to God and how God has broken sins power so regardless how far a person has fallen I believe there is hope to get back to God. There is forgiveness available regardless of the past life. Let's not think it is hopeless to get right with God. I have a bible with foot notes explaining those chapters I just mentioned and it makes it so much plainer. I wrote to you about Lewises & Monroes moving here so in thinking over these things I thought it might be worth mentioning to you that maybe if you had some ill feelings of the church there where you lived & were baptized you might consider coming here to our community and start a new life in a totally different place from your old environment. Now if you would rather go back to your own area and live there I'd have no regret but thought coming here might be easier and am sure we would want to do all we can to help you. Really eternity is sure to come and what could be more joyful than being right with our maker that day. I would advise you to not put it off any longer. The scripture says "Heit so ihr meine stimme höret so verstocket eure hergen night"

We here in our community we are not perfect but we do like living here and feel we have a lot of honest and faithful people in the community.

I had no intention of writing this much when I started so I again ask for your forgiveness if I wrote too much. Als wonder what your folks will do yet. They have had a lot of family concerns in their life time. Am sure that they've probably not always made the right decisions but who has? We all fail at times but what counts is if we admit our weakness to God and repent from evil.

I believe your folks are sincere and want what is right so lets Pray for each other.

Aus Liebe
Andy

One final birthday card arrived in early August 2005. It was blue with the word "Son" written over a cut-out that showed a scene with boats in a bay. In the inside of the card, my mother had written "*Dear William*" over the text that was printed:

For every thoughtful thing you've said...
For every loving thing you've done...
For every happy smile you've given...
you're loved just that much more.
Happy Birthday, Son

My mother added:

Love and Prayers
Dad – N – Mom
God Bless You!

Inside was a letter.

8 – 3 – 05
Dear Son,
Greetings of Love and Cheer sent your way from way out here at the
Health Mines in Montana. Where the mountains are. We saw so many
awesome mountains & scenery on our way here. Traveled with a van of
others Consisting of John Yoders, William Yoders, Larry, & Rosanna
(grandchildren) us 3 & Ammon Borntregers of the McComb, Il area others
all from Bloomfield.
Did you go over to Adlai's by now to see them? You should – you could
go one nite while they are choring if you don't want to go when other
people are there.
We are here & Keeping busy Going hiking to the mountains & talking
walks, doing laundry, doing 3 mine visits each day Except on Sun. we were
to church at the White Hall Amish settlement. Our drivers were Floyd &
Vera Martin of Cantril, Ia. & they went on to see more mountains &
Glacier National Park before coming Back.
We were glad to have the priveledge to see you when we were in
Wautoma, now come visit us in Iowa. Just 1 mile west of Drakesville on the
left side of road by a T road.
Larry & Rosanna like Mountain Climbing ☺ !
Well its about bed time & maybe I should write more so I can take the
things to the post office in Boulder tomorrow to mail.
So take care. We all love you and God does too!
Love & Prayers
Dads

They would never stop trying to get me back.
I knew it.
Maybe there was a part of me that was glad.
As long as they kept trying to get me back, it must mean that they still
loved me.
It meant that they hadn't forgotten me.
Maybe.

Or maybe it was only a selfish act.

Making certain that they were fit for heaven. Like my mother apologizing after yelling to me that I was going to hell in order to save her own soul.

Either way, it didn't matter.
I was out.

Once I realized that my marriage was over, there was no reason for me to go back.
The divorce made everything final.

I was out.
I would stay out.

Forty-one

Karrie

It was August 12, 2005.
I was having a crappy day.

After getting up early that morning to do some chainsaw carvings, a new hobby that my mom had lured me into, I had to quit before completing anything. By nine o'clock, it was already too hot to work outside. So I came inside, thinking that I would catch up on my email, only to find out that my Internet connection was down.

Over-heated, both inside and out, I was not in any mood to be bothered by anyone, but Bill happened to wander into the room at that moment.

"What are you doing this afternoon?" he asked.

"Well, it's not like I can check my email!" I snapped.

"I was wondering if you wanted to go get a marriage license."

My eyes flew to his face. He was serious.

It was August 12, 2005.
I was having a wonderful day!

"You bet! When?"

"We could go get it now, if you wanted."

"Let's go!" I said, out of my chair in a flash.

It had been a little over a year since we had become a couple. During that time, I sometimes wondered if marriage was something either of us would ever want to try again. The fact that I was even considering marriage surprised me. While I hadn't sworn it off, after the failure of my first marriage, I was in no hurry. No hurry at all.

Things are different after you go through a divorce. There were my kids to consider. Even though Kelsey and Clayton were teenagers, a stepfather is very different than dealing with a mother's boyfriend, even one who lived with us.

Also, I was happy with the way things were. Why change?

But there was a part of me that wanted to remarry.

As long as it was Bill.

But I wasn't going to be the one to bring it up.

Just as I had waited for him to make the first move romantically, I was determined to let him bring up marriage. So much crap had been said about me over the years. Gossip that I lured him away from his wife and daughter. That I lured him away from the Amish. That I was having sex with both him and David. That I had my hooks in him and was controlling him.

All of it was bullshit.

Nothing ever happened until after his divorce.

Nothing.

After he left, there was no way that I was going to complicate his life any more than it was already. Our getting involved would not have helped his situation. He didn't need any more to worry about. I wanted Bill to figure out for himself what he wanted. Did he want to go back and find a way to make his Amish life work? Did he want to find a way to make his marriage to Ruby work? Could he accept banning and ex-communication from his family and community?

Those were big decisions. It was a lot, a *lot*, for anyone to figure out. The last thing he needed was to get distracted by a love affair. He had more than enough to deal with.

In addition to that, there was no way I was going to be a distraction or an excuse. If Bill wanted to leave the Amish, then he needed to do it for himself, and only himself. I supported him with both my friendship and with a place to stay. I helped him while he learned to adapt to non-Amish life, no matter how distracting those bedroom eyes of his were. I was committed to being only his friend until he got settled into his new life.

After we became a couple, we admitted that we had each been attracted to the other for a long time, but neither of us had ever acted on it. Bill is too honorable and not the sort of husband who would ever cheat on his wife.

Ruby didn't believe that.

That's her loss.

On August 26, 2005, I went down to the river. Everything was green and lush. The tall reeds and grasses hid the tiny streams that trickled from the hillside, but I could still hear them whispering to me. Just a short distance away was my fishing rock, waiting patiently for me to come for a visit, but it would have to wait for another day.

I had other plans today.

Today I was getting married.

It wasn't the elaborate river wedding of my childhood dreams. There were no chairs set along the rows of trees to seat my guests. There were no flowers and white ribbons tied along the ice road trail. But I was older and didn't need an audience or anything artificial to enhance the beauty that Mother Earth provided us.

A momentary sadness came over me as I thought about my dad. I was thankful that he and Bill had gotten to know each other, if only briefly, before there had been no more time. Then, like moving from the cold shadows into a patch of sunlight, sadness was replaced with calm. I could feel my Dad's presence. He was still here with me on this special day. The day that I would marry the man who agreed that the Mecan River was the perfect place for a wedding.

No formal wedding invitations were sent.

No announcements issued.

Waiting by the water's edge was: our wedding official, Joni; our friends and witnesses, Scott and Jodi; my kids, Kelsey and Clayton; my brother and his family; and my mother.

Seeing my mother reminded me when she first met Bill, one of the times Bill went with me to visit my dad.

"Would you like a beer?" she offered.

"Sure," Bill replied.

Mom headed toward the kitchen, but stopped, "Oh...are you old enough to drink?"

"Ma, he's got a beard, that means he's married!" I told her with exasperation.

"Well, I don't know how young they start marrying them off!"

Who would have imagined that one day my bearded, married Amish co-worker would be standing on the bank of the Mecan waiting to marry me. But there he was. Waiting for me. And everything seemed to fit together.

Clayton and Kelsey smiled as I walked by them with my bouquet of wildflowers. They both liked Bill and were happy for us, but not without giving me some typical teenage attitude.

"You know he's closer to my age than yours, don't you?" Kelsey made a point of asking at least once. There are almost exactly fourteen years between me and Bill and there are ten and a half between Bill and Kelsey.

"Oh shut up, you smart ass!" I told her, but couldn't resist adding, "Just think, if you take after your mother, that means your future husband is wearing diapers right now!"

"That's disgusting, Mom."

Both Kelsey and Clayton excelled in school...not at all like their mother. Most mothers are prejudiced, but I really have great kids. And now I would have two more: Frieda and Paul. The Amlettes, as I call them.

The ceremony was simple and over quickly. We were wed. After that, everyone walked up the hill to the house for a barbecue and an ice cream wedding cake. It was very different from my first wedding that took place in the church, with the bridesmaids, the white dress, and the big reception with guests that I was obligated to invite and didn't even know.

My first wedding was nice but very traditional and fancy. But having a fancy, traditional wedding does not ensure a good marriage.

This time, the wedding was non-traditional and simple. We invited only our closest family and friends...the fewer the better. Best of all, it took place in a location that was meaningful to us.

It was our wedding.
It was a special day just for us.
A day we marked the beginning of our new life together.

Epilogue

Karrie

Nothing changed after Bill and I got married. We had already been living together and had been committed to each other long before it was legally recognized and official.

I got a kick out of signing my name "Mrs. Bill Herschberger," especially if Bill's family or the other Wautoma Community Amish would see it. They had all put me through enough hell. This was my vindication.

Being a stepmother to Frieda and Paul was a bit daunting at first. Kelsey and Clayton had intentionally been born close together because I wanted to do the diaper stage all at once and be done with it. It had been ten years since I had dealt with little ones, but here I was, changing dirty diapers again for Frieda and Paul. Not that I was complaining, the Amlettes quickly captured my heart, even before I was legally their stepmother. There was a transitional phase at first, when neither one of them seemed comfortable being at our house, but it didn't last long. Kids are so adaptable.

Now when we have them for visitation, Frieda runs to her dresser as soon as she gets in the house and starts changing clothes. She might go through ten outfits in a day. She loves the freedom.

"Take my hair down, Karrie," she says nearly the instant she enters the kitchen. She has beautiful long, wavy, blonde hair that will never be cut as long as she is Amish. It takes me forever to get the tight braids out.

"I will tonight, honey, after bath."

Frieda is full of energy. She's a free spirit and ready to try anything. When she goes for a snowmobile ride, she'll giggle the whole time and yell, "Faster! Go faster, Karrie!" while struggling to hold on.

Paul is quiet and reserved, just like his daddy. His big brown eyes take in everything and reveal very little. I'm never quite sure what he's thinking. He's the one who is more likely to ask when it will be time to go home. Back to his mom.

Ruby's attorney made it clear in the divorce that only Bill can pick up or drop off the kids. I am not allowed, not even after I became their stepmother. Most of the time it isn't a problem, but there are times when it causes difficulties.

It would be so much easier, the nights when Bill has visitation, if I could get the kids. Even if I could just drive up to the house. I wouldn't need to get out of the truck. The kids could be sent out to me. If we had that arrangement, Frieda and Paul would be at the house when Bill got home. He wouldn't have to leave work early to get them on time. He is never late either getting or taking them home. His kids are too important. He would never do anything to jeopardize his visitation, even if it is sometimes an inconvenience with work.

There's a sign in Ruby's store, I've been told, that states:
We reserve the right to refuse service to anyone.
My name isn't mentioned, but there's no doubt that it is displayed so prominently with me in mind.
They don't have to worry about me. I have no desire to go anywhere near the place. There is no way in hell that I will ever set foot in it. I don't want anything to do with a place built on maintaining a lie. The "poor Ruby, suffering victim" charade.
But I know the truth.
Ruby left Bill.
Ruby refused to go back to him, even with special permission.
I should thank her, since now he's mine.

Every once in awhile, Bill will have a bad day and joke that maybe it's time for him to go back to his "simple" life.
"That's fine. You can go back," I tell him, "but if you do, I'm going with you!"
"You'll go be Amish?"
"If you're going, I'm going. I'll just get myself a bonnet and start pinning up my clothes!"
Bill smiles and shakes his head when I tell him that. He knows that I would do it. And maybe, maybe without even realizing it, he is checking to see if I would abandon him...like Ruby did.
The worst part of dealing with Ruby is the way she acts when we happen to see each other in town. Frieda will run up to me and give me a big bear hug while Paul will look at me from under his hat brim, waiting for me to say something to him. Sometimes, before I get a chance, Ruby will haul them away, and not a gentle "we need to go" tug. No, she jerks them away, as if they were about to step in front of a train.
I don't get it. I definitely don't like seeing her treat the kids that way. If the kids were with us, and we bumped into her or another Amish they knew, I wouldn't yank them away with nearly enough force to dislocate a shoulder.

The Amlettes are with Bill and me one night a week and every other weekend. I bathe them. I cuddle and play with them. I brush out Frieda's long hair. It breaks my heart when I've had to scrub crud out of their scalps that had been there for who knows how many days. Frieda and Paul have become as much my own as the two that I bore.

I love those kids.

I often wonder what will happen in the coming years. Will they decide to leave as their father did? How much pressure will they face? How much pressure are they already facing to get them to stay Amish? The typical Amish brainwashing that the English can't be trusted begins at birth. At least Frieda and Paul know the truth, and when the time comes, Bill and I will support them in whatever decision they make.

"At least they'll have a choice," Bill says, when we talk about it, "At least they know that they've got someone on the outside who'll help them. That's more than I had."

Frieda has started school...Amish school, and it's hard knowing that she and Paul will only be educated to the eighth grade. Both of them deserve a chance to be whatever they want to be and not held back by their limited education. Not held back by low expectations. They are both so smart and have the capability to do so much more than to be kept simple and ignorant.

All of Bill's family, except his brother Adlai, have moved away from the Wautoma Community. Adlai's farm is only about five miles away from ours, but it might as well be five hundred or five thousand. We seem to have settled into pretending that we don't know that the other exists.

It will never seem right that Bill had to lose nearly all of his family when he left. It isn't fair that he was given an ultimatum: his family or his self-respect. But it only proves how terrible his life was as an Amish, that he would make such a sacrifice.

At least Bill has Rachel. Sometimes his sister Amanda, who is still Old Order Amish but in a higher and less restrictive community, will get in touch with him. It's good that he has them.

But the one I wanted to find for Bill, more than anyone, was his brother Lynn.

It took several years, years when I had nearly given up hope, but I finally tracked him down. Lynn was found. When the two of them saw each other, for the first time in more than twenty years, it was worth all the hard work and frustration. All that time I wanted to find Lynn for Bill's sake, but it turned out that Lynn was the one who needed his brother even more.

Living in fear and in shame, Lynn had no one in his life to help him get out of the pit that he had sunk deep into. We tried. We did what we could to help him get clean and to put things right with the law. Unfortunately, something even stronger than a reunited brother already had a fierce grip on him. Lynn was pulled back down into the muck.

We were both terribly disappointed with Lynn's decision. We can only comfort ourselves with the fact that at least now Lynn he knows that he has family. Family who care about him and want to help. Maybe one day. When he's ready. At least he knows there is someone out there who will throw him a sturdy rope to grab onto. Maybe someday soon, he will realize that he can get to a place that's healthy. Maybe knowing that he has a brother on the outside will help.

All we can do now is hope.
Hope is what I have.
For Lynn.
For the other girls like Mary Byler.
For Frieda and Paul.
For any Amish.

We hope they can all find help when they need it. We hope that by sharing our story, more people will realize that there are too many Amish who are trapped. Trapped by lies and misinformation. Trapped by their lack of education. Trapped by years of pressure and coercion that wears them down and breaks their spirits. Trapped by the reins that are tightly controlling them.

And the rest of us allow it to continue.

We look at them with admiration and respect. We hold them up as pillars of virtue. This has to stop. Not enough people realize what the Amish are really like.

When four Amish schoolgirls were shot by a deranged man, the Amish quickly expressed their forgiveness of the killer. How many times did I hear what an amazing example they set for the rest of us? Those noble Amish who can forgive a killer.

Except I know the truth.

I know how the Amish think.

To the Amish, those poor girls getting shot was no different than when Bill was told that it would have been better for Ruby to die when she was pregnant than for Bill to go against the *Ordnung* and leave his cell phone at home for her to use.

It was no different than that "lucky little lad" who died when he was ten in the farming accident. It was no different than too many others who should not have been put in unsafe situations.

Forgiving so easily isn't what bothers me. What bothers me is that the Amish seem so preoccupied with leaving this world. They rejoice in it, regardless of the circumstances. They seem to be in such a hurry to get to the next life that they see death as a good thing, no matter how unnecessary or brutal.

This is what the Amish believe.

Think about that the next time you buy their jams and quilts. Ask yourself if there might be a girl like Mary in that household who is being raped by her brothers and cousins. Is there is a young man driving by in his buggy who is like Bill? Someone who wants to escape but doesn't know where he can turn for help since he has always been told that the English are liars and can't be trusted? How many of them are out there who need our help?

We may never know.

We allow them their separateness and overlook far too much because we would rather put them on a pedestal. We think they have the answers to life's questions. We think they have retained something that we've lost. Many of them are good people, but even the good ones keep the wheels of their cult turning. They don't allow their children to be educated past the eighth grade. They don't report terrible crimes. They apply incredible pressure to anyone who leaves. They believe that no one is supposed to leave. These are all definitions of a cult and they perpetuate it.

They are all carriers of the terrible disease called Amish.

Author's Afterword

Karrie and I met in kindergarten. I don't have any specific memory of her that year, but I have very vivid memories beginning the following year. In first grade, and possibly in second, she and I got into so much trouble giggling that our teacher, Mrs. Verthein, assigned us each our own time-out corners in the classroom. Karrie's corner was at the front of the classroom and had a wiener dog height chart. My corner was the back, opposite corner and had a sink with mirror...and a trap door. While I never did find out where that trap door led, I would sometimes fantasize that I could sneak down to a secret tunnel that would take me under the large schoolyard and under the highway to the basement of my house. While standing in my time-out corner, I could see Karrie in the mirror's reflection. Sometimes she would sneak a glance over her shoulder, make a face, and we would start giggling again. Then Mrs. Verthein would scold her for turning around.

The summer before we began seventh grade, Karrie and I had a birthday party on July 26th, the day between our birthdays. Karrie's family had installed a swimming pool that summer, and she got us to create a whirlpool by getting everyone to walk around the inside perimeter of the pool as fast as possible. It's a trick that has been passed down in my family.

Karrie is part of a small group of my childhood friends who started school in kindergarten and were together all the way to high school graduation. Karrie and I lost touch after high school, as much as that is possible when you grow up in a small town such as Coloma...a town that doesn't have any stoplights and was barely reaching a population of 400 at that time.

Over the next few years, my mother would give me updates on Karrie. I remember hearing that Karrie was a jockey at some area horse races and later that she was becoming quite successful showing dogs. But even in such a small town, I remember our paths crossing only once during the Coloma Chicken Chew while I was helping my parents in the beer tent. The "Chew" is a typical small town weekend event with ballgames, dancing, fireworks, a parade, and excellent barbequed chicken.

After graduate school, I left Wisconsin and moved to the Finger Lakes area of New York, and not quite two years later, I moved to Arkansas. While in Dallas for a regional conference, I had a blind date with the man who would become my husband. We long-distance dated a year before I joined him in Dallas and after our son was born, we moved to Austin.

It was while we were living in Austin that Karrie contacted me via Classmates.com. We reconnected thanks to the internet, even though my parents still live in the house they built when I was two and Karrie is only a few miles away.

The winter after Karrie and I had begun emailing, we went up to visit my family in Wisconsin. Karrie invited us out to her farm so my son, then a toddler, could see the enormous pig she had gotten from the Amish. It had been the runt of the litter. That was the first time she and I ever discussed the Amish. Neither of us knew at that time the impact the Amish would soon have on her life.

It was a few years after that visit, after we had moved back to my husband's hometown of Little Rock, that I remember hearing the gossip that Karrie had "shacked up" with some Amish guy who left his wife and child.

I had a feeling there was more to the story. I know how small towns are. But I didn't ask.

A few years later, after we had exchanged "Happy Birthday" messages, Karrie told me she was considering telling the true story of Bill's leaving the Amish. She told me that she had saved all the letters the Amish had sent and told me some of the unbelievable events.

There was so much more to the story.
Much more than I had ever imagined.
I knew their story needed to be told.

I was excited when Karrie asked if I would be interested in writing their story. I didn't hesitate to give her an affirmative answer. Bill and Karrie's story offers a rare and unprecedented glimpse into the secretive world of the Amish, but I have always felt that it is a story that can speak to anyone. There is also something universal about finding your own path and being the person you want to be, no matter what the challenges may be.

I am thankful and honored that Bill and Karrie trusted me to tell this incredible, true story. I appreciate their openness and their patience. Everything has been set down as honestly as possible to the best of their recollection.

I would like to express my deepest appreciation to Mary Byler for the small portion of her own special story that is shared in this book. I am privileged to know her.

I would also like to thank my parents, family, and friends for their support, with special thanks to Denay and Meredith for offering editorial suggestions on the entire book, to Mary, and to Tina who has been encouraging me and waiting...sometimes even patiently!

Finally, I would like to express my love, appreciation, and gratitude to my husband, Mark, and our son, Cayman. There is not enough room on this page for me to tell them how much they mean to me.